THE SYNAGOGUE SURVIVAL KIT

JORDAN LEE WAGNER

JASON ARONSON INC.
NORTHVALE, NEW JERSEY
JERUSALEM

The author gratefully acknowledges permission to reprint the following:

"Partners," by Marc Gellman, in *Does God Have A Big Toe?* (1989): 1-3. Copyright © 1989 by Marc Gellman. Reprinted by permission of HarperCollins Publishers, Inc.

Selected excerpts from *Sifre, A Tannaitic Commentary on the Book of Deuteronomy* by Reuven Hammer (1986): 58,358. Copyright ©1986 by Yale University Press.

Excerpt from *"Jacob the Baker"* by Noah ben Shea (1989). Copyright © 1989 by Villard Books/Random House.

This book was set in 11 point Hiroshige Book by Alpha Graphics, Pittsfield, New Hampshire.

Library of Congress Cataloging-in-Publication Data

Wagner, Jordan Lee.
  The synagogue survival kit / by Jordan Lee Wagner.
      p. cm.
  Includes bibliographical references and index.
    ISBN 1-56821-967-9 (alk. paper)
    1. Siddur   2. Judaism—Liturgy.   3. Prayer—Judaism.   4. Judaism—
  Customs and practices.   5. Synagogue etiquette.   I. Title.
  BM 674.39.W34   1997
  296.4'5—dc21   96-39695

Printed in the United States of America on acid-free paper. For information and catalog write to Jason Aronson Inc., 230 Livingston Street, Northvale, NJ 07647-1726, or visit our website: www.aronson.com

Contents

Acknowledgements

I would like to thank Professor Lisa Kaczmarczyk, my parents Carol and Bernard Wagner, and my brother Daniel Wagner for reviewing the manuscript in its early stages and suggesting improvements in content, structure, and tone; and to my brother Mark Wagner and Dr. Naomi Weinshenker whose careful editing improved the readability and friendliness of the manuscript in its later stages; and finally to the editorial and production team at Jason Aronson Inc. who caught so many more errors after I thought it was all done. Any remaining faults are entirely my own.

The inspirational thoughts and historical facts presented throughout this book were found over the years in diverse sources too numerous to recall here, including other books about Jewish prayer, Jewish magazines and newspapers, pulpit sermons, and Torah classes. Like the *siddur* (prayerbook) itself, this manuscript grew organically. Other than my structural approach to mapping the liturgy, very little is original. My selection and arrangement of material bespeaks a debt to these many authors, rabbis, and scholars.

Finally, due thanks over the completion of this work must be expressed to the ultimate source of everything *she-he-che-ya-nu v' ki-y' ma-nu v' hi-gi-a-nu la-z' man ha-zeh*.

Preface

A non-Jewish friend who was considering becoming Jewish was tempted to attend a synagogue service. I knew that an unprepared solo visit to a traditional service would be confusing. Although there are many books on the historical development of the liturgy, and many books of insights into the prayers, I found none that could function as a survival kit for those disoriented at a traditional synagogue service.

I set out to write my friend an "orientation letter" to make initial attendance comfortable and intelligible. This letter developed into a lengthy document, plus a complete transliterated siddur for Friday evening and Saturday morning. I also gave a few copies to individuals who seemed lost at services. Awareness of the letter spread by word of mouth, and requests for copies began to come from many places.

This book is a reorganized and expanded version of that letter. It is addressed to:

Jews by choice, and potential Jews by choice

Jews by birth, rediscovering their tradition from an adult
     perspective

Russian Jews, deprived of access to their heritage

Female Jews, many of whom were not taught about con-
     gregational prayer as children

It may also interest non-Jews that participate in some of
the life-cycle events of their Jewish friends. It will enable
them to appreciate what they witness in a synagogue.

This book differs from other books in several ways:

It covers synagogue customs and features, not just the
     liturgy.

It begins with the most basic instructions, like putting
     on a *kipa* (head covering), assuming no prior knowl-
     edge. But it is written for adults, not for children. It
     assumes the reader is interested in mature interpre-
     tations of these customs.

It explains the significance and history of each custom,
     feature, and prayer. The intent is to show the reader
     both how to participate and how to appreciate.

It systematically develops a structural diagram of the
     liturgy, to give the reader an appreciation of the order
     of the service, and an understanding of where the
     service is going that is based on theory rather than just
     familiarity.

The discussions of the liturgy use nontheistic terminol-
     ogy to explain the central ideas of each prayer. Inter-
     pretations are carefully worded to be acceptable to the
     widest possible spectrum of Jewish philosophies,
     although that effort itself may render the result unac-
     ceptable to some Jewish communities. The book neither
     denies nor enforces anthropomorphic conceptions of
     God.

Jacob's Vision

At the end of the school day, the children came and sat on the flour sacks. Jacob would sit across from the children, and they would talk.

As Jacob told his stories, he would from time to time shut his eyes. It was as if he were remembering what to say, not by searching through his mind, but by remembering what he saw. Somewhere, he had a perfect picture, and the words he spoke were a description of this vision.

"What do you see when you shut your eyes, Jacob?" asked a little girl.

"Well," Jacob said, "once upon a time there was a man who had a vision and began pursuing it.

"Two others saw that the first man had a vision and began following him.

"In time, the children of those who followed asked their parents to describe what they saw.

"But what their parents described appeared to be the coattails of the man in front of them.

"When the children heard this, they turned from their parents' vision, saying it was not worthy of pursuit."

Jacob leaned toward the little girl that had asked the question.

"So what do we discover from this story?"

The children were quiet.

"I'll tell you," said Jacob.

"We discover children who deny what they have never experienced.

"We discover parents who believe in what they have never experienced.

"And, from this, we discover the question is not 'What do I see when I shut my eyes' but 'What do you see when you open yours?'"

Excerpt from *Jacob the Baker*
by Noah ben Shea

Following the Service

This book is an orientation to Jewish synagogue services and can serve as a roadmap for you. No matter what kind of synagogue you attend, the roadmap is the same. Less traditional synagogues may read some prayers in English translation rather than the original Hebrew, may replace some traditional prayers with newer versions, and may even omit some prayers; but the service will still touch on the same topics in the same order for the same reasons. So if you know the structure of the traditional service, you can readily find your place in any other service.

The converse is not true. The translations, replacements, and deletions made by one synagogue may be different from those made by another. Knowing one procedure does not prevent confusion when encountering another, because the underlying structure common to them both might not be obvious. This book maps the complete traditional structure, observable in practice at Orthodox synagogues, and also points out the differences commonly encountered in other synagogues. This will be the most useful method for most readers to become comfortable following a service and appreciating its various components, even if they don't ordinarily attend an Orthodox synagogue.

To really be comfortable at a service, you'll need to recognize the "signposts" as they pass. Since the Bible says that the language of the divine revelation at Sinai was Hebrew, Hebrew has been regarded as a holy language in Jewish tradition. Therefore most of the traditional liturgy is in Hebrew.[1] According to tradition, when praying in Hebrew, one need not understand every word as long as there is proper intent.[2] Furthermore, the common use of Hebrew in liturgy and religious discourse has bound Jews together even as we have been dispersed around the globe.

Unfortunately, Hebrew represents a significant obstacle for many. Although personal prayers can be made in any language,[3] congregational prayer is mostly in Hebrew. This book does not presume that the reader knows Hebrew. You can borrow a traditional prayerbook from a synagogue and study it using this book. (Nearly all American synagogues use prayerbooks that include English translation.) For that purpose, this book has cross-references to page numbers in the most commonly used prayerbooks. If you do not know the Hebrew alphabet, transliterations of the prayers are available. Transliteration means that the Hebrew sounds are written using the English alphabet. This will enable you to follow along with a traditional service.

Once you are comfortable following the structure of the service, you may want to participate. The liturgy is quite long, and this might make it seem like there is too much to learn. Don't worry about it. Pick one or two tunes that you really like, and enjoy those.

Although it might seem as though a melody constitutes additional information to memorize, it is actually easier to learn prayers with a melody than without. Some prayers will take many hearings before you can sing the words and melody. But others are simple because of their responsive and repetitive nature. They can all be approached the way a singer learns any piece of music in a foreign language.

Most of the prayerbooks that you'll find in American synagogues include English translations. Occasionally, a translation is great in its own right. But the translations never capture the beautiful rhythms, imagery, ambiguity, compactness of ideas, and rhyme of the original Hebrew. By experiencing the rhythms of the original language while singing the melodies, one gets a feeling not fully discernable when reading the English. This is true even if one doesn't understand the Hebrew that one is singing!

In fact, many of the prayers are chanted at a lightning speed that is beyond all comprehension. This surprises many newcomers. There are conflicting traditions regarding this practice. Some hold that the meaning of every word should be a focal point for concentration, while others regard the high-speed chant as a "mantra" facilitating worship through meditation.

The following Chasidic story finds merit in both traditions.

"Reb Yisroel of Ruzhin used to take a long time over his prayers; Reb Shalom of Belz would recite his prayers hastily. On this, one of their contemporaries commented that both of them cherished every word of the prayers; the former loved them so much that he could not bring himself to part with them, while the latter—for the same reason—could not restrain his eagerness to make them his."

    from *A Treasury of Chasidic Tales,*
    as reported in L'Chaim, issue #229, August 21, 1992
    published by Lubavitch Youth Organization

Many of the melodies used in traditional synagogues were composed in the Middle Ages. *Sefer Chasidim* (a twelfth century book on piety), said, "If you cannot concentrate when you pray, search for melodies and choose a tune that you like. Your heart will then feel what you say, for it is the song that makes your heart respond."[4]

The Alphabet

An ignorant villager, knowing that it was a *mitzvah* to feast well before *Yom Kippur*, drank himself into such a stupor that he missed *Kol Nidre* services. When he awoke late at night, he wanted to pray, but he didn't know any of the prayers by heart. So he began to recite the alphabet over and over again.

"Dear God!" he cried. "I am giving You all the letters. You arrange them in the right order!"

The next day he went to the Kotsker Rebbe's *shul* for services. As soon as the *Neilah* was over, the Kotsker summoned him to explain his absence at *Kol Nidre* the night before.

"Holy master!" he cried. "So eager was I to welcome the holy day with joy that I overdid it a bit and slept through the service. When I awoke late last night, I tried to pray, but I did not know the proper words. For, you see, all I know by heart is the *aleph-bet*. So I just recited the letters and asked God to make words out of them. Were my prayers acceptable?"

The Kotsker smiled. "More acceptable than mine," he said, "for you spoke them with your whole heart."

> excerpt from *The Classic Tales,*
> *4,000 Years of Jewish Lore,*
> by Ellen Frankel,
> published 1989 by Jason Aronson Inc.

Notes

1. The exceptions are in Aramaic, which reflects a text's nonliturgical origins or some other special consideration.

2. c.f., Mishnah Sotah 7:1; Talmud Sotah 33b; Berachot 15a.

3. as long as one perfectly understands every word. (c.f., citations in previous footnote.)

4. This observation and translation is by Birnbaum, from a note in his siddur.

Pronunciation

There are two major Hebrew dialects, Ashkenazic and Sephardic. Ashkenazic originated in Germany, and spread throughout Northern and Eastern Europe and then to America. Sephardic originated in Spain, and spread throughout Southern Europe, North Africa, and the Middle East.

The Jews who speak these dialects are called Ashkenazim and Sephardim. There are minor variations in customs, halacha (Jewish Law), and liturgical rites between them. In America, most Jews are Ashkenazic. But the trend in pronunciation is dramatically shifting toward Sephardic, because that is what is spoken in Israel.

In transliterating the prayers, I have adhered to Sephardic pronunciation. But in naming familiar ritual objects, I'll often use Ashkenazic designations. This will be the most useful method for most American readers. Where Sephardic and Ashkenazic rites differ, we follow Ashkenazic rite.

Until recently, Hebrew was reserved for prayer and religious discourse. It is "the holy tongue." The "mother tongue" of Ashkenazic Jews is Yiddish, and that of Sephardic Jews is Ladino. Yiddish means "Jewish." It is a blend of German, Hebrew, and local influences. Its vocabulary and grammar is nearly German, but it is written using the Hebrew alphabet. In naming familiar ritual objects and prayers, I'll often note popular Yiddish terms as well as the Hebrew.

There is no uniformly applied system for Hebrew transliteration. Here is a guide to my use of English letters:[1]

a	as in	"Ma"
e	as in	"Ted"
i	as in	"Bambi," or occasionally as in "pit"
o	as in	"Moe"
ai	as in	"Shanghai," "haiku," and "jai alai"
ei	as in	"neighbor" and "chow mein"
u	as in	"dune," or occasionally as in "push" or "bunt"
'	as in	a neutral short vowel sound, like the "a" in "ago"
ch	as in	the sound you make when you get a hair stuck to your adenoids

This last sound is not usually found in English, but "Johann Sebastian Bach," "mach 6," and "Loch Ness Monster" are phrases that use this sound.

I use a hyphen to indicate a stop between vowels. For example: *"Ma-a"* is like "Mama" but missing the second "m." I also use a hyphen to separate syllables if pronounciation is unclear, or if a word is long. For example: *"Yotseir"* is pronounced "yo-tseir," not "yot-seir," and "vimnuchateinu" is not as easy to read as "vim-nu-cha-tei-nu."

Unlike English, the last syllable of every Hebrew word usually gets the emphasis (excluding suffixes). Instead of sentences sounding like "one fish, two fish, red fish, blue fish," rhythms sound like "I went to dine on fish and wine."

In the transliterations, underlining is used to mark accented syllables that violate this rule. I also occasionally underline an accented final syllable, if the word is one that many congregants accent incorrectly.

These four examples:

> *Adon olam asher malach.*
> *Ein ke-lo-kei-nu.*
> *Adomai yimloch l'olam va-ed.*
> *v'shi-nan-tam l'va-ne-cha v'di-bar-ta bam,*

are pronounced:

> a-DON o-LAM a-SHER ma-LACH.
> EIN ke-lo-KEI-nu.   ["nu" is a suffix]
> a-do-MAI yim-LOCH lih-o-LAM va-ED.
> v'shi-nan-TAM l'va-NEH-cha, v'di-bar-TAH BAM.
>   ["cha" is a suffix]

When you attend services it is possible that congregants around you will be speaking Ashkenazic dialect rather than Sephardic. If you are following a service, and hear some of the congregants pronouncing some of the "*T*"s as "*S*"s, and some of the "*ah*"s as "*aw*"s, that is Ashkenazic.

For example:

> *L'cha do-di li-krat ka-la*
> *P'nei Sha-bat n'ka-b'la.*

would be pronounced in Ashkenazic dialect as:

> *L'chaw do-di li-kras ka-law*
> *P'nei Sha-baws n'ka-b'law..*

Note

1. Those who know Hebrew may object to my transliteration on several grounds. First, it does not correspond (except perhaps coincidentally) to any other transliteration system. Second, it fails

to maintain a one-to-one correspondence between Hebrew symbols and transliterated symbols. Third, it is sometimes phonetically imprecise (e.g., my use of "i," " '," and "u").

Several groups of Hebrew letters make similar sounds, and four Hebrew letters are silent in some contexts. Some transliterations use unfamiliar (i.e., non-English) notation to preserve one-to-one correspondence between Hebrew symbols and transliterated symbols (often by putting strange symbols above or below h, s, and i). Some Hebrew letters can make two different sounds depending on context (like b and v, p and f, k and ch, s and sh, o and u). Some transliterations advertise these structural relationships between sounds by using unnatural letter choices (like underlining b and p to make v and f sounds). And some transliterations maintain the slight distinctions between similar sounds, (like "ch" and "kh," or *ayin* and *alef*).

My transliteration makes no attempt to do any of this. I assume that the reader will use the transliteration only because they want to follow along with a service. So I have tried to make everything feel as familiar as possible. A linguistically accurate transliteration would be more difficult to use. Hopefully my system of transliteration will help the reader for whom this book is intended. And hopefully Jewish readers will learn Hebrew (or at least the Hebrew alphabet) and outgrow my transliteration fairly quickly.

The Siddur

The siddur is the Jewish prayerbook. "Siddur" is pronounced "see-DOOr" (rhymes with "tour") in Hebrew; or "SIDDer" (rhymes with "bidder") in Yiddish. The word comes from a Hebrew root, meaning "order"; and indeed Jewish worship occurs at fixed times, with fixed prayers, in a fixed order. Once you are comfortable with the siddur, you can be comfortable at any service anywhere, for the liturgy has varied only slightly around the world and over the last 1,000 years.

The first impression of a service is that it is a confusing hodgepodge of activity. At first, the various tunes and events are indistinguishable from each other, but after sitting through several services, the melodies and events will become distinct. It is possible, however, to attend services for years, become completely familiar with the sequence of events, become comfortable pronouncing the prayers and performing the tasks that congregants are called upon to publicly perform, and yet not perceive that there exists an underlying structural pattern common to every service!

This is because the service was not designed all at once. Some of its contents are 2,400 years old. The basic framework was fixed in the first century. The service started out simple, but steadily gained appendages and insertions. Over time, these additions masked the simple underlying form. But once aware that a form is present, you will readily notice it, and appreciate the systematic logic behind the patterns of the liturgy. From then on, you will have a roadmap good for every type of service, rather than just a set of specific directions.

Although the order of worship was defined in the first century, it was forbidden to put the liturgy into written form. People knew the prayers because they recited most of them frequently. The learned knew more than the unlearned. The first siddur was written in the eighth century. The prior development of the liturgy is deduced from the discussions among sages reported in ancient collections of rabbinic teaching.

The siddur is more than an order of worship. It is also a collection of great Hebrew literature. For at least 3,000 years, religious themes have been central to Jewish culture. Some of the best sacred poetry has found its way into the siddur. In the siddur, one finds the experiences of Jewish hearts from many lands and times.

THE LANGUAGE OF THE SIDDUR

Hebrew is unlike any modern language. Its grammar renders rhyming trivial. Therefore Hebrew poetry is often more concerned with recurring patterns of sound within the lines. Consonants are used to construct tempos that ebb and flow.

Furthermore, it is common to build communication into the poetic form itself, by using number harmonies, acrostics, and calligraphic techniques.

In Hebrew, words and numbers are written with the same symbols.[1] Numbers are not represented using places held by zeros, but are formed by adding the values of all the symbols that appear in the representation. (This is like Roman numerals rather than Arabic.) Therefore every Hebrew word can also be interpreted as a number. Conversely, almost every number can be represented very many different ways, and so become associated with words. By extension, different words having the same numerical value become related to each other. These correspondences between words and numbers are used to extract additional meaning from text. The application of these ideas is called *gematria*. *Gematria* is a fertile playground for mental gymnastics.

The most widely known *gematria* is that eighteen is "life." *Chai* is the Hebrew word for "life," as in the toast, *"L'Chaim!"* (To Life!). *Chai* is spelled in Hebrew with two letters. They are the eighth and tenth letters of the *alef-bet* (Hebrew alphabet) and are the symbols commonly used to represent the numbers 8 and 10. Hence the word *chai* and the number eighteen look identical. (This correspondence is why Jews frequently give donations in multiples of $18.)[2]

In Hebrew, hidden communication can be built into a poetic form by using particular quantities of sentences, words, and letters to represent, through *gematria*, a message beyond the simple meaning of the words.

Acrostics are messages that are formed when letters are plucked out of context, based on a pattern. Acrostic messages are found throughout the siddur. Messages may be formed from the first letters of each stanza, or sentence, or even every word. They are also sometimes found based on the last letters, or on every seventh, fiftieth, or 613th letter. Messages are also sometimes formed by skipping fixed numbers of words rather than letters.

Calligraphic techniques include changing the sizes of letters[3] or changing the shapes of letters[4] in certain contexts.

In Jewish mystical tradition, each letter has its own personality, and the shapes of letters have significance. Religious
exegesis (homiletical interpretation of scriptural and liturgical texts) can be based on the shapes of letters and their
juxtaposition, as though the plain meaning of the text had
not required this arrangement.[5]

Hebrew is a very compact notation compared with any
modern language. It can be more ambiguous than any
translation can be. (For all its rich poetry, the *Tanach* [the
Jewish Bible] only has a vocabulary of about 7,000 words.)
This compactness also has another result: words are rich in
value-laden conceptual interconnections.

ANTHROPOMORPHISM AND GENDER[6]

Judaism declares that the concept of "God" completely tran-
scends material reality and human comprehension. Yet the
Bible and the siddur are filled with concrete imagery. God
goes "walking in the Garden" although God has no feet. God
"stretches out his right arm" although God does not have
arms. God "speaks," "smells the pleasing odor," and "hears
their cry"; but has no mouth, nose, or ears. God is described
as "remembering" things, and as possessing human emotions, but has no brain. God is called "Father" but has no
genitals.

This imagery is not limited to human characteristics.
God's "wings" cast a "shadow" but God is not a bird. God
"lifts his horn" but is not a ram. In Jewish tradition, these
divine concessions to limited human capabilities for comprehension and communication need not imply restrictions
on each person's unique concept of God. In fact, the traditional Jewish limitations require an absence of materiality.

In Jewish tradition, God is neither male nor female. God
has all nonmaterial aspects of both and no material aspects
of either. But there is no neutral gender for Hebrew nouns.

Breasts are male. Hands are female. God (as a noun, not as an entity) is male.[7]

We sense the inadequacy of human language in general (and even the human mind) to accurately express or contain the Jewish God-idea and hence the totality of ideas within the Torah. All humanly expressible God-ideas are limited metaphors for that which contains them all.

LITURGY AS PERFORMATIVE SPEECH

In traditional Jewish thought, words and reality are intertwined, utterances have a material substance. The Hebrew word for "utterance" and "thing" are the same. All that we say is critically important and irrevokable.

Speech does not merely describe something. We do not merely agree or disagree with the words as a depiction of reality. Speech establishes a transformation of reality by its affirmation. A classic example is a wedding ceremony. After the words are spoken, nothing has really changed. But everything has changed.

Nearly all of the siddur's contents are performative speech rather than descriptive speech. If you are experiencing difficulty relating to certain contents, don't try to evaluate the accuracy of the text as a description, for that is not how the words are spoken. Try to see what the worshippers are using the text to do.

DIVINE NAMES IN THE SIDDUR

In the Bible, several names are used for the Deity. One name is usually translated as "Almighty," another is usually translated as "God," and so on. Jewish tradition associates the various names with the exercise of different divine attributes.

The most personal Name is the one that is represented by four Hebrew letters. This is what Jews simply call "the

Name." It is more widely known as the Tetragrammaton, from the Greek language, meaning "four letters." In ancient times, the Name was pronounced only by the High Priest, and only within the Holy of Holies within the Temple, and only once a year on Yom Kippur (the Day of Atonement) in the context of prayer. Today, and for at least 1,000 years, no one knows how it was pronounced.

Because of the holiness ascribed to the Name, media on which the Name is written (including prayerbooks) are treated in special ways. Many prayerbooks print widely recognized conventional codes rather than the Name itself.[8] This makes it easier to properly dispose of the writing when it has outlived its usefulness. You will notice this only by examining the Hebrew text of the siddur. It does not affect the translation.

In English translations of the Bible and of the siddur, the divine Name is usually translated either as "the Lord," or as "the LORD," or as *"Hashem"* (pronounced hah-SHEM). *"HaShem"* is Hebrew for "the Name." The word "Lord" appears in the Bible and siddur with reference both to the Deity and to others. Full capitalization of "LORD" is used in some translations to distinguish the Name from the word "Lord." Idiomatically, it would be better to translate the divine Name as "LORD" rather than "the LORD" since it is a personal name, but this is not done. Those who translate the Name as *"Hashem"* use Hashem as a personal name, preserving the Hebrew idiom.

Since we do not know how the Name was originally pronounced, there is a conventional substitute pronounciation used during prayer.[9] For all intent and purposes this unique word is treated as the divine Name. Observant Jews do not use the Name to refer to God in conversation, only in prayer. Observant Jews are very careful not to pronounce this word in other contexts. The pronounciation is a unique variant of the Hebrew word for "lord." It bears no relationship to

the four Hebrew letters on the printed page, nor to any conventional printers' substitution. If you are following the
progress of a service in Hebrew rather than in transliteration,
you will notice this convention.

Throughout this book, we will transliterate the Name as
you would pronounce it during prayer.[10] To comply with
tradition, do not pronounce the following transliterated word
except in prayer. During prayer, occurrences of the Name
are pronounced: *A-do-nai.*

Most Orthodox Jews treat the Hebrew word for God as
a Name warranting similar respect. Unlike the four-letter
Name, the correct pronounciation of this word is well
known, but is used only in prayer. The pronounciation in
prayers is: "*E-lo-hei.*" When not praying, the respectful
pronounciation is "*E-lo-kei.*" This may be compared to the
habit some people have of spelling the English word "God"
as "G-d."

HANDLING AND USING A SIDDUR

Because a siddur contains the Name of God, it is treated with
reverence. Do not carry a siddur with you into a bathroom.[11]
Do not put it on the floor. If you drop a siddur, pick it up
immediately. After dropping it, the tradition is to kiss it as
you pick it up. Close the siddur before leaving it unattended.
Some people also kiss the siddur as they finish using it, and
take care to always put it down with its front cover up. When
a siddur is worn beyond repair and has outlived its usefulness, it is not thrown away. It is buried respectfully, like a
human corpse.[12]

When you enter a synagogue, the *siddurim* (plural of
siddur, pronounced "see-du-REEM") may be near the
entrance piled in stacks, or lined up on shelves, or in a rack;
or they may be already distributed at the seats.

There may also be a second book, called a *Chumash.*

"*Chumash*" comes from the Hebrew word for "five." The *Chumash* contains those parts of the Bible that are occasionally read as part of the liturgy (i.e., all of the first five books of the Bible, plus excerpts from the Prophets). It enables the congregation to follow along with the Bible readings that occur at certain services. The *Chumash* will only be used on Saturdays, Mondays, and Thursdays (and on festivals), so you won't need to take one on a Friday night. (Some editions of the siddur add all the weekday Bible readings at the back, so the congregation only needs a *Chumash* for special occasions.)

The most commonly found *Siddurim* are:

The Art Scroll Siddur, by Rabbi Nosson Scherman
    a traditional siddur; includes Psalms, weekday Bible readings, and commentary
    available in both Ashkenazic and Sephardic editions

Daily Prayer Book, by Philip Birnbaum;
    a traditional Ashkenazic siddur
    also exists in an out-of-print Sephardic edition

Siddur Tifereth David, by Hyman Segal
    a traditional Sephardic siddur

Siddur Tehillat Hashem, by Rabbi Nissen Mangel
    a traditional siddur; uses the rite of the Lubavitcher community, similar to Sephardic[13]
    available with Russian or English translation, with common page numbering

Siddur Sim Shalom, by Rabbi Jules Harlow
    the latest siddur authorized by the Conservative movement
    less traditional than its predecessor

Sabbath and Festival Prayerbook, by Rabbi Morris Silverman
    the older siddur of the Conservative movement, still widely used
    a separate siddur is needed for weekday services

Gates of Prayer, by Chaim Stern
  the latest prayer book authorized by the Reform
    Movement
  more traditional than its predecessor
The Prayer Book, by Ben Zion Bokser
  used at some Conservative synagogues
  includes the weekday Bible readings
Siddur Chadash, Likrat Shabbat, and *Mincha Shabbat,*
  by Greenberg and Levine
    separate siddurim for all morning, evening, and
      afternoon services respectively
    has more transliteration than most others
The Authorized Daily Prayer Book, by Joseph H. Hertz
  The late Rabbi Hertz was Chief Rabbi of the British
    Empire.
  Too bulky for synagogue use, but widely studied for
    its commentary.

As you read this book, you may wish to look in your own siddur for the prayer being discussed. Appendix B contains a concordance to the page numbering of many siddurim.

In Jewish services, a single prayer may be used on several occasions. A prayer may even recur within the same service. Many prayerbooks require you to flip around to find the right prayers at the right times. They do this to reduce the number of pages that must be printed. The newer prayerbooks do this less than the older ones. Because so much of the service is said silently, and because the sounds of the language may be unfamiliar to you when chanted rapidly, it is possible that you will lose your place at times. It may help to look over a neighbor's shoulder.

THE ORGANIZATION OF THE SIDDUR

When you must use a siddur with which you are not familiar, start by assuming that the most frequently occurring events are treated first. Next, assume that events having similar frequency appear in the order they occur. (This organizational principle is found throughout Jewish tradition; the siddur is just one example.)

First come the daily morning, afternoon, and evening services. Then come the weekly Sabbath evening, morning, and afternoon services. Judaism has three annual festivals, called *Pesach* (Passover), *Shavuos* (Weeks), and *Sukkot* (Booths). All three festivals use the same liturgy, so the next items in the siddur are the thrice-yearly festival evening, morning, and afternoon services. Next come the annual services for the High Holy Days, first Rosh Hashannah then Yom Kippur. Lastly come services for even less frequent occasions.

Many of the services share common components. To save pages, the less frequent services often consist mostly of references to various components of the more frequent services. To avoid having to skip around, many Jews use separate special prayerbooks organized for each festival or High Holy Day. Such a prayerbook is called a *machzor*.

Notes

1. The Hebrew *Alef-Bet* (alphabet) has 22 letters. Their 22 symbols are all used to represent numbers as well.

To understand this better, imagine using the symbols A through J to represent 1 through 10. The written representation, "Jeff is not bad," might mean that Jeff wasn't born seven (b+a+d) years ago; or that twenty-seven (j+e+f+f) of something isn't a bad amount to have; or that 27 (10+5+6+6) does not equal 7 (2+1+4); or that I like Jeff.

2. Why associate giving charity with 'life?' Because "charity saves from death" (Proverbs 10:2).

3. For example, enlarging *Ayin* and *Dalet* in the fist line of the Sh'ma, to call attention to an obscure acrostic (discussed in the section beginning on page 144).

4. Examples include: crowns on letters in a Torah scroll, a final *Mem* in the middle of a word in *parashah B'shalach.*

5. One of the most famous examples of this is the "*Aggadic* Alphabet" in the Talmud, Tractate Shabbat, folio 104a.

6. This section is adapted from observations found in notes in the siddur by Ben Zion Bokser.

7. Even so, there are some mystical liturgical texts that explicitly refer to God as female. The most notable example is "*Ka-gav-na Di-nun,*" which is recited at sephardic *shuls* on Friday night.

8. Such as a double-*yud*, or a *hay* followed by an apostrophe.

9. C.f., Talmud Pesachim 50a, which suggests that the restoration of unity between spelling and pronouncing the Name is a touchstone of the coming redemption and the experience of utopia, and that this is what is meant by liturgical references to the Name "becoming one."

10. except for occurrences prior to this page. For example, on page 8 we used *A-do-Mai* and *E-lo-Kei.*

11. c.f., Sifre Deuteronomy Piska 258.

12. c.f., Deuteronomy 12:3–4; Sifre Deuteronomy Piska 61.

13. In the context of this list, "Sephardic" refers to the rite known as *Nusach Sephard* rather than *Minhag Sephard.*

The Synagogue

The family is the traditional Jewish institution for religious expression, education, performance of ritual, and sanctification of life's events. The practice of traditional Judaism is centered around the home. The home is the Temple, the parents are the priests, and the dining table is the altar. Eating (and just about everything else a Jew does) is transformed into a holy act, augmented by rituals and related to fundamental values. The core practices that traditionally define Jewishness[1] are all home-centered.

A synagogue is an institution where Jews gather for congregational prayer and study. A synagogue may also be called a *shul*. This is a Yiddish word meaning "school," and is pronounced "shool." The original Hebrew term is *Beit Ha-Knesset*, which means "House of Assembly." "Synagogue" is originally Greek, and also means "assembly." Reform Judaism calls its synagogues "temples," and to some extent this usage has been adopted by other congregations.[2] But traditionally "the temple" refers to the original Temple in

Jerusalem described in the Bible, and is not used to refer to a synagogue.

A synagogue is not required for congregational prayer, and many Jews meet for congregational prayer in homes, campus auditoriums, or wherever appropriate space can be found. A full service can be conducted anywhere. Physical space is not made holy in Judaism; only time can be sanctified, and that is effected by our intent. So the congregation can be holy, but not the building. Synagogues are "dedicated" using the same procedure as any other building.[3]

A synagogue is supported primarily by annual dues from its membership. It is run by its members. The members elect officials and committees from among themselves. The synagogue hires employees (and organizes volunteers) as needed.

Most synagogues hire a cantor. Traditionally, the cantor leads the liturgical services on special occasions, such as Sabbaths and festivals. Usually, cantors' contracts with synagogues call on them to do much more. A cantor might be expected to teach classes, give concerts and perform at weddings, and prepare children individually for observance of their *Bar Mitzvah* or *Bat Mitzvah*.

Most communities also support a rabbi.[4] A rabbi is a repository of Jewish learning, functioning as a resource to the community and as a judge in disputes between Jews. Traditionally, the title "rabbi" is a credential, not a job description. Although anyone may educate or preach, only a rabbi can issue a definitive ruling to answer a question in a binding way or formally resolve a legal dispute. Classical rabbinic education involves study in four areas and specialization in one: arbitration, food inspection, education, and preaching. Being a "rabbi" need not imply any financial relationship with a synagogue; rabbis work in all trades and professions. A congregationally-supported rabbi is usually expected to preside over services on special occasions such as Sabbaths and festivals and to preach on those occasions, to represent the congregation to the non-Jewish public, to provide adult education programs, and to perform pastoral duties.

In America, most synagogues are affiliated with one of three philosophical movements: Orthodox, Conservative, or Reform. Other philosophical movements (e.g., Reconstructionist) don't have as many synagogues, although they meet for congregational prayer.

Judaism places great value on forging and nurturing independent personal religious philosophies. Judaism's expectations are much more rigorous about deed than creed. Therefore separate movements are only recognized when their adherents change the prescriptions for how Jews ought to deport themselves in prayer and/or in life.

There are minor differences in liturgical practices and synagogue customs that are characteristic of the three movements. These differences will be noted throughout this book.

For most congregants, Jewish communities are more clearly defined in terms of differing practices than in any elements of faith. That is to say, most Jews shop around for a community that practices Judaism the way they want to practice it (including holding services they are comfortable with). Then they move to that neighborhood and/or join that synagogue. They are part of that congregation, even though others who practice similarly may do so for different reasons, and possess very different philosophies.[5]

Notes

1. *Shabbat* (Sabbath observance), *kashrut* (dietary laws), *taharat ha-mishpachah* ("family purity").
2. The Reform movement's original intent in calling its synagogues "temples" was to call attention to their rejection of traditional Zionist aspirations. Their synagogues were the new "temples," entirely replacing the function of the original in their hearts. This intent no longer prevails although the name has stuck.

Notice that all the liturgy that the movement's founders associated with the Temple is still excised from Reform prayerbooks, including the Psalm of the Day, the Priestly Blessing, and the Musaf Service.

3. The word "temple" comes from the Latin word "*templum*" which refers to a consecrated holy place, which a synagogue is not. Thus "temple" is a misnomer.

4. Rabbis are not employees. C.f., Ketubot 105a; Shulchan Aruch Choshen Mishpat IX,5; Bechorot 29a; Nedarim 37a; Rambam Mishneh Torah Talmud Torah III,10 and on Nedarim IV; Nedarim 62a; Rambam on Pirke Avot IV,11; R. Asher, on Bechorot IV,6; Responsa "Radbaz" 84; Tur, Aruch Chaim 242; Responsa Tashbatz I,148; Moari, Be'er Ha-Tave Yoreh Deah 245,12; Responsa, Moses Sofer, Choshen Mishpat 164; Vide itchai T'shuva, on Choshen Mishpat IX,12.

5. Newcomers may initially find the movements philosophies hard to distinguish, just as many Jews can't perceive any distinction between Protestants and Catholics (which is a much greater distinction than any within Judaism).

The Reform movement was originally an assimilationist movement. (This is no longer the case.) It began in nineteenth century Germany in response to newly granted emancipation. Philosophically, the founders of the Reform movement rejected the idea of Torah as revelation, and the idea of Torah as a basis for behavioral law (halacha). They regarded the Bible as a valuable folklore, abandoned Jewish nationalism, and repudiated all religious practices that were felt to be peculiar to traditional Judaism in contradiction to secular European society. Thus praying in Hebrew and wearing a head covering were prohibited. At one point, moving Sabbath observance to Sunday was debated. It was the new behavior (rather than the philosophy) that necessitated a separate community.

The wave of Jewish immigration to America in the early 1800s consisted largely of Reform Jews. In the twentieth century, Reform philosophy and liturgical practices have grown much more traditional. Zionism is now mandatory, praying in Hebrew and covering one's head are permitted as options, and ritual appears to be making a comeback. Reform liturgy has many features that are based on the dominant non-Jewish culture, such as organ music, mixed choirs, prayers in English, lighting flames on the Sabbath, and so on. The American Reform movement has a proud record of social activism and charity work.

The Conservative movement was originally a nineteenth century reaction to Reform, from within the Reform community. They returned to accepting both Torah and halacha as authoritative. But because this was a distinct community, their application of halacha to contemporary situations took an independent course from the Orthodox application of halacha. Nevertheless, differences in prescribed behavior are actually quite small. The waves of Jewish immigration to America from the 1880s to the 1920s resulted mostly in enlarging Orthodox and Conservative congregations.

The Reconstructionist Movement is a twentieth-century reaction from within the Conservative movement. It generally accepts the conclusions of philosopher Mordechai Kaplan as its axioms. It rejects the concept of a deity, and regards Judaism as an evolving civilization; whereas Reform regards Judaism as a religion in the western sense, and Orthodox communities and the Conservative movement see Judaism as a people that is bound by a specific covenant with God.

These philosophies differ over how a mitzvah becomes a mitzvah, and conversely what makes any behavior a transgression. Reform theology regards each individual Jew as the sole arbiter of what Jewish tradition demands of them. Orthodox and Conservative theologies regard the community's rabbi as the authority. Reconstructionism regards the local Jewish community as the arbiter of what is (or is not) a mitzvah. But Reconstructionism does require the community to reach certain conclusions. For example, identical roles for men and women is a fundamental tenet of Reconstructionism. It was this movement that first introduced the public Bat Mitzvah celebration.

Most American Jews identify themselves as Conservative. But most of these Jews are not observant of Conservative halacha and are unfamiliar with it. This is the most significant practical distinction between Orthodox and Conservative. Thus most American Conservative Jews practice Reform Judaism in deed and philosophy, but join Conservative synagogues because that is the style of service they prefer. Their affiliation has become a matter of community more than a matter of philosophy or of forms of observance. The leadership of the movement recognizes this as a significant educational challenge.

'Orthodox' is a term originally invented by the 'non-orthodox' to put a label on the Judaism they were rejecting. By now, most American Jews who are observant of halacha have resigned themselves to being so labeled. Some resent it, but others wear the label with pride. In any case, there is no actual organized 'Orthodox movement.' Unlike Reform Judaism, Conservative Judaism, and Reconstructionist Judaism, 'Orthodoxy' has no all-encompassing synagogue umbrella organization; no central rabbinic body; no authoritative seminary; no annual budget. Each Orthodox community follows its own authorities and practices Judaism accordingly. Some have formed umbrella associations for mutual support and to advance common goals, but there are very many such associations. The Orthodox segment of the Jewish community is generally credited with a very high commitment to Jewish education, both for children and adults, and is currently the only segment of the American Jewish community not plagued by disaffection culminating in intermarriage.

Fitting In

Before you leave home to go to the synagogue, the following considerations may help you to fit in more comfortably on arrival.

CLOTHING AND DECORUM

Some congregations get dressed up while others are more casual. Generalizations are difficult, as each Jewish community has its own character. At many Reform and Conservative synagogues, congregants tend to dress up. Many Orthodox congregations are more casual. A jacket and tie for a man, and a long skirt[1] for a woman, should be a safe bet at most synagogues. If you haven't been someplace before, it never hurts to err on the side of formality.

You will be standing up for much of the service, so choose shoes accordingly.

If you are going to an Orthodox synagogue, be aware that Jewish women wearing pants or with exposed shoulders, and

Jewish men wearing shorts or shirtless, will be offensive to most congregants (both male and female). These restrictions only apply to Jews, but should be followed by non-Jews who wish to appear inconspicuous.

On Sabbath (Friday at sundown to Saturday at sundown), Orthodox or observant Conservative Jews do not carry a purse or handbag. Again, this is only expected of Jews, but non-Jews may wish to follow local custom.

On *Yom Kippur* (the tenth day of the Jewish month of *Tishrei)* and on *Tisha B'Av* (the ninth day of the Jewish month of *Av)* do not wear leather shoes.[2] On those days, you may see people dressed in suits and ties and sneakers.

The decorum of Conservative and Reform services is often more formal than that of many Orthodox services. This can be more striking than any differences in matters of dress. (A student-oriented Reform or Conservative service would be less formal. Most colleges have a "Hillel House" that holds services on campus.)

CHILDREN

In most communities, small children go up to the reading desk when kiddush is chanted, and are given a small amount of sweet wine to drink. Children might also clamber up to the open Ark when the Torah is being taken out; where they often show interest in kissing the Torah or peeking inside the Ark. (These liturgical events are described later in detail.)

Orthodox Jews are usually comfortable and "at home" in synagogue—the children as well as the adults. Children are often free to enjoy the service in their own playful way. I have been to Orthodox services where children ran around the legs of the men on the raised platform as the men chanted Torah, and also played house under the reading desk. Each group continued undisturbed by the other.

In all kinds of congregations, children are permitted, and in many congregations encouraged, to lead the closing hymns of the service. Congregations with large numbers of children may operate a "Tot Shabbat," a parallel children's service on the Sabbath.

DATES AND TIMING

Jewish dates begin and end at sundown. The convention for Gregorian (so-called secular) calendars is to assign Jewish labels to Gregorian dates based on their corresponding daylight hours. So if your Gregorian calendar says that Tuesday is a Jewish holiday, the evening service that inaugurates the holiday is Monday night. Thus the Sabbath begins Friday at sundown and continues through Saturday at sundown.[3]

The Sabbath evening (Friday night) service typically lasts about forty-five minutes. The Sabbath morning services typically last around two and a half hours, ending around midday. Thus the Jewish Sabbath morning services are much longer than many Christian services.

On Sabbath mornings and on Festival mornings, many congregants come late to synagogue. When they arrive, they catch up with the congregation silently at their own faster pace. Non-Jews that don't want to be one of the few worshippers present at the very beginning should note this and arrive about a half hour "late."

Punctuality should be observed at all other services. On these occasions the service has to finish on time; therefore congregants must arrive punctually. (After weekday morning services people must eat breakfast and go to work. Afternoon services, usually scheduled for just before sundown, must finish by nightfall. After early evening services people want to go home to dinner, and after late evening services they want to go to sleep.)

FOOD

Unless you are very familiar with Jewish dietary laws, do not bring food or beverages into a synagogue. Although there is nothing wrong with bringing food, many synagogues have facilities for the preparation and serving of kosher meals, and you might make an error that would cause your hosts great inconvenience and expense in restoring the premises to a kosher condition.

Many congregations eat together after Saturday morning services, and many do so on Saturday evenings also. Those synagogues that have late (i.e., after dinner) Friday night services will often serve desserts after services.

Wait until the appropriate brief prayers are said before partaking. If someone hands you wine or food, these items are to be held until the appropriate prayer is concluded. If unsure, just wait until everybody else starts drinking before you drink, and wait until everybody else starts eating before you eat.

The Jewish grace is said after meals, not before. This is in accordance with Deuteronomy 8:10. The Grace After Meals is called *Bir-kat Ha-Ma-zon* (The Blessing for Sustenance) in Hebrew. Saying grace is popularly called *"bentching"* (Yiddish). It takes about two minutes; but much longer if one is not in the habit.

After Saturday morning services, many congregations do not serve bread, no matter how elaborate the feast may otherwise be. Technically, this makes the event a "snack" rather than a meal. (Cakes and crackers don't count as bread.) Not only does this avoid the need to *bentch* (i.e., the grace after a snack is very short), but it enables congregants to return home to enjoy a traditional Sabbath "second meal" ritual.

Other congregations will serve bread, say grace, and spend much of the afternoon singing *z'mirot* (Sabbath table songs); essentially transplanting the Saturday afternoon home ritual to the synagogue.

SABBATH OBSERVANCES

If you are going to synagogue on Shabbat (Sabbath), then additional customs apply. Shabbat is a special time when Jews enjoy separation from the everyday. We listen to our "still small voices,"[4] and delight in the Sabbath Peace of Shabbat. We focus our attention on our historic role in the future by analogy with the past. We rededicate ourselves to the mission of fulfilling the intent of creation. We become refreshed. We spend the time with family and community, delighting in the pursuit of fundamental values. We look forward to it all week, and lament its passing.

The Sabbath rest is not limited to human beings and animals. An underlying philosophical principle behind Sabbath customs is that the physical world itself is not to be worked by us. Thus once a week, Orthodox and observant Conservative Jews enjoy the recognition that no part of creation is in existence just for us to exploit it. All exploitation of material reality is subservient to higher goals.

This is an extension to the concept of a benediction. Every time you "take" from material reality, you "owe" a blessing.[5] All week long, observant Jews say blessings constantly. On Shabbat we go further. We refrain from "taking" to the greatest possible extent.

When among observant Conservative or Orthodox Jews you should avoid flaunting violations of the Sabbath peace. (These customs are not limited to the synagogue.) Do not handle money or talk business. Hide the pen in your pocket,[6] since both writing and carrying are not done on Shabbat. Do not remind people of troubles, since this would mar the festive mood. Do not turn lights on or off, or operate appliances. Maximize joy in yourself and others. Do not smoke.[7] Do not bring a purse or handbag.[8] Do not bring photographic or recording equipment.[9] Do not bring a musical instrument.

There are several minor differences between the Shabbat practices of Orthodox Jews and observant Conservative Jews. In Orthodox *shuls*, do not offer someone a ride home, since operating a car or riding in one is not done. Observant Conservative Jews will drive or ride on Shabbat if necessary (but only for the purpose of attending congregational prayer). In Conservative synagogues, do not adjust the microphone; it should be left on and in a pre-set position throughout Shabbat. (Orthodox *shuls* will not use a microphone.)

Although these forms of Shabbat observance are only expected of Jews, non-Jews who wish to be inconspicuous may wish to follow them. Be aware that Reform theology rejects, or makes optional, many of these traditions. And many Conservative Jews are unaware of much of their heritage. So you will probably see wide variations in observance of these traditions at a Conservative or Reform synagogue. The Orthodox tend to be both aware and observant of such matters. Follow local custom.

Some people unfamiliar with these traditions forget that those who consciously adopt these practices as part of a religious or philosophical system cherish and delight in them, or that those who grew up with these practices experience them as the natural way of life.[10] They are joyfully spent festive family days. The discipline of rituals is easy compared to the discipline needed to deal ethically with the trials of daily life and to maintain awareness of the profound moral implications buried in all our actions.

Jews are uniquely blessed with 25 hours of joyous holiday once every 7 days! The oppressive burdens of the week vanish, and there is plenty of time to enjoy beloved luxuries such as Torah study and prayer with friends, an extra meal (called *Shalosh Seudos*), and games of chess. To those who celebrate this holiday in traditional ways, the calendar and time itself seem to revolve around Shabbat, which becomes a weekly foretaste of the utopian world-to-come.

THE BAR MITZVAH AND BAT MITZVAH

There is no such thing as a "Bar Mitzvah service" or a "Bat Mitzvah service." If you are invited to a "Bar Mitzvah" or a "Bat Mitzvah," you will be attending a "regular" synagogue service.

A *Bar Mitzvah* is a boy who has attained legal majority under Jewish law (at age thirteen[11]). A *Bat Mitzvah* is a girl who has attained legal majority under Jewish law (at age twelve). These terms literally mean "Son of Commandment" and "Daughter of Commandment," but are better understood as "Man of Duty" and "Woman of Duty."

The attainment of adulthood is traditionally celebrated by publicly performing some of the commandments that are newly incumbent upon the young adult. This is then followed by a *se-u-dat mitz-vah* (a festive meal, the traditional way to celebrate a very significant fulfillment of commandment).

Since a boy becomes responsible for attendance at daily congregational prayer, the traditional form of the *Bar Mitzvah* celebration (since the fourteenth century) is to have him participate prominently in leading part of a service, which is followed by the festive meal. The participation usually takes the form of reading the Torah or Haftarah. (These parts of the liturgy are described later, on pages 237 and 273.) Participation may also include a discourse to display learning.

In congregations where women participate in daily congregational prayer in the same manner as men, the *Bat Mitzvah* will celebrate similarly to a *Bar Mitzvah*. In Orthodox communities, a wide variety of forms are employed to demonstrate the attainment of responsibility. The festive meal afterward is the only element guaranteed to be a part of the celebrations of all communities.[12]

You may also find yourself invited to a "confirmation." This innovation of Reform Judaism[13] is a religious school graduation event for students of high school age. Judaism has no concept of confirmation in any belief or creed. Even converting to Judaism does not require confirming a creed. Although the name of this graduation event may be confusing, the goal of encouraging through recognition events the continuing education of girls and boys is meritorious.

GREETINGS AND RESPONSES

Here is a lexicon of Jewish greetings and their appropriate responses. Their use is not confined to synagogues.

Used at all times:

Sha-*lom*	peace	greeting and response
Sha-*lom* A-*lei*-chem	peace unto you	greeting
A-*lei*-chem Sha-*lom*	unto you, peace	response
ya-sheir *ko*-ach	strength	variations of a blessing
ko-ach		meaning "may you be
Yi-*ya*-sheir Ko-a-*cha*		strengthened," or "may you
ko-ach l'*ko*-ach		go from strength to strength." Typically said with a handshake to someone who has participated in synagogue ritual or performed some other *mitzvah* (good deed)[14]
Ba-*ruch* T'hi-*yeh*	blessed may [it] be	the Ashkenazic response to "Yasher Koach"
Cha-*zak* u-va-*ruch*	[moral] strength and blessing	the Sephardic exclamation and response, analogous

		to both *ya-sheir koach* and its response, *baruch t'hiyeh.*
Ma-<u>zal</u> Tov	good luck	(Hebrew) used especially for weddings, but applicable
<u>Ma</u>-zel Tuv	(Yiddish pronounciation)	wherever the English phrase would be; including sarcastic usage (literally "good flow," an astrological reference). Often connotes "congratulations," such as at a *Bar Mitzvah celebration.*

Used on the Sabbath:

Sha-<u>bat</u> Sha-<u>lom</u>	Sabbath peace	greeting and response on *Shabbat* (Hebrew)
Gut <u>Shab</u>-bas	good Sabbath	greeting and response (Yiddish)
Sha-vu-a Tov	a good week	greeting and response after *Shabbat* ends (Hebrew)
a <u>gut</u>-e <u>vo</u>-che	a good week	greeting and response (Yiddish) at the conclusion of Saturday evening services and on Sunday morning regarding the week just begun

Used on Other Holidays:

Chag Sa-<u>mei</u>-ach	happy holiday	greeting and response on *Purim* and *Chanukah*, as well as on the three festivals, *Pesach, Shavuot,* and *Sukkot*
Gut <u>Yun</u>-tif	good festival	greeting and response (Yiddish) on the three festivals (*"Yom Tov"* means

		"festival" in Hebrew, literally "good day")
Mo-a-_dim_ L'sim-_cha_	joyous festival-days	greeting and response on the intermediate days of the festivals
a _gu_-ten _mo_-ed	a good festival-day	greeting and response (Yiddish) on the intermediate days of the festivals
Sha-_na_ To-_va_	a good year	abbreviated[15] greeting and response during the Days of Awe (from _Rosh Hashana_ through _Yom Kippur_).
a _gu_-ten yahr	a good year	same as above, but Yiddish.
ge-_mar_ tov	[may you be] sealed	greeting and response, used from _Rosh Hashannah_
ge-_mar_ cha-ti-_mah_ to-_va_	for good	through _Yom Kippur_, or even until _Hoshannah Rabbah_ (the end of _Sukkot_)
Tzom kal	[may you have] an easy fast.	greeting at _Kol Nidre_ (before the _Yom Kippur_ fast)

Notes

1. Yes, I do mean a long skirt, not a "midi," especially in Orthodox congregations. This need not imply dressing up, since Orthodox women wear long skirts routinely.

2. Leather shoes are associated with comfort and luxury. Thus one way to represent 'afflicting one's soul' on these fast days was to prohibit wearing leather shoes.

3. The Sabbath (i.e., the seventh day of creation; the day of the week about which the Bible gives commentary and commandments) is Saturday, not Sunday. Prior to the fourth century, the Church observed what its theologians called "the Sabbath of the Decalogue" (Saturday) and also met on what they called "the Lord's Day" (Sunday, which they associated with "resurrection"). In the fourth century they decided to observe the latter "in honor of the Sabbath," as well.

4. c.f., Elisha in Kings.

5. c.f., Talmud Berachot 35a to b (reconciling Psalm 24:1 with Psalm 115:16).

6. Or better yet, leave it at home.

7. Lighting a fire is a prohibited form of work.

8. Implies both carrying and money-handling.

9. But it is permissible to record and photograph services on weekdays, when operating appliances is allowed.

10. Imagine a "primitive" family of eight. They are seated on the ground, surrounding a big pot, serving and eating with their hands. To them, the idea that eating requires eight plates, each assigned to a particular individual; plus three different utensils, each assigned to its own exclusive set of functions, must seem an extraordinarily complex (and pointless) burden. Yet many of us conceive of western manners as ennobling (in addition to normal). Similarly, the dietary laws and Sabbath traditions of Judaism are natural, and are associated with spiritual elevation, not burden. (Their absence can appear degrading, in the same sense that eating with one's hands can.) The possession of commandments is therefore a source of great joy.

11. Theologically, there is a distinction between the earthly court and the heavenly court. Each acts independently, with different jurisdiction over particular transgressions and applying a different range of penalties. Although males are liable for consequences in the earthly court at thirteen, and females at twelve, they become liable for deeds that are punished in the heavenly court only at age twenty.

12. The Orthodox form of the celebration for girls is unstable now. One increasingly common practice is for the *Bat Mitzvah* to lead services in a women's prayer group (at which only nine or fewer men may be present, all of whom must be close relatives of the *Bat Mitzvah*). Subsequently, the *Bat Mitzvah* gives a discourse to display learning before the entire community, at the conclusion of the community's ordinary service. Although everyone remains present, the end of the service (the dissolution of that minyan) is effected, or evidenced, by the men removing their prayer shawls.

13. Early Reform Judaism rejected the concept of a Jewish people, and therefore rejected the idea that a distinctive Jewish system of law should be maintained or have any authority, in favor

of turning Judaism into just a religion. At that time, the Reform
movement found it necessary to prohibit observing a change of
status at Bar Mitzvah age. (Please note that this is of historical
interest only. The Reform movement no longer represents this
position.) It introduced a "confirmation" event. Like the Christian
tradition it emulates, this event takes place at a slightly older age,
marks the completion of a program of study, honors both boys and
girls, and is observed by the entire class together (on the Festival
of *Shavuot*) rather than celebrated individually. The movement
regarded each of these features as an improvement over the Bar
Mitzvah observance.

14. c.f., Talmud Shabbat 87a and Yebamot 62a.

15. The abbreviation stands for:

L' sha-na to-va ti-ka-tei-vu *v'tei-cha-tei-mu*	"May you be inscribed for a good year" (to a man)
L' sha-na to-va ti-ka-tav-na *v'tei-cha-tam-na*	"May you be inscribed for a good year" (to a woman)
L' sha-na to-va ti-ka-tei-vi *v'tei-cha-tei-mi*	"May you be inscribed for a good year" (to women)
L' sha-na to-va ti-ka-teiv *v'tei-cha-teim*	"May you be inscribed for a good year" (to men)

Synagogue Customs

If you are going to a Jewish service for the first time, you will see some unfamiliar behavior even before the service begins. So before outlining the structure of the service, let me describe the customs of the synagogue and their significance. They are listed below in the order that you might notice them.

THE KIPA

A *kipa* (KEE-pah) is a head covering. The plural is *kipot* (kee-POT, rhymes with "boat"). In Yiddish it is called a *"yarmulka"* (YAH-mih-kuh; note that the pronounciation does not resemble the English spelling). They are available in many different sizes, shapes, materials, colors, and patterns.

In ancient times a covered head was the mark of a servant. Wearing a *kipa* can signify that you are taking upon yourself the role of a servant, dedicating yourself to something beyond your own self; or it can be a ritualistic way to remain conscious of all the associated values and behaviors; or it can just be an act of solidarity, belonging, and participation; or it can be just politeness, like removing your shoes when going into a Japanese friend's home.

These different levels of meaning can also be applied to the act of reciting prayers or participating in any other aspect of Jewish ritual. Many synagogue attendees are there primarily to support a tradition, or as a courtesy to family, or to get a warm sense of identification, or for the musical tradition, or many other reasons.

Note that the Jewish tradition of covering the head as a sign of modesty and respect for higher authority is different from the Christian tradition of removing a hat as a sign of respect.

Most synagogues will have a bin filled with *kipot*. The men will put one on. (In Orthodox communities, men wear them all the time, not just in synagogue.) Sometimes you may find an inscription on the inside of a *kipa*, commemorating someone's wedding or attainment of Bar or Bat Mitzvah status.

There may also be a bin or tabletop with hair pins and lacy head coverings. These are for women to pin on their hair as an alternative to a hat.[1] Traditionally, married women cover their heads, unmarried women do not. In many synagogues, either choice women make will be fine.

In many Reform synagogues, and in some Conservative synagogues, both men and women will wear the same *kipot*. In the most extremely nontraditional Reform synagogues, there may be no *kipot* at all. Be alert to local custom.

Non-Jews are expected to wear head coverings in accordance with local Jewish custom. The covering need not be a *kipa*; a hat is fine.

There is no ritual or blessing associated with donning a head covering; you just put it on. Head coverings are a tradition, not an explicit Torah law (biblical commandment).[2] They are not removed when going to the bathroom.

THE TALLIS

A *tallis* (TAH-liss) is the Yiddish name for a prayer shawl. The plural is *taleisim* (tah-LAY-sim). In Hebrew it is a *tallit* (tah-LEET), and the plural is *talitot* (tah-li-TOT).

At the synagogue prayer shawls will be hanging on a rack, or folded in stacks on a table. These are for shared public use. Regular synagogue attendees often have their own *tallis* that they leave on their seat in a decorated rectangular *tallis* bag. These should not be used without permission.

If you are at a morning service (*Shacharit*) the men will put on *taleisim*. Traditionally, only married men wear them. But in many modern synagogues, all men put them on. Most women probably will not, although there is no prohibition. (In Orthodox synagogues, a woman's *tallis* should be distinctly different from a man's *tallis*.)

In many Reform synagogues, and in some Conservative synagogues, both men and women will wear *taleisim*. In extremely nontraditional Reform synagogues, there may be no *taleisim* at all (or only those leading the service might be wearing them). Be alert to local custom.

At an afternoon service (*Mincha*), only those leading the service wear *taleisim*.[3] Some synagogues also have the leaders wear them at evening services (*Ma-ariv*) on special occasions such as Shabbat, festivals, and other holy days. So when you enter a synagogue on those occasions, do not hastily don a *tallis* just because the most prominent figure in the room is wearing one.

Non-Jews should not wear a *tallis* when visiting a synagogue.[4]

Do not wear your *tallis* into a bathroom. Remove it and

leave it outside, along with your siddur. Put it on again after leaving the bathroom.

THE SYMBOLISM OF THE TALLIS

A *tallis* can be made of linen or wool, but not both.[5] A *tallis* has four corners, and each corner has fringes.[6] These four fringes are what make the *tallis* a *tallis*. In ancient times, *taleisim* had a blue thread bound up in the fringes. In modern times, it is common to find a blue stripe in the fabric. The fringes are called *tsi-tsis* (TSIH-tsis) in Yiddish, or *tsi-tsit* (tsee-TSEET) in Hebrew.

The mitzvah of wearing a *tallis* lies in the wearing of the fringes. The fringes are reminders to do all of the Torah's 613 commandments. The commandment to wear fringes for this purpose is explicit in the Torah.[7] Orthodox men wear a small fringed garment under their outer clothes every day, all day long.

The word "*tsi-tsit*" has a numeric value of 600. (The letters of the word are also the symbols used to represent numbers that when added together equal 600.) Each fringe has eight threads and five knots. When added together, that makes 613. This is the number of *mitzvot* (biblical commandments) incumbent on Jews. The Talmud[8] (an authoritative repository of Jewish tradition) associates wearing the fringes to observing the entire Torah.

A blue thread is no longer found among the fringes, because the prescribed dye is no longer available. But a blue stripe is commonly used in the cloth as a reminder. In the ancient world blue had special significance. The dye came from a rare snail[9] (now extinct) that came from the western coast of Africa. It took thousands of snails to get a tiny amount of dye, and the process was terribly foul-smelling. The result was incredibly expensive. The process produced a range of dyes from reddish purple to deep blue. That is why purple (or royal blue) has been the color of royalty in western civilization (much the same way that yellow is reserved for royalty in China).

The Torah makes a radical political and theological statement when it directs that every Israelite is to wear a blue thread. This indicates that every person, not just divine pharaohs and kings, shares a spark of the divine. The stripe says that every individual is of infinite worth. Thus the fringes that remind us of all the commandments are intertwined with the blue thread that represents the central idea and reason for following all the commandments. This fundamental faith in the infinite worth of each individual is built into the tallis. It is the basis for what is secularly (but sexist-ly) known as the "brotherhood of man."

HOW TO PUT ON A TALLIS

Because the fringes are worn in fulfillment of biblical commandment, there is a blessing that one says before donning a prayer shawl.[10] Many prayer shawls have this blessing embroidered on the collar of the shawl. You may see people kiss the ends of the collar as they put it on.

If you remove your *tallis* briefly (for example, to go to the bathroom) you do not need to recite the blessing again when you put the *tallis* back on.

The complete traditional ritual starts with a meditation consisting of the first two verses of Psalm 104. We are about to emulate the metaphoric behavior of God in the Psalm, as we try to act in partnership.

> My soul, praise *HaShem*;
> *HaShem*, God, You are exalted;
> in splendor and beauty You are clothed.
> You cover yourself with light like a garment,
> You spread the heavens like a [tent] curtain.

This is followed by a mystical meditation, in which we recognize the need to act on behalf of the community, to unify the male and female aspects of God (represented here by the two halves of the four-letter Name). This reconciliation is one of several mystical models of the process Jews use to perfect creation. (Releasing materially-trapped sparks of divine light so they can return to their source is another.) The meditation then cites number harmonies between our human bodies and the divinely given *mitzvot* (commandments), which together are the tools for this task, and are the respective contributions of the two partners (God and Israel). The meditation then expresses the hope that we will be privileged to participate in the utopia that will ultimately result from this work. The relationship of the *tallis* to prayer and redeeming acts is compared to an eagle fluttering over its chicks.[11]

Then we say the blessing (and optionally kiss each end of the collar).

> *Ba-ruch a-tah A-do-nai, E-lo-<u>hei</u>-nu <u>me</u>-lech ha-o-lam,*
>   *a-sher ki-d'<u>sha</u>-nu b'mitz-vo-tav, v'tzi-<u>va</u>-nu*
>   *l'hit-a-teif ba-tsi-tsit.*

> Praised are You, LORD, Our God, King of the Universe,
>   who sanctified us with His commandments,
>   and commanded us to enwrap ourselves with
>   *tsi-tsit.*

Then we don the *tallis* like a shawl, covering the head, and wrap it around us like a cocoon (if it is big enough).

Another meditation, consisting of Psalm 36:8–11, then occurs in appreciation of the kindness and protection now felt, and expressing the hope that kindness and righteousness will be experienced by good-hearted people everywhere. It echoes the eagle metaphor of the second meditation and then the light metaphor of the first meditation.

How precious your kindness, God!
The children of Adam
   in the shadow of your wings take refuge.
They will be filled from the abundance of your House
   and the stream of your delights they will drink.
Because with You is the source of life,
   in your light we see light.
Send your kindness to those who would know You,
   your righteousness to upright hearts.

Finally the *tallis* slips off the head, onto the shoulders, where it is worn like a cape. (If it is the large square kind of *tallis*, reach down at your sides and grab the edge of the *tallis* in the middle on both sides. Lift your hands to near your ears and deposit the edges high on your shoulders.)

THE MECHITSA

In Reform and Conservative synagogues, men and women sit together. In Orthodox synagogues, men and women sit separately.[12] The separating partition is called a *mechitsa* ("Meh-CHEE-tsah"). There is no required floor plan for a *mechitsa*. For example, it could split the congregation from side to side, or front and rear. But the traditional architectural feature is a balcony for the women. If you are visiting an Orthodox *shul*, note the arrangements and follow local custom.

THE T'FILLIN

T'fillin are two small black leather boxes attached to black leather straps.[13] In English, they are sometimes called "phylacteries" (from Greek). One is worn on the upper part of the left arm, near the heart, and is called "*Shel Yad*" (of the hand). The other is worn on the forehead, and is called "*Shel Rosh*" (of the head).

The *t'fillin* have internal compartments that contain parchments. The "head" *t'fillin* has four compartments, containing Exodus 13:1–10 and 11–16, and Deuteronomy 6:4–9 and 11:13–21. The "heart/arm/hand" *t'fillin* has a single compartment, containing the same four biblical passages written in four columns on a single parchment.

By donning *t'fillin* on the head and near the heart, the wearer aspires to employ his thoughts and emotions in divine service. This is a different purpose than wearing the fringes, which remind one to follow the commandments.

The *t'fillin* are signs of the covenant between Jews and God. They are not worn on Shabbat (the Sabbath) or festivals because Shabbat and the festivals are themselves signs of the covenant, so nothing further is needed. (Non-Jews should not put on *t'fillin* when visiting a synagogue.)

The act of putting on *t'fillin* is a metaphoric betrothal between the Jew and God. (Part of the ritual for donning the *t'fillin* is the recital of Hosea 2:21–22 while wrapping the strap of the "heart/hand" *t'fillin* around your finger, like a wedding ring.)

The "head" *t'fillin* has a three-pronged *shin* (a Hebrew letter) on one side, reminding us of the merits of the three Patriarchs; and a four-pronged *shin* (an odd variant) on the other side, reminding us of the merits of the four Matriarchs. Since *shin* has a numeric value of 300, it reminds us that *t'fillin* are worn 300 days out of the 354-day Jewish calendar. *Shin* is also the first letter of, and an abbreviation for, one of the Names of God (the one usually translated as "Almighty").

On weekday mornings (i.e., not Sabbath and not another holiday; in most Jewish contexts Sunday is a weekday), the men will put on *t'fillin* that they bring with them from home. The *t'fillin* are donned before beginning the morning service and are worn throughout the service.[14] Although some Jewish women wear *t'fillin*, most do not attend weekday morning services and do not wear *t'fillin*. Orthodox women have traditionally not worn them.[15, 16]

Many synagogues provide a place for people to leave their *t'fillin*. Unlike prayer shawls, head coverings, and prayer books, you should assume that any *t'fillin* are the personal property of individuals and should not be borrowed without asking permission.

There is a very complex ritual associated with donning *t'fillin*. The details are in Appendix A.

Wearing *t'fillin* is a symbolic act of binding. It proclaims that, like the slaves from Egypt that stood together at Sinai, we have permanently exchanged human masters for the duty of divine service. Thus the leather straps of the *t'fillin* may remind one of the leather straps that were used to beat Israelite slaves.

Remove your *t'fillin* before entering a bathroom and leave them outside.[17]

THE MEZZUZAH

There will be a small container mounted to the doorpost at the entrance to the synagogue (and to the doorposts at the entrances to most rooms). You will find it on the upper third of the right-hand doorpost as you enter.[18] It will be mounted at an angle, with the top toward the inside. The word *mezzuzah* literally means "doorpost," but it is most commonly used to refer to the container.

The container holds a parchment on which is written Deuteronomy 6:4–9 and 11:13–21. This text (which is also inside the *t'fillin*) is the beginning of the *Sh'ma* prayer. The full significance of this text is described later, in the discussion of the *Sh'ma* prayer.

Many Jews follow the custom of kissing the mezzuzah when they enter and leave. This is done by touching their fingertips first to the mezzuzah and then to their lips.

The mezzuzah has nothing to do with the synagogue. It is present in all Jewish homes (and most buildings owned by Jews). Affixing a mezzuzah is an explicit biblical commandment.[19]

In addition to its significance as an emblem of the values contained in the *Sh'ma* prayer, a mezzuzah evokes warm sentiments as a symbol of a traditional home, and as an appeal to divine sheltering protection (because it is reminiscent of the protection from the last plague of the Exodus).

Judaism employs many beloved objects in the performance of ritual, but objects are not holy in Judaism. Objects, or the ritual acts that use objects, cannot cure, protect, or magically strengthen in any way. Objects enable people to experience their own holiness, which they in turn can use to sanctify time. In contrast, the words of the Torah are considered holy. Therefore objects that contain them, such as Torah scrolls, t'fillin, and Mezzuzot are treated with reverence.

The Mezuzah of Onkelos

When Onkelos ben Kalonymous (author of the Targums[20]) became a Jew-by-choice, Caesar sent a militia to take him back to Rome. But Onkelos persuaded the militiamen to become Jews. Caesar sent another militia, warning them not to engage Onkelos in conversation. As they were escorting him in proper Roman order, Onkelos asked, "Who carries the light for whom?" They replied, "The torch-bearing slave leads, then comes the *lecticarius* carrying the light for the *dux*, the *dux* carries the light for the *hegemon*, the *hegemon* for the *comes*." "Does the *comes* then carry the light for the people?" asked Onkelos. "No," said the soldiers. Said Onkelos, "Our Leader is different. The Holy One, Blessed be He, carries light for the people Israel, as it is written, '**And the LORD went before them in a pillar of cloud . . .**' (Exodus 13:21)." And the soldiers became Jews.

Caesar, now completely enraged, ordered another militia

to take Onkelos, and ordered them not to speak with him at all. They handled Onkelos roughly, bound him, heaved him over their shoulders, and began to carry him out of the house. Yet he managed to kiss the mezzuzah on his doorpost as he was being carried off. This curious behavior aroused the soldiers to ask what the strange object was. He answered: "It is customary with a human king that while he is sitting inside his palace his servants guard him outside. With our King, The Holy One, Blessed be He, it is the opposite. His servants are inside, and He guards them from the outside, as it is written, 'The LORD will guard your going out and your coming in . . .' [Psalms 121:8]." These soldiers also became Jews. And Caesar did not send any more after him.

From the Talmud, tractate Avodah Zara, folio 11a-b; retold in *Chibbur Yafeh* and many other places.

Mezzuzot (plural of mezzuzah) can also be works of art. Because Jewish tradition emphasizes the art of living and deemphasizes representative art, Jewish visual artistry has traditionally focused on calligraphy and on beautifying ritual objects. There is a principle that commandments should be fulfilled in the most beautiful way possible.[21] We should maximize the delight in their performance. A counterbalancing principle holds that the intention of doing a mitzvah (fulfilling a divine commandment) should itself be the greatest possible delight.[22] In any case, Jews appreciate beautiful ritual objects, even though the simplest examples have unequalled beauty in their purpose. *Mezzuzot* can be found in a variety of shapes, sizes, materials, and designs—from playful ceramic animals for children's rooms, to exquisite silver and glass creations for adult appreciation. The parchment inside a mezzuzah always reflects the holy intent and concentration of the scribe. Mezzuzot on exterior doorposts and in public buildings are likely to have simple inexpensive cases.

TSEDEKAH BOX

On regular weekdays and on minor holidays (e.g., Purim, Chanukah, Rosh Chodesh), there will be a container near the synagogue entrance to accept charitable donations. This is called a "*tsedekah box*"; or a "*pushke*" in Yiddish. There may be several *tsedekah* boxes, each labeled with a different charity, so that you have several choices. There will be no *tsedekah* box set out on major holidays (for example, Shabbat and the festivals) since handling money and recollecting troubles are off-limits on those days.

Donating alms is a traditional act of preparation for prayer. Every observant Jewish home has at least one *tsedekah* box. Often each child has their own box and gets to select the charity. The synagogue and home *tsedekah* boxes are not there to raise large sums; only to facilitate more meaningful prayer.

Donating alms is also an important part of preparing for many Jewish occasions, most especially Shabbat, Purim, Days of Awe, and funerals. (Additional donations follow memorial services on the annual holidays of Yom Kippur, *Shemini Atzeret*, and *Shavuos* once one's parents are no longer living.)

Tsedekah

Tsedekah is a Hebrew word that means "justice" and "righteousness." *Tsedekah* is the Jewish term for giving alms. There is no Hebrew word having the same connotations as the Christian word "charity." Justice and almsgiving are metaphorically one in Jewish thought. The rights of the recipient are paramount, rather than the merit of the giver.

Jewish law requires every Jew to give between ten and twenty percent of their income to needy or disadvantaged people. This is not an act of compassion. This is *tzedekah*.

In Christian tradition, one who does not give charity lacks compassion. In contrast, a Jew who does not support the needy commits a positive act of social injustice, and delays the coming of the Messianic Age.

To understand this better, consider that "the earth is the Lord's and the fullness thereof"[23] and that numerous biblical laws direct us to transfer specific amounts of the bounty we possess to support the poor. Therefore these laws effect transfer of legal title, and failure to obey is misappropriation of assets that rightfully belong to others.[24] After the performance of "charitable" acts, one should not say, "I have dealt with my fellow man benevolently," but rather, "I have dealt with my fellow man justly, as I must do."[25]

Giving more than twenty percent is prohibited. This is viewed as irresponsible dissipation of wealth which may, in the long run, cause the giver to become dependent upon society.

Giving less than ten percent is considered miserly under normal circumstances, but Jews who are themselves dependent upon *tzedekah* may give as little as five percent. Even the most destitute Jews must give five percent of what little they get—even if all they get is *tsedekah*. Thus even the poorest maintain their self-worth and their societal role by being able to help others.

Jewish tradition maintains that *tsedakah* is best given in such a way that neither the giver nor receiver are aware of the other. Thus no one can feel dependent on, or indebted to, another individual. And no one can feel in control of, or owed by, another. Thus there have always been Jewish organizations acting as go-betweens for anonymous donors and anonymous recipients.

Tsedekah is an integral part of the traditional observances associated with most events of the Jewish calendar and life-cycle.

Notes

1. In some orthodox communities, many women prefer to wear wigs or shawls.

2. c.f., Talmud; Kiddushin 31a; Nedarim 30b and Shabbat 156b; Aruch HaShulchan 2:10 Iggerot Moshe, Orach Chaim 3:2; Choshen Mishpat 1:93.

3. Some Orthodox congregations do not have those leading the service wear *taleisim* in the afternoon.

4. The purpose of the *tallis*, and the symbolism of the fringes, are related to the unique relationship between Jews and God. Non-Jews are bound to God by seven commandments, not 613. Whereas the function and symbolism of a *kipa* (head covering) relate to all human beings, the *tallis* does not. A *tallis* is one of the distinctive signs of the Jewish people.

5. c.f., Leviticus 19:19; Deuteronomy 22:11; Mishna Kilayim 9:2, 5, 8; Sifra Leviticus Kedoshim Perek 18 (CC:IX).

6. c.f., Sifre Deuteronomy Piska 234.

7. c.f., Numbers 15:37–41; Deuteronomy 22:12; Zechariah 8:23; Sifre Numbers CXV:I to CXV:V.

8. in tractate Nedarim, folio 25a.

9. c.f., Tosefta Menachot 9:6; Tosafot Menachot 42b; Rambam Hilchot Tzitzit 2:2.

10. The obligation is incumbent only on Jewish men, so observant Jewish women omit the blessing or reword it to avoid the Hebrew word "*v'tsi-va-nu*" ("who has commanded us").

11. This is a metaphor taken from Deuteronomy 32:11.

12. This ancient practice may originally have been instituted to emphasize Judaism's rejection of paganism, whose rites sometimes culminated in frenzied sexual activity. Later, the practice came to be considered as an aid to concentration in worship.

Mixed seating was first introduced to Jews in 1825, when a Reform synagogue in Albany borrowed a Baptist church for services. The very influential rabbi of that congregation (Isaac Mayer Wise) liked it and retained this feature. Its introduction was not based on any philosophical considerations. He wrote about his experience with it, and the practice spread throughout American Reform congregations.

From a traditional perspective, congregational prayer is something people do alone, together. Men in the presence of women, and women in the presence of men, are not free to be alone inside. That is, they are not in intimate contact with their most natural ways of thinking and expressing themselves. Some Jews see separation as a way to reduce consciousness of one's public self so we have freedom to be ourselves and to reveal and examine ourselves.

Most American Jews reject this view and prefer mixed seating. And many of them pray effectively. But at least as many view mixed seating as a good in itself. It has become a touchstone of their liberalism. They do not argue that it makes deep introspection easier to achieve or more effective.

13. The boxes and straps are made from the skin of a kosher animal. The parchments are also made from the skin, and specially written by a scribe. They are tightly rolled and then bound with animal hairs. The boxes are sewn together with fiber from the hip muscle of a kosher animal.

14. the *Shacharit* Service only. They are removed for *Musaf*, e.g., on *Rosh Chodesh*.

15. c.f., Shulchan Aruch Orach Chayim 38:3.

16. Rashi's daughters were notable exceptions.

17. c.f., Sifre Deuteronomy Piska 258; Shulchan Aruch Yoreh Deah 43:1.

18. c.f., Sifre Deuteronomy Piska 36 "of thy house. . .".

19. c.f., Deuteronomy 6; Shulchan Aruch Yoreh Deah 291:1.

20. An important series of Aramaic interpretive translations of the Torah.

21. The principle of inner glorification is called *hiddur mitzvah*, of outer beautification *noi mitzvah*. C.f., Kitzur Shulchan Aruch 9:1 re: Exodus 15:2.

22. c.f., Sifre Deuteronomy Piska 36 "precious are Israel . . ."

23. c.f., Psalm 24:2; Midrash T'hillim 24, 2; T.Berachot 35.

24. c.f., Leviticus 19:9–10; Deuteronomy 24:21; Mishnah Peah chapters 2, 4, and 7; Sifra Leviticus Kedoshim 1:6 to 3:7 (chapters 196–8) CXCVI:I to CXCVIII:I.

25. This sentence taken from "Family" edited by Hayyim Schneid, *JPS Popular Judaica Library*, 1973. The quotes about the word "charitable" are my own.

Synagogue Features

ARCHITECTURE

There are no stylistic guidelines for synagogue architecture. Synagogues have diverse forms and styles throughout the world. Nevertheless, there are some features common to nearly all synagogues.

The most fundamental components of congregational prayer are said while facing toward Jerusalem.[1] Since Jerusalem lies due east from America, the front of most American synagogue interiors will be the eastern wall.[2] Traditionally, a synagogue must have at least one window facing east (i.e., Jerusalem). If the synagogue is in a multi-story building, the synagogue will be on the top floor.[3]

A traditional synagogue might have twelve windows, one for each of the twelve tribes. Some traditional synagogues also employ other architectural elements in quantities of twelve. For example, there might be twelve columns holding up the roof.

THE ARK

At the front of the synagogue (on the east wall) will be the Holy Ark (*Aron HaKodesh*). Like the original Ark, this is a cabinet. The Ark contains the Torah scrolls. The scrolls will be hidden behind a curtain (called a *parochet*), or doors, or both. This is reminiscent of the arrangement in the Temple, where the Ark containing the pact between Jews and God was kept behind a curtain in the "Holy of Holies."

It is the presence of the Torah scrolls within the Ark that gives the synagogue whatever measure of specialness it has. Specialness radiates outward from the letters on the scrolls, to the scrolls, to the Ark, to the congregation, to the synagogue.

THE BIMA AND THE AMUD

There will be a raised platform, called the *bima* (BEE-ma). In traditional synagogues, the *bima* will usually be in the midst of the congregation.[4] This arrangement emulates the assembly of tribes around the traveling Ark in the wilderness.[5] This can also create an intimate communal setting for prayer.

On the *bima*, there will be a reading "desk" facing the Ark (i.e., Jerusalem). This is actually a large inclined table, designed for several people to use simultaneously while standing. In Sephardic synagogues, the entire service is led from the reading desk on the *bima*. In Orthodox Ashkenazic synagogues, Torah scrolls are read from the desk on the *bima*, but the rest of the service is led from a lower podium, called the *amud* (pronounced "ah-MOOD"). The amud is located between the *bima* and the Ark, facing the Ark (i.e., Jerusalem).

The centrally located *bima* is becoming rare in America. In most non-Orthodox synagogues the *bima* will be at the front. In this case the Ark will be on the *bima*. There will be no *amud*; and the entire service, not just the Torah readings, will be led from the reading desk. In most Reform synagogues, and in some Conservative ones, the reading desk (and the reader) faces the congregation.[6]

THE READER

The reader is the congregation's representative and leader in prayer. The reader is called the *She-li-ach Tsi-bur* (the agent of the community) in Hebrew. This is sometimes abbreviated to "*Shats.*"

At a traditional service, the musical interplay between the chanting of the congregation and the chanting of its agent can be close, interdependent, and somewhat improvisational. This exciting musical proposition is possible because shared tradition provides a stable framework within which the reader's improvisation happens. Each type of service has its own particular sound—its own musical scale with characteristic cadences and melodic gestures. This enables Jews around the world to improvise together. The congregation can sense the moment to respond, and how to respond, based on the reader's cues. Congregants develop this sense naturally over time, just by participating.

In traditional communities most of the congregants are capable of functioning as reader on ordinary occasions. It is a traditional act of hospitality to invite unknown newcomers to lead the service. (Don't worry. It's OK to decline. You are being honored, not tested.) Unlike the *Leiturgos* of Christian tradition, the reader is not someone possessing a peculiar spiritual endowment so as to be a qualified intermediary between the community and God. The reader needs no special training, wears no special garb, and is not clergy. Congregants are identical in relationship to God. Each congregant can represent the entire nation and be entitled to speak in its name.[7]

A professional reader is called a *chazzan* (cha-ZAHN) in Hebrew, or cantor in English, meaning "singer." A reader that is not a cantor is referred to as a *Ba-al T'filah*, meaning "prayer leader." Traditionally, congregations hire a cantor to lead services on special occasions, such as Sabbaths, festivals, and High Holy Days. A cantor should have a beautiful voice,[8] an intimate knowledge of all the special services, and (because the cantor represents the congregation regularly) an excellent moral character.

THE RABBI

There will also be a lectern at the front of the synagogue, facing the congregation. This may be used for words of guidance during the service (e.g., "Psssst . . . we're on page 38 now"), for announcements, and for a Torah lesson (a sermon). At special services (such as Sabbath, festivals, and other holidays) this will usually be done by the rabbi of the synagogue (if it has one).

A rabbi is an optional feature at a service. So is the sermon. Centuries ago, traveling preachers were a popular form of Saturday afternoon entertainment, having nothing to do with services.

THE MENORAH AND THE ETERNAL LIGHT

A menorah is a seven-branched candelabrum. The original Menorah had an important function in the ancient Temple.[9] Today, the Menorah is the official emblem of the State of Israel as well as the most traditional symbol of Judaism. A menorah is often present as a decorative motif. It has no liturgical function whatsoever.[10] (There is an unrelated nine-branched candlabrum used on Chanukah. It is properly called a *chanukiah*, although it is colloquially called a Chanukah menorah.)

". . . all Jews are essentially the same. They are not just separate entities that may later link themselves together. This is
why the Menorah in the Holy Temple was made out of one
piece of solid gold, which was beaten into seven branches. The
different branches of the menorah symbolize the diversity and
broad spectrum of the Jewish community. Each Jew shines and
expresses the light of Torah in a different way. We may represent different aspects of Jewish life, yet deep down we're all
made of the same substance."

from *Blossoms*
by Rabbi Yisroel Rubin
as excerpted in L'Chaim #270.

Suspended above and before the Ark is the *Neir Tamid*
(Nayr Tah-MEED), an eternal light. It has no liturgical function. In the Temple, this was the western-most light of the
Menorah.[11] It is a reminder of the *Shechina*, the Divine Presence.[12] In Jewish mysticism, the *Shechina* is the surface of
contact between material reality and the divine; the female
emanation from the unknowable; and the Bride Sabbath.

Israel is a wick; Torah is oil; and the Shechina is light.

Tikkune Zohar, T.21

THE STAR OF DAVID

A six-pointed star may appear as a decorative motif. This is
called *The Star of David*. In Hebrew it is called *Ma-gein David*
(Ma-GAYN da-VEED), which means "Shield of David." In
Yiddish it is *Mogen Dovid* (MAWgen DUVvid). The Star of
David is commonly thought to be the symbol of the Jewish
nation (or tribal federation) since King David (circa 1,000
B.C.E.).[13] It is not analogous to a cross; it does not represent
a means to salvation, and is not a focal point for worship.
(In a synagogue there is no object upon which thoughts or
eyes focus in worship.)

SYMBOLS OF THE TRIBES

Each of the twelve tribes is associated with a symbol.[14] These appeared on their military banners in biblical times. Each is also associated with a particular gemstone in the breastplate of the ancient High Priest and with the color of that gemstone. As a result, you may find these symbols and colors used as decorative motifs in synagogues. Ancient sources promote several different associations between tribes and stones, and between stones and colors. If you see twelve of anything, chances are they correspond to the twelve tribes and bear appropriate design elements.

The symbol of the tribe of Judah (a lion, or two lions) often appears by itself. Note that the word *Yehudi* (Jew) comes from *Yehudah* (Judah). The Bible describes how the tribes split into two kingdoms after King Solomon's death. The ten tribes that comprised the northern kingdom of Israel did not survive the Assyrian conquest about 2,600 years ago. This left only the kingdom of Judea, which (as its name implies) consisted most prominently of the tribe of Judah (along with the tribe of Benjamin).

Symbols of the Twelve Tribes

Re-u-ven	mandrakes	carnelian/ruby	flesh/red
Shi-mon	Shechem (city)	topaz/chrysolite/ emerald	green
Lei-vi[15]	urim & thumim	smaragd/emerald	white/black/red/ green
Ye-hu-dah	lion	carbuncle/ chalcedony	sky blue
Issachar	sun & moon	sapphire	red/dark blue
Ze-bu-lun	ship	beryl/emerald/ amethyst	green/ white
Dan	snake	jacinth/carbuncle	orange/dark blue

Naf-ta-li	deer	agate	light red, wine/ striped gray
Gad	encampment	amethyst/crystal	violet/black & white
A-sher	tree	beryl/chrysolite	bluish green/ olive green
Yo-sef	ox/bull	onyx/lapis-lazuli	black
Bin-ya-min	wolf	jasper	multi-colored

OTHER DECORATIVE MOTIFS

The two tablets bearing *A-se-ret Ha-Di-brot* (The Ten Utterances, The Decalogue; popularly but somewhat inaccurately[16] called "The Ten Commandments") represent *Mattan To-rah* (the giving of the Torah at Sinai). They are common in synagogue decoration. They are sometimes held by the lions of Judah (*Ye-hu-dah*). A crown is another common motif. It can represent the Torah, the Kingship of Heaven, or *Keter* (one of the *sefirot* in the Jewish mystical model of the divine). These concepts are described later.

Calligraphy usually appears, sometimes in panels and medallions, other times in artistic shapes. Calligraphy in the guise of a burning bush (as in chapter 3 of Exodus) is common. The first line of Balaam's blessing (Numbers 24:5) often appears. And the first line of *Ashrei* (Psalm 84:5) is also common. (These passages are discussed later, on pages 302 and 185, respectively.)

Another common decorative motif is a hand, with a wide spread between the middle and ring fingers; or a pair of such hands. This is the ancient handsign of the *ko-ha-nim* (priests) in the Temple. The priestly handsign is symbolic of divine immanence. The handsign was used by the *kohanim* when they pronounced The Priestly Blessing on the congregation. This ritual is still a part of the service, and is discussed later.

This Jewish ritual has been popularized by the Star Trek TV show, which used it as the Vulcan ritual of greeting. The Vulcan ritual consists of the handsign accompanied by a blessing: "Live long and prosper," which is an abbreviated paraphrase of the original Jewish blessing.[17] The modern Hebrew greeting ("Shalom") is a still shorter version of this blessing.

Decorative motifs may also be based upon the seven fruits, or the four wild animals, traditionally associated with *Eretz Yisroel* (The Land of Israel). The fruits are grapes, figs, pomegranates, wheat, barley, olives, and dates.[18] The animals are the leopard, eagle, deer, and lion.[19]

Some synagogues display the flags of the United States and *Medinat Yisroel* (The State of Israel).[20] Notice that the Israeli flag is a *tallis* (prayer shawl), including two blue stripes! Thus the conceptual unity of humankind is built into it via the blue stripes. (The light blue is also the color of Judah.) The Israeli flag also has a Star of David, the symbol of the Jewish nation. The conceptual unity of mankind arises from the transcendental aspect of the divine. The uniqueness of the Jewish people arises from the immanent aspect of the divine. So the universal and the particular, the transcendental and the immanent, are combined in the Israeli flag.

SYNAGOGUE FACILITIES

Outside the sanctuary, many synagogues have a giftshop with books and ritual objects for sale. All synagogues have a library, and some have a small museum. All this will be closed when you are there for Shabbat services. However, some artwork may be visible.

Most synagogues have a function room where food can be served, and many have a kitchen. Synagogues sometimes have an associated school, and always have educational programs. In some larger communities, the synagogue may take on the character of a "community center" with sports facilities.

Notes

1. c.f., Daniel 6:11; I Kings 8:30 and 8:48; II Chronicles 6:26, 6:32, and 6:34; Sifre Deuteronomy Piska 29; Mishnah Berachot 4:5–6; Talmud Berachot 31a and 34b.

2. In Northern Israel, the synagogue will face south. In Jerusalem, the synagogue will face the Temple Mount.

3. This is rare in America. But it was common in parts of Europe where Jews were forced by law to live in small overcrowded walled-in ghettos. (Three magnificent examples of synagogues in multi-story buildings can still be seen in Venice, in the original ghetto.)

4. c.f., R. Moshe Isserles' gloss on Shulchan Aruch Orach Chayim 150.5; Tosefta Megillah 4:21; R. Yosef Karo in *Kesef Mishnah* to Rambam's *Hilchot Tefilah* 11:3.

5. It also emphasizes the democratic nature of Judaism. Whoever is leading the service is representing the congregation of which he is a member and in whose midst he stands. And it indicates that the Torah (which is read from the *bima*) is equally the possesion of every Jew.

6. c.f., Talmud Sotah 40a; Tosefta Megilla 4:21; Yosef Karo "Kesef Mishneh" to Hilchot T'fillah 11:3; Moshe Isserles on Shulchan Aruch Orah Chayim 150.5; The Hafetz Chayim "Biur Halacha" Tomeich ka-Halacha v.1 p.4.

This innovation often promotes cantors who act like they are performing for an audience rather than praying with, and on behalf of, a congregation; and congregations of staid nonparticipants who watch the cantor's "performance," rather than interacting with the cantor's improvisation.

7. by virtue of the presence of a quorum, called a "minyan."

8. c.f., Talmud Ta-anit 16a.

9. According to some scholars, it symbolized the planetary motions, and embodied a notion that the Shechina (Divine Pres-

ence) was represented by the west-southwest direction. The Menorah appeared as a symbol on ancient Jewish coins. The Arch of Titus in Rome shows him carrying off the Menorah along with other spoils of the second Temple. References to the Menorah in the siddur are sometimes a metaphor for the seven continents (i.e., all the world's inhabitants). This occurs in the ritual for donning *t'fillin*.

The classical sources for a study of the Menorah are: Exodus 25:31 and 27:20, Leviticus 24:2–4, Numbers 8:2, Nehemiah 9:6, Josephus Anitiquities III:144, Philo Moses II:102–3, Mishnah Tamid 3:10 and 10:2; Sifre Numbers LIX:I to LXI:I; Talmud Shekalim 24b, Megillah 21b, Menachot 98a-b, Rosh Hashana 24a-b, Avodah Zarah 43a-b; Beraita d'Melechet ha-Mishkan X:65, Sifre on Numbers 59, Tosafot Menachot 11:8, Numbers Rabbah 12:16 and 15:5, Rashi to Numbers 8:2, and Rambam on Mishnah Tamid 3:9 and 6:1.

10. There is a nine-branched candelabrum that is lit on *Chanukah*. It is properly called a *Chanukiah*, but most Jews colloquially call it a *"Chanukah menorah,"* or "menorah." It is not actually related to the menorah.

11. c.f., Exodus 27:20–21; Leviticus 24:2–4; Sifre Numbers 59.

12. As described in Exodus 14:21–22, 25:16–17, 33:15, and 40:34–38; and Numbers 9:15–23.

13. In actuality, universal acceptance of the six-pointed star as a symbol of Judaism is a twentieth-century phenomenon. Its widespread association with David's shield begins in the eighteenth century. It entered Judaism by way of superstition, magic, and mysticism, in which pentagrams and hexagrams had always been powerful protective symbols. Its original use on Jewish banners stems from fourteenth century Prague, where the star surrounded a representation of the peculiar hat that discriminatory laws required Jews to wear. The banner symbolized the royal protection that the Holy Roman Emperor extended to the Jewish community of Prague. Pentagrams and hexagrams about discriminatory Jewish hats were similarly used later in other communities. By the seventeenth century, the star had been adopted by the Jews of Prague as the symbol of their community and as the Shield of David. It spread from Prague to Vienna, and with the expulsion

of the Jews from Vienna, it reached the rest of Europe and Russia. The first juxtaposition of the star with the cross, as comparative symbols of two communities, was in the seventeenth century. It first became a widespread symbol of Judaism itself in nineteenth century Germany. (c.f., *The Magen David*, by Gunther Plaut, published by B'nai B'rith, 1991.)

14. c.f., Exodus 28:17–21; Exodus Rabbah 38:8–9; Numbers Rabbah 2:7.

15. Levi got no territiory, but Joseph's sons Ephraim and Mennashe separated, so there were still twelve territories. In lists that exclude Yosef and Levi in favor of Ephraim and Mennashe, Ephraim is associated with striped onyx and Mennashe with yellow topaz.

16. The biblical passages at Exodus 20:2–14 and Deuteronomy 5:6–18 are popularly, but innaccurately called "The Ten Commandments." According to some traditional Jewish commentaries, the plain meaning of the text contains only nine commandments. Other traditional Jewish commentaries demonstrate (via complex textual analysis) that these passages can be understood as a "shorthand" notation containing all six hundred thirteen commandments.

The Hebrew term for these passages is "*Aseret HaDibrot*." This can be translated as "The Ten Utterances" or "The Ten Things" (or more idomatically as "The Ten Statements"). Thus the best English word for them is The Decalogue, which comes from Greek for "Ten Utterances."

In any case, the traditional Jewish view is that the whole Torah was divinely revealed to Moses at Sinai. Therefore every commandment, word, and even letter, of Torah is of infinite, hence equal, importance. Thus the Decalogue is not more important than any other part of Torah.

The most ancient form of *K'riyat Sh'ma* (Recitation of the *Sh'ma*) stood on its own as a separate liturgical event. Two thousand years ago, this liturgy consisted of the Decalogue and the *Sh'ma* together; with a blessing before and after (c.f., Josephus, Antiquities 4:8:13; Mishnah Tamid 5:1).

At that time, the focus of the *Sh'ma* was love for divine service. Reciting the Decalogue was the primary daily ceremony of covenental renewal. So *t'fillin* may have functioned as early prayer-books. The presence of the Decalogue is also hinted at by a line in *Ahavat Rabbah*, which may have been the blessing preceding the Decalogue/Sh'ma pair at that time.

By late Tannaitic times (i.e., the third century, c.e.), the Decalogue had been removed from the liturgy. (c.f, Yerushalmi Berachot 1:5 [venice 3c, vilna 9a] and 1:8 [3c, 9b]; Bavli Berachot 12a; and Bavli Tamid 35a.)

This may have been done to support the authority of the entire Torah against claims from some non-pharasaic sects that only the Decalogue had come from Sinai; and/or to challenge the later claims of the Church, which sought to invalidate all of the Torah except for the Decalogue. The traditional Jewish view is that every commandment, word, and even letter, of Torah is of infinite, hence equal, importance.

Many Protestant Christian denominations still believe that the Torah is no longer valid, except for "The Ten Commandments." This belief is what the Catholic Church calls the "Doctrine of Supercessionalism." The current Catholic view, which is relatively new, rejects this doctrine, and recognizes it as a primary cause of antisemitism. According to the Catholic view, Torah is not needed by faithful Christians because Christians enjoy an ability to fulfill God's will in a new and surprising way: a covenant based on their faith, as transmitted to and interpreted by Christians. But according to the new Catholic theology, the original covenant between God and Jews is also a loving gift of divine grace and remains effective. So the Torah, as transmitted to and interpreted by Jews, still represents a viable way for Jews to fulfill God's will. With this declaration, Catholicism has quietly taken a giant leap forward for humankind.

The struggle to maintain the authority of the Torah as opposed to just the Decalogue may also have affected the *Amidah* Section. On Sabbath morning, the Sanctification of the Day (the benediction that replaces the thirteen intermediate petitions of the weekday *Amidah*) extolls Sabbath observance as a sign of the covenant. The introduction begins:

> Moses rejoiced at the lot assigned . . .
> a faithful servant . . .
> He brought down the two tablets of stone
> on which was written the observance of the Sabbath,
> as it says in your Torah: . . .

The most logical biblical prooftext might seem to be to quote the Decalogue: "Remember the Sabbath day to keep it holy." But *V'sha-m'ru* was chosen instead. This careful demotion of the Decalogue seems deliberate.

Without the Decalogue, the *Sh'ma* section was reoriented over time. (c.f., Mishnah Berachot 2:2; Yerushalmi Berachot 1.8.3c.) The attendant blessings gained insertions related to accepting the yoke of heaven. For example:

> *Ga-al Yisraeil* (c.f., page 000) acquired The Song at the Sea, reenacting ancient Israel's acceptance. (c.f., Tosefta Berachot 2, 1; Tosefta Berachot 1,10; Yerushalmi Berachot 1.9.3; Bavli Berachot 14b)
> *Yo-tseir Or* (c.f., page 000) gained a modified *K'dushah*, reenacting the angelic acceptance.
> And reciting the first line of the *Sh'ma* publicly represented contemporary Israel's acceptance. (c.f., page 000)

As a result of this transformation, reciting the *Sh'ma* in a congregational service is often referred to as "accepting the yoke/kingship of heaven" in ancient literature, and is still thought of that way. (c.f., Shulchan Aruch, Orach Chayim 70:1)

Generally, the places in the *Sh'ma* Section where the reader and congregation break silence and chant antiphonally are exactly those passages that affirm allegiance. (c.f., Philo, Contemplative Life 88; Tosefta Sotah 6, 2–3; Bavli Chullin 91b; Deuteronomy Rabbah 2, 31; Tosefta Pesachim 2, 19).

(For a detailed description of the excision of the Decalogue from the service, see *The Shema and its Blessings: The Realization of God's Kingship*, by Reuven Kimmelman, an essay contained in *The Synagogue in Late Antiquity*, edited by Lee I. Levine, a centennial publication of the Jewish Theological Seminary of America.)

17. Star Trek's use of the Jewish ritual is not coincidental. Leonard Nimoy, the actor that portrayed the original Vulcan, Mr. Spock, got his first acting jobs in Yiddish Theater, and has been *Baal Koreh* (Torah reader) at his synagogue.

18. As per Deuteronomy 8:7–10. (The "honey" of the Bible is date syrup, not bee honey. Samson's riddle is an exception.)

19. As per *Pirke Avot* 5:23.

20. The Meanings of "Israel":

Hebrew	English	Refers to:
Yisroel	Israel	the Jewish People.
B'nei Yisroel	The Children of Israel	the Jewish People (with emphasis on shared past)
Am Yisroel	The People Israel	the Jewish People (with emphasis on shared national destiny)
Beit Yisroel	The House of Israel	the Jewish People (with emphasis on our interdependence)
Eretz Yisroel	The Land of Israel	a geographical place name; the eternal property (though not the possession) of the Jewish People.
Medinat Yisroel	The State of Israel	a modern political state; located on a small portion of Eretz Yisroel and some land that is outside Eretz Yisroel; sometimes depicted as a secular democratic local state (that happens to have a Jewish majority), and at other times as a Jewish state (the political expression of world Jewry).

Jewish Worship

STUDY AS WORSHIP

The Jewish people have built Temples twice. The first was built by Solomon about the tenth century B.C.E. It was destroyed by the Babylonians in 576 B.C.E. The second was built on the same site in 444 B.C.E., and was destroyed by the Romans in 70 C.E.[1] Both times, the destruction created a dilemma. Our ancient sages disagreed over how to worship in the absence of the Temple. Some suggested study. Others suggested prayer. At first, the idea of worship through study might seem strange. But the sages regarded worship as bidirectional. Somehow, the Temple processes included communication in both directions. Therefore study (i.e., listening to God) was as likely as prayer (i.e., addressing God) to be the essence of worship.

These two forms of worship have been equal partners, and central to Jewish culture, for millenia. Study as a form of worship appears at several points in synagogue services.[2]

And the Jewish preoccupation with study is not limited to the fixed liturgical settings.

FIXED PRAYERS

While individuals can pray spontaneously anywhere, Judaism also has fixed prayers for specific circumstances. These circumstances occur all day long, so fixed prayer is not limited to congregational services. All fixed prayers follow the same formula, whether said in an individual or congregational setting. Knowing the formula makes it easier to follow along with the synagogue service. (This formula applies to the prayers only, and has nothing to do with singing the many hymns and psalms that are part of the service.)

The formula is called a "benediction" in English, or a *"b'racha"* in Hebrew. Colloquially, it is often called a "blessing." (Technically, "blessings" are actually the boons we experience—which are often appreciated, or hoped for, through benedictions.)

All fixed prayers end with a climactic formal statement, called a *"chatima."* This usually summarizes the primary idea of what has been said. It may help you pick the primary idea from several that have been mentioned in passing. Or it may help you recognize the central idea that relates the preceding thoughts to each other. Some very brief fixed prayers consist only of the *chatima*.

A *chatima* is a single sentence. It begins with: *"Baruch atah Adonai . . ."*[3] which is often translated as an accolade, "Blessed (are) You, Lord, ..." This is followed by a specific ending, depending on the function of the prayer.

In addition to having a concluding *chatima*, all fixed prayers are supposed to begin with: *"Baruch atah Adonai, Eloheinu Melech Ha-olam, . . ."* The second phrase means "Our God, King of the Universe."[4] But when a series of fixed prayers occur in succession, only the first one begins this way. The rest can drop the opening. So we frequently encounter[5] structures like this:

Three Fixed Prayers in a Row:

1. *Baruch atah Adonai,*   Blessed art Thou, Lord,
   Eloheinu melech ha-olam,   Our God, King of the Universe,
   .... [topic of first prayer starts]
   ....
   ....
   Baruch atah Adonai,   Blessed art Thou, Lord,
   .... [one line summary]

2. .... [new topic starts]
   ....
   ....
   Baruch atah Adonai,   Blessed art Thou, Lord,
   .... [one line summary]

3. .... [new topic starts]
   ....
   ....
   Baruch Atah Adonai,   Blessed art Thou, Lord,
   .... [one line summary]

Examples of prayers using this structure: *Birkat HaMazon, Amidah,* blessings after *Haftarah,* blessings attendant on the *Sh'ma.* (For discussions of these prayers, see pages 30, 102, 247, and 148, respectively.)

The formula described above is reserved for the fixed prayers. Personal prayers do not use this formula. Personal prayers typically begin with phrases like "Our Father . . ." "Master of the World . . ." or "May it be your will . . ." They address God in the second person, and contain references to the worshipper, such as "I" and "my."

"*Baruch*" is also commonly translated as: "Praised (are),"

or "Worshipped (are)"[6], which still makes the sentence an accolade. But the blessing can also be understood as an imperative, because *Baruch* could be taken to mean: "Increase," "Expand," or "Intensify." We actually direct the divine to magnify its influence. This gives the blessing new significance as a statement: The involvement of goodness in the world depends on people dedicated to maximizing it. When we say that God is "blessed," "praised," or "worshipped," we are not describing a situation. We are acting upon reality, taking a small step in the transformation of the world.

> R. Simeon ben Yochai says: A parable: A man bought two ships, tied them to anchors and iron weights, stationed them in the middle of the sea, and built a palace upon them. As long as the two ships are tied to each other, the palace stands firm. Once the ships are separated, the palace cannot stand. . . . Similarly scripture says: *This is my God, and I will glorify Him* (Exodus 15:2)—when I acknowledge Him, He is glorious, but when I do not acknowledge Him, He is [not] glorious, if one may say such a thing—*For I will proclaim the name of the Lord; ascribe ye greatness unto our God* (Deuteronomy 32:3)—when I proclaim His Name, He is great, but when I do not, [He is not great,] if one may say such a thing—*Therefore ye are my witnesses, saith the Lord, and I am God* (Isaiah 43:12)—when you are My witnesses, I am God, but when you are not My witnesses, I am not God, if one may say such a thing—*Unto Thee I lift up my eyes, O Thou that art enthroned in the heavens* (Psalms 123:1)—were it not for me, Thou would not be enthroned in the heavens, if one may say such a thing.
>
> excerpt from *Sifre Deuteronomy*, Piska 346
> (the earliest extant commentary on Deuteronomy)
> translated by Reuven Hammer,
> published by Yale University Press, 1986.

Reconsider the formula used to begin every fixed prayer, paying close attention to the second phrase:

Baruch atah Adonai,	Blessed art Thou, Lord,
Eloheinu melech ha-olam, . . .	Our God, King of the Universe, . . .

The word "*olam,*" translated here as "universe," refers to time as well as space. The specificity of modern English words requires that "*olam*" be imperfectly translated as either "eternity" or "universe." Sometimes the context suggests one or the other, but often both are meant. The modern physicist's word, "space-time," would be a most accurate translation, but more confusing than inspiring for many worshippers. Thus the phrase could be translated: "Sovereign of Space-Time." A title more transcendent over material reality would be difficult to imagine.

Similarly extreme is the first half of the phrase, namely "Our God." The only more immanent title imaginable would be "My God," but we shall see later that Jews do not recite fixed prayers in the singular, only in the plural.

Therefore the two halves of the second phrase, "Our God" and "King of the Universe," stress two diametrically different aspects of the divine, the national and the universal, and assert their unity by their juxtaposition. The unity of the immanent and the transcendental will be a common motif in Jewish worship.

When an act is being performed in fulfillment of commandment, the benediction preceding the act has a third phrase in its opening: ". . . *a-sher kid-sha-nu b'mitz-vo-tav, v'tzi-va-nu* . . ." This means, ". . . who makes us holy by His commandments, and commanded us to . . ." We encountered an example of this when we discussed putting on a *tallis* (on page 43).

Benedictions of this kind are most frequently encountered as preparation for performing certain actions which involve the use of ritual objects. The popular names of these benedictions often make it seem as though the food or ritual objects are being blessed by us. For example: "the blessing over wine," "blessing the candles," etc. Such names are misnomers. The text of the benediction makes it explicit that it is we who are sanctified by the rite, through which we experience our holiness. The status of the food or the ritual object is not materially transformed in any way. We are transformed.

On the other hand, Jewish mystical perspective suggests that, by revealing any object's potential for use in divine service, we have elevated it. This process will be described in more detail later (on page 178).

Notes

1. c.e. stands for "Common Era," and "b.c.e." stands for "Before the Common Era." Non-Christians (and many Christian scholars) specify Gregorian dates in this fashion.

This avoids the theological and historical problems associated with the terms "*Anno Domini*" which means 'The Year of [the reign of] Our Lord,' and "b.c." which means 'Before the Anointed.' ('Christos' is Greek for 'Anointed'.)

At best, a.d. and b.c. are inaccurate terms, since the Gregorian year one doesn't actually correspond to the birth or death of the man anointed by Church tradition. And at worst, these terms may offend non-Christians, since they presuppose a theology not shared by all who must, for practical reasons, use the Gregorian numbering system.

From a Jewish perspective, every year since creation is another 'year of the reign of our Lord,' and our current years are also 'before the Anointed.'

2. c.f., The Talmud Torah section and the *Korbanot* Section of the Preliminary Morning Service (daily), the *K'riat Torah* Sec-

tion (four times a week), and sometimes the Sh'ma (only when started before sundown). These liturgical events are all discussed later.

3. taken from Psalm 119:12.

4. taken from Jeremiah 10:10.

5. See for example: the *Amidah*, the Blessings after Haftarah Reading, *Birkat Ha-Mazon*, etc.

6. as used at Psalm 95:6.

Congregational Prayer

Under Jewish law (halacha), prayer can be "congregational" or not. Prayers become "congregational" when a specified minimum attendance is achieved or exceeded. The Hebrew term for "congregational prayer" is *T'fi-lah b'Tsibur*. The minimum attendance required for "congregational prayer" is ten "Men of Duty" (Bar Mitzvah; literally "Son of Commandment"). This quorum is called a "minyan." (Ten is the number of righteous men that would have justified saving the communities of Sodom and Gomorrah as the result of Abraham's negotiation with God. Ten is also the number of men who caused the forty years of wandering in the wilderness.[1])

In all Reform synagogues, and in most Conservative synagogues, women now are counted to "make a minyan." It seldom makes a difference at Sabbath services, since those communities tend to build large synagogues. The congregation usually gets far more than a minyan with no difficulty. (Large synagogues also mean that most congregants can't expect to be called up to participate, which is an honor.) But many communities have problematic "close-calls" on weekdays.

Under Jewish law (halacha), congregational prayer has special significance. In this setting, a person who does not know how to pray can listen to the reader and respond "*A-mein*" after each benediction. "A-mein" signifies agreement[2], and corresponds to "amen" in English. One does not say "A-mein" after reciting a blessing, only after listening to one. Halachically, it is the same as if they were praying themselves. The presence of the community enables the individual to pray effectively. (In addition, there are certain prayers that can only be said when a minyan is present.[3])

Thus it is a *mitzvah* (good deed) to go out of your way to help make a minyan when a group needs help reaching ten. This typically happens at the homes of mourners, or occasionally in synagogue on weekday mornings. If you are a member of a synagogue, you can expect occasional "minyan calls." This is like jury duty.

Jewish tradition emphasizes congregational prayer in glowing terms:[4]

> "When a one leaves the synagogue, one should not take hasty steps . . . but in coming, it is right to run."[5]
>
> When an individual prays, God sees the faults of the individual; when the community prays, God sees the merits of the community.[6]
>
> "One who does not pray in the synagogue of one's own town is called a bad neighbor."[7]
>
> "In a community of not less than ten, one makes up for the forgetfulness or error of the other."[8]
>
> It is good luck to be the tenth at a minyan.[9]
>
> "The prayer of the community is always heard."[10]
>
> "Nine *tsaddikim* (saintly men) cannot make a minyan, but if one common man joins them, he completes the minyan."[11]
>
> Even when praying alone, one benefits from praying simultaneously with one's community.[12]

When you go to services, you will notice three recurring patterns that reflect this emphasis on community.

PERSONAL PETITIONS ARE
NOT MADE INDIVIDUALLY

All fixed prayers are in the plural. Even when praying alone, a Jew says prayers in the plural. For example, when a sick person recites a prayer for healing, they do not say, "make me well." They say "heal the sick." Furthermore, everyone recites such prayers, even when they are not affected. A Jew is always part of the community. Even if a particular prayer doesn't apply to oneself, there are others for whom the prayer does apply.[13]

COMMUNAL BENEDICTIONS

When fixed prayers are sung in the context of congregational prayer, the congregation prays communally by relying on the reader. You will recognize this pattern after hearing it a few times.

Prior to reaching the *cha-ti-ma* (the climactic formal concluding statement[14]), the reader may be chanting the prayer solo. Or the congregation may be praying "silently" (actually quietly mumbling independently). In either case, the reader chants the climactic *cha-ti-ma* aloud and solo. The reader says: "*Ba-ruch A-tah A-do-nai. . . .*" The congregation then interjects: "*Ba-ruch [hu u-v'ruch] Sh'mo*" which means "Blessed [is he and blessed] is his Name." Then the reader completes the benediction with its specific ending, depending on the function of the prayer, and the congregation sings "*A-mein.*" This is the classic form of "congregational prayer."

It is important to understand that, in very traditional synagogues, all Jews follow this formula even though most know how to recite the blessings themselves (and many are comfortable leading the service as reader). Otherwise, someone's lack of learning might be exposed by reliance upon the communal formula. This could cause public shame, or even discourage someone from joining in future communal prayer. So everyone constrains themselves to saying "a-mein" (or repeating the words after the reader sings them).[15]

In modern times, the congregation is often singing along with the beginning of the prayer, but stops singing before reaching the *cha-ti-ma*. Many synagogue melodies take this into account, with the cadence coming just before the *cha-ti-ma*. A less traditional modern practice is to have the congregation read an English adaptation of the prayer aloud, and then have the reader sing just the *cha-ti-ma*.

THE SOUND OF "NU"[16]

To understand the third pattern, we will need to look at Hebrew grammar. Hebrew is brief and condensed. Example: "*Ein Keloheinu*" means "There is none like our God." ("Ein" rhymes with Spain.)

The core of a Hebrew word is in the middle, surrounded by a prefix and/or suffix. When you see a Hebrew word that has a long English translation, look at the middle part for a key to the central idea. Here is a table of a few Hebrew prefixes and suffixes:

Prefixes:		*Suffixes:*	
H	this, the	Y	mine, my
B	in, on	Cha	yours, your (singular)
K	like	O	his
Ch	like	Nu	our (attached to noun)
L	to	Nu	us (attached to verb)
M	from	Chem	your (plural)
V	and, but, so		
U	and		

Look again at "Keloheinu," and you'll now see: "K-Elohei-Nu" = "like our God." (There are no words for "is" in Hebrew. "Ein" means "none"). In Hebrew, consonants and vowels are not of equal importance. In prefixes and in root words, vowels may change according to complex rules of grammar. This does not change the meanings of words. But consonants and vowel suffixes are decisive.

In synagogue, you will notice that the sound "*nu*" ("noo") permeates the atmosphere of the liturgy. This is more than a point of grammar. It is a Jewish ethnic and ethical message— an assertion of our mutual interdependence. The life and hopes of the individual are intertwined with those of the community.

Jewish prayers are full of "we" and "our." There are very few instances of "I" or "my" in the prayer book. It is nearly all communal prayer aimed at effecting visible transformations in the world. This is very different from classical Christian tradition, which emphasizes a personal salvation evidenced by an inner transformation. We speak more frequently of "our" God than of "my" God. Jewish prayer comes mostly from the Jewish community.

HOW TO COUNT A MINYAN

Jewish tradition prohibits counting Jews. So rather than pointing at people and counting to ten, an attractive mechanism has developed for determining if you have a minyan. You recite (or sing) Psalm 28:9, allocating one word for each person that you see:

Ho-<u>shi</u>-a et a-<u>me</u>-cha,	*Save your people,*
u-va-reich et na-ha-la-<u>te</u>-cha,	*Bless your inheritance,*
u-r'eim v'na-s'eim ad ha-o-lam.	*Tend them and uplift them for ever.*

This song has ten words. If you can successfully complete it then there is a minyan.[17]

STANDING AND SITTING

At certain points in the service, the congregation (or a specific part of the congregation) will stand or sit.[18] This will often catch a newcomer by surprise. Many of these points in the service are not labeled in most prayerbooks. They are noted in the following discussion of the structure of the liturgy. But there may still be minor variations in local custom. Be alert.

In traditional synagogues, many Jews pray semi-independently, and will stand or sit based on their own progress rather than the congregation's. So if you find yourself out of phase with the rest of the congregation, don't panic. You can calmly alter your posture without embarassment.

When the congregation is reciting a prayer that requires standing, you need not stand unless you are actually participating in that prayer. You may always elect to stand when the congregation stands even if you are not worshipping. There are only three exceptional events that require standing by all present (excluding health-related limitations). These are when a Torah scroll is being carried, when the summons to public assembly (the *Bar'chu*) is recited, and when the *K'dushah* is recited. These liturgical events are described in detail later (on pages 234, 159, and 119, respectively).

SEATING

It is traditional for Jews to adopt a fixed place for their daily prayer. This regularity in their ritual helps them achieve proper meditative intent (*kavannah*). They will take the same seat every day. If you do not come regularly, and a disappointed expression on someone nearby makes you think that you might be occupying another person's regular place, ask if this is so and offer to move.

WOMEN AND CONGREGATIONAL PRAYER

Since halacha (Jewish law) only requires fixed congregational prayer of men, the nature of male and female obligations in prayer are different. This results in different practices at different synagogues. (Classical Reform theology rejects the concept of halachic obligation. Reconstructionist theology values halacha but considers it nonbinding. Orthodox and Conservative theologies acccept the sovereignty of halacha but apply the law and legal precedents differently in rendering decisions.)

At nearly all services in Orthodox *shuls*, women do not lead the service as reader and do not chant Torah. In all Reconstructionist congregations, nearly all Reform synagogues, and in the great majority of Conservative synagogues, the women participate in the same manner as the men. The derivations of these practices, and the parts of the service that are exceptions to these practices, are discussed in note 19.

NON-JEWS AND CONGREGATIONAL PRAYER

Non-Jews that are visiting a synagogue are welcome to participate in any of the prayers whenever they wish. Most non-Jews will find that many Jewish prayers express thoughts they can affirm despite being expressed in an unfamiliar idiom.

Non-Jews should wear a head covering in accordance with local custom, but should neither wear a *tallis* (prayer shawl) nor *t'fillin* (phylacteries). Non-Jews should not permit themselves to be counted toward a minyan (prayer quorum).

The rules for standing and sitting are the same for non-Jews as for Jews. When a particular prayer requires all its reciters to stand, non-Jews that elect to recite it should stand. Non-Jews may elect to stand when the congregation stands even if they are not participating in the prayer. Usually, this is the most comfortable option. The three events[20] that require all to stand (even if not reciting) also expect non-Jews to stand.

THE BIBLICAL ANTECEDENTS
TO CONGREGATIONAL PRAYER

All of us have experienced the feeling that we are not what we should be. We often fail to live up to our own expectations. We are not always at peace with the source of our fundamental values.

Sometimes people respond to this experience by surrendering something of value in an effort to restore intimacy between themselves and their values. The greater the value surrendered the more effective the reconciliation. In many ancient societies one's firstborn male offspring (a key part of one's own posterity) was of the highest value. In some pagan societies, this was surrendered if the gulf between self-image and ideal warranted such drastic surrender. The key component in this sacrifice was not in the killing, but rather in the act of great sacrifice. The Bible doesn't ascribe to the ancient Israelites a system that normally did this. But we do know that prior to the revolutionary events at Sinai, the first-born sons served as the priests of their clans.[21] They were thought of as having been given up, donated to the service of God.

When Moses instituted the sweeping changes mandated at Sinai, he not only taught new laws, installed a new judiciary system, switched to a new calendar, commenced a war on paganism, and so on. He also revealed a new system of social administration and divine service. Henceforth, Moses's own tribe (the Levites) would be the administration, and his own clan (headed by the oldest brother, Aaron, as its patriarch) would be the priests.[22]

The firstborn sons of the Israelites (when they reached the standard age of viability for newborns, which was one month) would be "redeemed" by paying money. This supported those who would now perform the services that the firstborn sons had "owed" in the past. This new system was adopted in memory of the slain Egyptians. The ritual known as *Pid-yon Ha-Ben* (The Redemption of the Firstborn) is still observed (and Jewish firstborns still fast on the day before Passover). The Redemption of the Firstborn was just one way that the new social administration was supported. Tithes[23] and sacrifices were additional ways, but were not new ways.

Most modern people have misconceptions about the sacrificial system. Most sacrifices did not involve an animal. Donors brought fleece, gold, incense, wagons, silver, votive offerings, and useful objects. Donors also brought fruits, vegetables, grain, dough, wine, and oil. These objects and foods were all put to use. In early times the foods were "waved" (offered symbolically) and then eaten. In later times, a token amount was burned before using the rest. In both cases, the participants thought of this as "sharing," an act of self-sacrifice. The subsequent joint use established communion with the other participants and with God.

There were also sacrifices of rams, bulls, goats, sheep, pigeons, and turtledoves. The climactic point of most animal sacrifices was the eating of the offering. The offerings were not wasted.[24] Priests and Levites had to eat.[25] In that time and place, this meant that animals were going to be donated and slaughtered. The rituals transformed what might have been a routine necessity into a source of spiritual and ethical elevation (just as *kashrut* transforms today's methods of food production, preparation, and eating into an effective tool for improvement).

There is no Hebrew word having the same connotation as the English word, "victim." The Hebrew word for a sacrificial offering is *korban*. This comes from a Hebrew root[26] meaning "to come closer [to God]." The plural of *korban* is *korbanot*. The donor's selfless contribution of a *korban* transformed the donor. By participating in the ritual, or in the maintenance of the system, the donor expressed repentance concretely, contemplated the meaning of his life and deeds, sensed himself to be a part of divine plan, and (hopefully) experienced atonement (the reconciliation of who we feel we are with who we feel we should be).

Another common misconception is to view the sacrificial process as some sort of exorcism, wherein some moral infirmity is carried off by the "victim." This is based upon a modern confusion between the Jewish concept of ritual purity (preparedness to participate in Temple rites) and non-Jewish notions of moral failure as a condition of being.[27] In Judaism, no ritual is efficacious in and of itself. The donor's act (and intent), not an animal's death, is paramount. Therefore there was no vicarious sacrifice. One could not bring a *korban* on behalf of another individual.

Some offerings were voluntary while others were required. Some offerings were communal while others were individual. Some were recurring while others were occasional. Some were penalties, like a combination of paying a fine and performing community service. But sacrifices were only available for involuntary or inadvertant transgression. Deliberate acts were not atoned for by sacrifices. And atonement required the reversal of any material effects of the transgression (to the extent possible) prior to the bringing of a sacrifice as the final step.

Thus participation in the sacrificial system had elements of our modern income tax, voluntary contributions to reduce the national debt, community service, fellowship, and patriotism.

But primarily, the sacrificial system fulfilled precisely the same need that is now fulfilled for pious people by prayer and Bible study and alms-giving. When we understand this, we understand what the loss of the Temple, in 586 B.C.E., meant to us. Imagine all prayer and Bible and alms-giving suddenly removed from the world. Our sages lived through that. In response to this loss, and based upon the characteristics of the "Service of the Altar," they constructed Jewish congregational prayer.

Notes

1. c.f., Bereshit Rabbah 24:13, and Numbers 13–14, respectively. See also: Exodus 18:21, Ruth 4:2, Nedarim 3a, Kiddushin 9b, Mishnah Megillah 4:3, Megillah 23b, Yerushalmi Berachot 7:3.

2. c.f., Sifre Deuteronomy Piska 320, "R. Dostai ben Judah says. . .".

3. c.f., Mishnah Berachot 4:3, 4:7; Mishnah Megillah 4:3; Yerushalmi Berachot 7:3; Bavli Berachot 21b, Megilah 23b, Sanhedrin 74b; Shulchan Aruch Orach Chayim 55:1; Mishneh Berurah Orach Chayim 55:2, 5, and 6.

The parts of the service that are omitted when a minyan is lacking include: the *Bar'chu*, the Kaddish, the Torah-reading and *Haftarah*, the repetition of the *Amidah*, and the benediction after the *Amidah* on Friday nights.

4. Talmud Berachot 47b; Mishnah Megillah 1:3 and T. Megillah 21b.

5. Talmud Berachot 6b.

6. c.f., Lamentations Rabbah 3:8; Sifre Deuteronomy Piska 27.

7. Talmud Berachot 8a.

8. Judah Ha-Levy, The Kuzari, 3:19.

9. a superstition from Eastern European Jewry.

10. Rambam, Mishneh Torah, Laws of Prayer 8:1.

11. Rabbi Nachman of Bratslav.

12. The Talmudic source is Berachot 8a, at the top of the page: "What is the meaning of the verse, *Let my prayer be . . . in an acceptable time* (Psalm 69:14)? When is the time acceptable? When the congregation prays."

Evidence that this advice was observed in practice is found in Deuteronomy Rabbah II,12; Josephus Against Apion 2:23; Judith 9:1; and in Christian scripture (Luke 1:10).

13. "One who doesn't include his fellow men in his prayers is a sinner." Talmud, quoted from a note in the *Hertz* siddur.

14. c.f., page 68.

15. c.f., Mishnah Bikkurim 3:7.

16. This section is taken, with minor adaptation, from *Ayn Keloheinu* by Noah Golinken, published by Sheingold Publishers, 1981.

17. Some congregations use Psalm 5:8 as an alternative:

Va-a-ni,	As for me,
b'rov chas-d'cha	through Your kindness
a-vo vei-te-cha,	I will come to Your House.
esh-ta-cha-veh, el hei-chal kawd-sh'cha,	I will bow to Your holy Sanctuary,
b'yir-a-te-cha.	in awe of You.

18. The chart below is for reference only. The parts of the service listed in it are not expected to be familiar yet.

STANDING & SITTING

All Stand:

The *Bar'chu* (The Summons to Public Assembly)

Whenever a dressed Torah scroll is being carried (e.g., The Announcement of the New Month, or the Procession)

The *K'dushah* (The Third Benediction of the Repetition of the Amidah)

Worshippers Stand:

The Half-Kaddish and The Full Closing Kaddish (except in some Sephardic congregations)

The silent *Amidah* and the first three blessings of the reader's repetition

Psalm 29 (*Hodu L'adonai*), Psalm 100 (*Mizmor L'Todah*), and Psalm 136

On Friday night: *V'sha-m'ru*, *Va-y'chu-lu*, and the last verse of *L'cha Dodi*

Aleinu, Hallel, Yizkor

The Fifteen Morning Benedictions
Baruch She-amar and Vay'vareich David and Yishtabach (in the
    Verses of Praise)
whenever the ark is opened (e.g., Anim Z'mirot)

Variable:
Mourner's Kaddish (those already standing remain, mourners rise;
    only mourners recite)
Kaddish d'Rabbanan (all are permitted to rise and recite, but
    usually only mourners do so. Wide local variations.)
Tsur Yisraeil, or earlier, in anticipation of the coming Amidah

All Sit:
The Sh'ma, and its attendant blessings

Optional:
The rest of the service may be said in any posture, and so is usually
    said sitting

19. In Jewish law (halacha), the legal mechanism of agency
requires that the agent and the individual represented be similarly
obligated with respect to the mitzvah being discharged by the agent
on behalf of the individual. And community authorization is required to establish the mechanism of agency. In Orthodox congregational prayer, the presence of the minyan authorizes the
reader to function as agent for the community.

Since the halacha only requires congregational prayer of men,
the nature of male and female obligations in prayer are different.
Therefore neither can represent the other in a minyan or as reader.
Most Orthodox congregational prayer groups are organized as a
male minyan with women attending, although women's prayer
groups are becoming more popular. At regular services in Orthodox shuls, women do not lead the service as reader and are not
counted to make a minyan.

These considerations alone would not prevent a woman from
leading portions of the service that don't require the mechanism
of agency, such as Kabbalat Shabbat (L'chu N'ran'na through L'cha
Dodi) on Friday night.

In addition, women are not called to Torah in regular Orthodox services. The Orthodox application of tradition regards pub-

lic Torah-reading by women as being dishonorable to the congregation although legally permitted. Presumably, this originated in a period when public Torah-reading by the women would have implied that there were not enough learned men in the congregation; and may also reflect a societal aversion to putting a woman, or her solo voice, on public display before men.

Furthermore, some Orthodox communities have multiple small synagogues, and enjoy knowing that a maximum number of congregants can be called to Torah, thereby maximizing the performance of mitzvot (plural of mitzvah) within the community. Some Orthodox and some Conservative Jews (both male and female) feel that calling women up to read Torah, although potentially rewarding, deprives the community of an opportunity to fulfill a mitzvah, since public Torah-reading may be legally incumbent on the men.

This objection would not apply to women chanting *Maftir* and/ or Haftarah, nor to a woman (such as a Bat Mitzvah) chanting Torah on Saturday afternoon at *Mincha*. These events are not mitzvot. (Other objections might be raised.)

In Reform synagogues, and in the great majority of Conservative synagogues, women participate fully in the same manner as the men. And both movements have female cantors and rabbis. (Reform philosophy rejects halacha (Jewish law), Conservative applies it differently.)

In a minority of Conservative synagogues, women do not lead the service and are not called to the Torah. They are sometimes involved in other rituals, those that the men are not explicitly commanded to perform. All these rituals (male and female) are considered honors. But Reform and Conservative congregations tend to be large, so most attendees (of both sexes) actually don't get to do anything on the *bima*. Reform and Conservative congregational prayer sometimes seems less participatory and less interactive, with a greater distinction between leaders and congregants. Many attendees might not care to do anything on the *bima*. Since the Reform movement rejects halacha, men as a class don't feel deprived of an opportunity to fulfill a religious obligation when a woman is called up.

Reconstructionism rejects the concept of a supernatural deity, and regards Judaism as an evolving human civilization. The

Reconstructionist movement has made egalitarianism a major tenet of its spirituality.

Orthodox women's prayer groups use a modified liturgy that reflects uniquely feminine spirituality and respects halachic norms. Under normal circumstances, men are not permitted to attend. (For the exception, see page 37.) These prayer groups are growing in popularity.

20. See page 80.

21. c.f., Numbers 8:23–26; Sifre Numbers LXII:I to LXIII:II.

22. c.f., Numbers 3:41 and 3:44–51.

23. Tithes are divinely mandated taxes in kind, commanded explicitly in the Torah. Tithes are due from harvests and the increase of flocks, usually at the time one's actions first evidence a claim of ownership over the result. Note that the householder who planted and harvested had a divine partner who did the actual growing.

24. Even the "burnt offering" provided the priests with useful hides.

25. c.f., Numbers 5:9–10 and 6:13–20.

26. *karov*

27. *Tumah* and *taharah* are often imperfectly translated as "ritual impurity" and "ritual purity" respectively, or even as "cleanness" and "uncleanness." This causes people to confuse *tahara* with physical cleanliness or with moral purity. It is actually ritual preparedness to interface with eternity, a readinesss to experience the *Shechina* (divine presence).

The Structure of Jewish Services

THE SERVICE OF THE HEART

All Jewish services are built out of three ancient components. Each component developed separately to fulfill a different function in Jewish society. They did not occur in association with each other. They were later combined into a liturgical rite, where they remain distinct sections. The three ancient components are: *Amidah*, *K'riat Sh'ma*, and *K'riat Torah*.

The *Amidah* was the original invention of prayer as a form of worship. Liturgy and worship are not the same thing. Liturgy is a textual formula that accompanies or facilitates worship. The original Jewish form of worship was the communal maintenance of a sacrificial service—the "Service of the Altar." This was displaced by the "Service of the Heart," or prayer.[1] The *Amidah* is a liturgical formula for worship, designed to replace the sacrificial system. Its original name, *T'filah*, has become the word for "prayer." The *Amidah* is recited at the times when sacrifices would have been offered.

The *Amidah* is the core of every Jewish congregational service, and is the reason Jewish liturgical rites are called services.[2]

The *Sh'ma* is a concise statement of the central principles of Judaism. It was (and is) recited frequently by individuals on a wide variety of daily occasions. The *Sh'ma* existed even before Judaism invented the idea that the "Service of the Altar" could be replaced by the "Service of the Heart." The *Sh'ma* was not associated with the functioning of the sacrificial system. *K'riat Sh'ma* (Reciting the *Sh'ma*) is an act of dedication.

The *K'riat Torah* (public Torah reading) was the original form of democratic universal education.

The *K'riat Sh'ma*, *Amidah*, and *K'riat Torah* (representing allegience, service, and education) are the ancient building blocks now used in synagogue liturgy. But services also have a Praise Section that precedes them, and a Closing Section that follows them.

There is also a daily morning Preliminary Service, and a different preliminary service on Friday night, for Welcoming the Sabbath. Thus six different kinds of building blocks can be used to make a Jewish service. Not all services include all six sections.

The most widely attended services are Friday night and Saturday morning, since they are Sabbath services. When you go to traditional services on a Friday night or Saturday morning, you can expect to see the liturgical structures shown below:

Friday night:	*Saturday morning:*
1. Preliminary Service	1. Preliminary Service
2. Praise Section	2. Praise Section
3. *Sh'ma* Section	3. *Sh'ma* Section
4. *Amidah* Section	4. *Amidah* Section

5. Closing Section

5. Closing Section
6. Public Torah-Reading
7. Miscellaneous Community Business
8. Praise Section
9. *Amidah* Section
10. Closing Section

We shall look at each component of the service in more detail. But we will not review them in the order shown above. We shall examine them in an order designed to help you understand the structure of all services, so that you will end up with a roadmap rather than a set of directions. The differences between Friday night, Saturday morning, weekdays, holidays, mornings, afternoons, and evenings, will all fall into place logically as the result of a small consistently-applied group of ideas. To this end, we will discuss the components in the following order:

1. *Amidah* Section
2. *Sh'ma* Section
3. Praise Section
4. Preliminary Sabbath Service
5. Public Torah-Reading (and miscellaneous community business)
6. Closing Section
7. Preliminary Morning Service

We will discuss the *Amidah* Section first because the *Amidah* is common to every service, and is at the heart of every congregational service. The need to recite the *Amidah* is actually what determines the occasions of congregational services.

If you are cramming in preparation for attending a service, just read the beginning of each chapter. When you've learned enough about one section of the service, skip to the next chapter. You can always go back for more depth later.

FIVE MOODS OF JEWISH WORSHIP

Jewish worship has five different moods. The moods are:

Study	Listening to the divine; like a diligent student at work
Joy	In praise of the good; like a child extolling a parent
Statement	A reflexive act affirming an idea, securing human confirmation; like a declaration
Petition (with praise and thanks)	Daily recognition of constant needs; like an upright citizen addressing a governmental authority
Supplication	Expresses abject humility, helplessness, and despair; like dust encountering Creator

There are differing opinions on whether study or joy constitutes the closest form of communion with the transcendental.

These five moods may be expressed in many ways (e.g., reciting for purpose of memorization, dancing to express joy, crying, etc.). When these moods are expressed in litugical text, different forms of writing are used for each mood. Each liturgical text functions in one mood exclusively. Congregational liturgy changes moods from section to section.

THE STRUCTURE OF THE JEWISH SERVICE

Now we will systematically build the structure of the service. By the end of this book (and after attending services a few times), you could be a well-oriented observer at any service.

Our beginning structure is an amorphous blob:

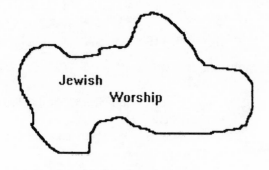

Notes

1. Psalms 141:2; Sifre Deuteronomy Piska 41.
2. *Slichot* is the exception. It's the only scheduled, fixed, con-gregational liturgical event that does not include an *Amidah*. (*Slichot* is a special midnight service in preparation for the High Holy Days, and is not discussed in this book. It consists of peni-tential poetry.)

The Amidah Section

SHACHARIT, MINCHA, AND MA-ARIV

Every Jewish service corresponds to ancient sacrificial practices prescribed in the Torah. The Torah prescribed two Temple offerings every day, one in the morning and one in the afternoon. At night, a secondary process took place on Temple grounds: The fat and leftovers from the daytime offerings were burned on the altar.

Prayer has replaced sacrifice.[1] The specific prayer to be used as the replacement was introduced about 2,400 years ago. This is called the *"Shemoneh Esreh." Shemoneh Esreh* means "Eighteen Benedictions." The *Shemoneh Esreh* is also called the *"Amidah." Amidah* means "Standing." The two names are often used interchangeably.

The *Shemoneh Esreh* is considered prayer "par excellence" on account of its importance and antiquity.[2] In fact, in ancient times, it was simply called *Tefilah* (the prayer), and was the entire conception of "prayer." It contains praise, confession, petition, and thanks.

It is said while standing, with one's feet together, facing Jerusalem.[3] (That's why it's called the "Amidah.") It is said inaudibly.[4] A low whisper or mumbling is appropriate. This is even more dramatic than the fact that all are standing. The Amidah is an easy signpost, because nothing else in the service remotely resembles several minutes of "silent" standing. Everyone recites independently. Do not interrupt someone who is reciting the Amidah.

The Shemoneh Esreh is recited in fulfillment of the commandment to "serve the Lord" in Exodus 23:25.[5] This mitzvah was originally fulfilled by the sacrificial service. The "service of the altar" was replaced by the "service of the heart." This is why Jewish liturgical events are called "services." Jews say "services" to mean "congregational prayer."

Thus observant Jews pray three times a day, and each daily service centers around the Shemoneh Esreh. The three services are called "Shacharit" (Shah-Cha-REET), "Mincha" (Meen-Cha), and "Ma-ariv" (Mah-Ah-REEV)—the morning, afternoon, and evening services. Shacharit means "of the dawn." Mincha literally means "gift." This was originally the name of the meal offering, a sacrifice of grain. It became the name for the afternoon service because a dramatic biblical event (I Kings 18:36) associates the meal offering with the afternoon. Ma-ariv is also called Ar-vit (ar-VEET), which means "of the evening." Ma-ariv means "causes to become evening," which is the key motif of the first blessing that is unique to the evening liturgy.

Because the evening process was not really a sacrifice, the evening service (Ma-ariv) did not originally include the Shemoneh Esreh. Eighteen biblical verses were recited instead.[6] The inclusion or exclusion of the Shemoneh Esreh at Ma-ariv was a subject of debate in the Talmud.[7] But by around 900 C.E., the Shemoneh Esreh had been included, although with a procedural difference. This procedural difference was a compromise, in which one side agreed to include the Shemoneh Esreh, if the other side agreed that the Shemoneh Esreh wasn't required.

This sort of compromise is typical of Jewish thought. Our sages emphasized the importance of uniformity in synagogue service. (Remember that Jews were dispersed around the globe). In order to link the people, they reconciled divergent forms of prayer. They often did this by incorporating several traditions, rather than selecting one and excluding others. We will see several examples of this.

For each of the three daily services, there is a specific time period during which the *Shemoneh Esreh* can be recited by individuals.[8] These windows of opportunity are very large. But in congregational schedules there is more regularity, resulting from practical considerations. *Shacharit* is typically said in the early morning before eating breakfast and going to work. (On days when Jews do not work, it will often start later.) *Mincha* is typically said just before sundown. *Ma-ariv* is typically said at sundown. That way, *Mincha* and *Ma-ariv* can be combined in one trip to the synagogue, by simply waiting a few minutes between them.[9] In some synagogues, this time will be occupied by a brief Torah lesson, called a "*daf.*" On Friday nights, the time is often filled by singing a song called *Yedid Nefesh*. If you show up at a synagogue on a Friday night to welcome Shabbat, and are having trouble finding your place in the service, you have probably walked in on the tail end of *Mincha*.

So now our daily liturgy looks like this:

Daily Schedule of Services

Shacharit (morning):	Mincha (afternoon):	Ma-ariv (evening):
Shemoneh Esreh	*Shemoneh Esreh*	*Shemoneh Esreh*

Although it is natural to think of the daily services in this order, Jewish calendar dates begin and end at sundown. So every holiday has a *Ma-ariv* service first, then *Shacharit* the following morning, and ends after the *Mincha* service. The Sabbath begins on Friday night and ends on Saturday night.

MUSAF (THE ADDITIONAL SERVICE)

The Torah prescribes an additional offering on Sabbaths, festivals, and other holy days. Each of these additional sacrifices have become an additional liturgical service built around an *Amidah*. The additional service is called *Musaf*.

Therefore Saturdays feature an extra service in observance of the Sabbath. Although the text of the *Shacharit* (daily morning) liturgy varies a bit on the Sabbath, it is only the *Musaf* service that is done in observance of the holy day. Because *Shacharit* and *Musaf* services are almost always combined in one trip to the synagogue, many congregants speak of Saturday morning services as though they were one service containing two *Amidah*s.

Reform congregations are an exception. They do not recite the *Musaf* service.

So now our liturgy looks like this:

Weekday:			*Shabbat:*		
Morning	Afternoon	Evening	Saturday Morning	Saturday Afternoon	Friday Evening
Shacharit	*Mincha*	*Ma-ariv*	*Shacharit*	*Mincha*	*Ma-ariv*
Amidah	Amidah	Amidah	Amidah	Amidah	Amidah
			Musaf		
			Amidah		

The above diagram shows the structure of Jewish liturgy. The left side of the diagram contains the three daily services. The components of each service are listed in a column. As we examine the internal structure of these services, and discuss additional components of the liturgy, we will expand this diagram and fill in details. The columns will lengthen. The right side of the diagram shows the Sabbath services.

Side-by-side comparison will make similarities and differences apparent, so that patterns are recognized.

THE ORIGINS OF THE AMIDAH (THE STANDING PRAYER, THE SILENT DEVOTION, *SHEMONEH ESREH*)

There is no definitive knowledge of the origin of the *Shemoneh Esreh*, but there are several competing traditions. In any case, the order of the benedictions, the general idea of each, and the exact wording of the last line of each, were not fixed until after 70 c.e.[10]

According to the RaMBaM[11] (Rabbi Moshe ben Maimon, also known as Maimonides, one of the most influential Jewish philosophers and legal codifiers of all time; lived in the twelfth century c.e.), when the First Temple (i.e., Solomon's) was destroyed (in 586 b.c.e.) the exiled Jews mixed with Persians and Greeks. The language of their children became a mixture of tongues. They could not express themselves fully and accurately in any one language. When they prayed in Hebrew, their vocabulary was too limited to articulate effective prayers. When Ezra and his council took notice of this, they instituted the *Shemoneh Esreh*. Their goal was to enable inarticulate people to pray as clearly as those who were eloquent in Hebrew. Everyone could memorize the standard blessings (and what they mean) so as to have them readily available even if unfamiliar with the language. 2,400 years later, this is still a good reason for having fixed prayers.[12]

FORGING A PERSONAL UNDERSTANDING

The same argument for standardization can be made for the entire liturgy, not just the *Shemoneh Esreh*. By breathing personal emotions and feelings (even new meanings) into the classical forms of the traditional prayers, the individual feels united with and a part of all Israel—past, present, and future. When one's voice is added to the other voices present, a give-and-take develops among the congregants, each supporting and being supported.[13]

There are as many personal ways of understanding a prayer as there are people. For each phrase of a prayer, there are many *midrashim* (homiletical textual studies) with new insights, many even conflicting with one another. By reading collections of other people's insights you get to pick and resynthesize, or create your own. And your own perceptions will not be stable over time. The only thing that remains stable is the outward form of the prayer.

This is true of the entire service and every prayer in it. In this book, descriptions of the prayers only scratch the surface. Judaism does not require or expect adherence to any particular insight or interpretation. In fact, the tradition desires the opposite. Traditionally, Jewish prayers do not have titles. They are simply referred to by their first or most distinctive words, or an objective description of their form (like the names *Shemoneh Esreh* and *Amidah*). Any title would necessarily reflect just one interpretation of the prayer, constraining the worshipper.[14]

For each prayer, this book describes at least one of the relationships that a worshipper might have with the prayer. The relationships described in this book have been chosen in the hope that they are ones that many readers will find useful in their initial way of approaching the service. In this book, all of the insights into the meanings of the prayers are taken from within the broad mainstream of the tradition, but the selection process is necessarily a personal one. Thus this book not only objectively describes the structure of the service but also subjectively describes the author's Judaism. Your Judaism will differ.

The opening words of the *Amidah* say "the God of

Abraham, the God of Isaac, and the God of Jacob," rather than "the God of Abraham, Isaac, and Jacob," because each Patriarch's approach and perception was unique. No two pathways are the same.

Many of our sages, inspired by Deuteronomy 32:2, gave diverse homiletical answers to the question, "How is Torah like rain?" One typical answer is: "Just as identical raindrops falling upon seeds cause them to grow, some red, some green, some black, and some white; so it is with Torah and people. Some become wise, others worthy, others righteous, and others pious."[15]

Here is one entry from *"Shemoneh Esreh"* by Abraham Feuer, a collection of insights on each of the benedictions:

> The introspective mood of prayer helps us discover our unique talents and qualities of character. The Talmud (Berachot 58a) observes that just as no two faces look alike, no two minds think alike. We are not meant to be clones of our forebears or carbon copies of our social peers.
>
> Rav Naftali Amsterdam once lamented to his teacher, Rav Yisrael Salanter, "If only I had the mind of the author of *Sha'agas Aryeh*; the heart of the author of the *Yesod V'Shoesh Ha'avodah*; and the sterling character of the *Rebbe* [Rav Salanter himself]!"
>
> Rav Yisrael retorted, "No, Naftali! Serve with your OWN mind; your OWN heart; your OWN character!"
>
> Four centuries ago, the Maharal of Prague [predicted] that, according to the Divine plan of history, most Jews in the pre-Messianic era will be irreligious and estranged from the Torah legacy. . . . Ultimately, these lost Jews will make independent decisions . . . to return to their heritage. This chain of events is necessary, explains the Maharal, because if all Jews would serve God only because they accepted the words of their parents, the service would be mechanical, routine, and lifeless.

God wants Israel to greet the Messiah with a level of enthusiasm that can be attained only through personal inquiry, struggle, and hard-earned discovery of the truth.

By the time an observant Jew reaches old age, he or she will have said the *Amidah* about 65,000 times. But, in a sense, a different person will have said it each time. The fixed thrice-daily liturgy can be a tool to chart a personal spiritual path. One's relationship with a text can be a measure of one's position. The evolution to different meanings, and more meanings, charts growth. The stable text is like a map.[16]

THE REPETITION OF THE AMIDAH

Although the *Amidah* is silent, it is repeated aloud by the reader. This was originally for the benefit of those who can't recite it for themselves. They can follow along with their agent, the reader, during the repetition and say "A-mein" after each benediction. The repetition enables them to fulfill their religious obligation. There is no repetition without a minyan, since it is the presence of the minyan that authorizes the reader to act as agent for the community.

Earlier I noted that the rabbis had reached a compromise, concluding that the *Amidah* was not a necessary component of *Ma-ariv* (the evening service). For this reason, there is no reader's repetition of the *Amidah* at evening services. But at *Shacharit* and *Mincha*, the entire *Amidah* is said silently first; then aloud from the beginning. The congregation might join in singing along with some parts of the reader's repetition.

If you finish the silent *Amidah* before the reader begins the repetition, you can sit down to rest. But you stand again when the repetition begins. The entire congregation sits after the third benediction of the repetition.

THE INTERNAL STRUCTURE OF THE AMIDAH

The Talmud suggests several reasons for there being eighteen blessings in the original *Amidah*.[17] God is mentioned eighteen times in the *Sh'ma*. "Abraham, Isaac, and Jacob" are mentioned eighteen times in the Tanach (Jewish Scriptures). It corresponds to the eighteen essential vertebrae in the spinal column (as it is said while standing, and is the backbone of the service). And God is mentioned eighteen times in Psalm 29 (*Havu L'Adonai*). Saadia Gaon (a great Jewish philosopher, and a leader of Jewry in the tenth century C.E.) suggested that there are eighteen prayers mentioned in the Torah and that there are eighteen festival days in the Jewish calendar. *Midrash Tanchuma*[18] (an ancient collection of insights derived from close analysis of scriptural text) cited the eighteen repetitions of the phrase "As God had commanded Moses" concerning the construction of the Tabernacle. Later, Jewish mystics associated eighteen with the word for "Life," the highest ethical value.

The *Amidah* follows a basic principle of Jewish worship: we proceed from praise, to petition, to thanks.[19] The first three blessings contain praise, the last three contain thanksgiving. The intermediate benedictions contain petitions for the most essential needs of the individual and the community.

Of the intermediate blessings, the first six relate to the needs of all individuals, the next six deal with the needs of the community. Of the first six, the first three deal with spiritual needs; the next three with material needs.

Synagogue prayers are meant to remind us of permanent fundamental values; to help us prioritize everything we perceive; to help us prepare for the complexities and ethical trials of daily life. The prayers should also motivate us to action—to effect changes in our behavior and changes in the world.

The intermediate benedictions of the *Amidah* plead for:

4 knowledge and understanding
5 the moral inspiration needed to be good
6 the ineffectuality of our past errors
7 delivering the disadvantaged from their troubles
8 health and healing of the sick
9 economic prosperity
10 reunion of the dispersed
11 establishing justice
12 suppression of tyranny
13 protection of the upright
14 rebuilding Jerusalem
15 establishing a utopia
16 the efficacy of these prayers

Note the theological progression.[20] The fulfillment of each step is a prerequisite for later steps, on a path to build a Utopia, thereby fulfilling the intent of creation, which in turn fulfills the Jewish mission. (Utopia is a modern word for the Jewish concept of a Messianic Age.)

The *Amidah* was originally written when all Jews were comfortable with anthropomorphic God-ideas, hence each benediction's standard wording is structured as a divine petition. But with each benediction, the congregation is expressing dedication to a principle, and is being inspired to undertake tasks that address the central issue of that benediction. For example, the third benediction of the middle section (numbered 6 in the list above) could enable one to admit a wrong done, and to formulate an intention and a plan to reverse its material effects. Each of the benedictions can catalyze a person if said in a certain spirit (not often achieved).

The ancients understood that only rarely might a person achieve the intended inner intent. (And prayer that is devoid of all intent is said to be of little worth.)[21] But people were urged to participate fully anyway, until, by habit and zeal, the person arrives at new understandings and comes to love the service. This may be the Jewish analogue of "Act as if ye had faith, and faith shall be given ye."[22]

Partners

Before there was anything, there was God, a few angels, and a huge swirling glob of rocks and water with no place to go. The angels asked God, "Why don't you clean up this mess?"

So God collected rocks from the huge swirling glob and put them together in clumps and said, "Some of these clumps of rocks will be planets, and some will be stars, and some of these rocks will be . . . just rocks."

Then God collected water from the huge swirling glob and put it together in pools of water and said, "Some of these pools of water will be oceans, and some will become clouds, and some of this water will be . . . just water."

Then the angels said, "Well God, it's neater now, but is it finished?"

And God answered . . .

"NOPE!"

On some of the rocks God placed growing things, and creeping things, and things that only God knows what they are, and when God had done all this, the angels asked God, "Is the world finished now?" And God answered . . .

"NOPE!"

God made a man and a woman from some of the water and dust and said to them, "I am tired now. Please finish up the world for me . . . really it's almost done." But the man and woman said, "We can't finish the world alone! You have the plans and we are too little."

"You are big enough," God answered them. "But I agree to this. If you keep trying to finish the world, I will be your partner."

The man and the woman asked, "What's a partner?" and God answered, "A partner is someone you work with on a big thing that neither of you can do alone. If you have a partner, it means that you can never give up, because your partner is depending on you. On the days you think I am not doing enough and on the days I think you are not doing enough, even on those days we are still partners and we must not stop trying to finish the world. That's the deal." And they all agreed to that deal.

Then the angels asked God, "Is the world finished yet?" and God answered, "I don't know. Go ask my partners."

from *"Does God Have a Big Toe?"*
by Marc Gellman,
published by Harper Collins, 1989.

THE NINETEENTH BENEDICTION

By now you may have noticed that I listed thirteen intermediate benedictions. But 3+13+3=19, so what happened? The answer is that a nineteenth benediction was added. There are two benedictions that are candidates for this distinction. One traditional opinion holds that the extra benediction is the one in the twelfth position, written in the first century.[23] But modern scholarship holds that the extra benediction is the one in the fifteenth position, added in Babylon in the third century.[24] In this case, the first-century composition of the twelfth benediction was only a replacement for a previous version. In any case, The Eighteen Benedictions actually consist of nineteen benedictions.

LORD, WON'T YOU BUY ME
A MERCEDES-BENZ?

Note that all the *Amidah*'s petitions are made on behalf of the community. But petitions for personal needs may be inserted after the most appropriate benediction.[25] Personal prayers may also be added to the end of the *Amidah* (which was the end of the service in ancient times). The weekday *Amidah* is the only place in the congregational liturgy where individuals may insert personal prayers and petitions.[26]

Personalizing the weekday *Amidah* is critically important. The use of a fixed liturgy has many virtues, but also creates challenges. Our sages wrestled with the problem of *keva* (fixedness) in worship. The Mishnah (a written compilation of ancient orally transmitted Traditions, redacted circa 200 c.e.) says: "Do not make your *Amidah* a *keva* (i.e., an appointed routine)."[27] The Talmud (redacted circa 600 c.e., structured as a commentary on the Mishnah) says that the *Amidah* becomes *keva* "whenever one cannot say something new in it."[28] The opposite of *keva* is *kavannah*. *Kavannah* is focused intention, consciously-directed meditation. The sages struggled to balance inward *kavannah* with external *keva*. "Do not be like one who mechanically unloads a burden and then departs." Personalizing the weekday Amidah was considered an effective tool for maintaining *kavannah*.

All of us spend a great deal of time cultivating careers, family relationships, education, and hobbies. Jewish prayer does not consider any area of endeavor to be mundane, irreligious, profane, or off-limits. If one is spending time and energy to get a promotion, find a mate, pass a test, care for a sick pet, win a contest, have a baby, earn more money, or learn a new skill, it is perfectly appropriate to recognize these goals in prayer.

Ideally, how we spend our time and what we talk about in prayer resemble each other. Sometimes something that we spend a lot of time doing (or worrying about) does not seem appropriate to talk about in prayer. This can be a warning that our actions are not aligned with our own most deeply-felt priorities.

THE SANCTIFICATION OF THE DAY
(K'DUSHAT HAYOM)

Since Sabbath and festivals are supposed to be entirely joyous days of rest, no personal requests may be made on those occasions. This is consistent with the practices of the Temple, where personal offerrings were not accepted on holy days. The central petitions of the *Amidah* could remind people of their failings and troubles, hence they too are not permitted on Sabbath and festivals. Therefore the 13 central blessings are replaced with one blessing that reflects on the significance of the day. This benediction is called "the Sanctification of the Day." Naturally, the "Sanctification of the Day" is different for each holiday.

The Sabbath is different from every other Jewish holiday. The Sabbath is the only demarcation between sacred and ordinary time that is not fixed by us. All other holidays depend for their timing on Israel's administration of the calendar. Each month, the Sanhedrin (the ancient Jewish "Supreme Court") heard testimony from witnesses concerning the timing of the new moon's appearance, and then fixed the day that would be the beginning of the new month, thus determining the length of the preceding month. This authority is mandated by the Torah, therefore their declaration establishes transcendental reality. For example, the Sanhedrin's monthly declaration, and not the astronomical testimony that led to it, is what makes a particular day be Yom Kippur (i.e., what turns a particular day into the tenth day of the month of Tishrei). Their declaration transformed ordinary time into sacred time. Thus the sanctity of the festivals is entirely dependent on the covenant relationship between Jews and the Divine. In contrast, the holiness of the Sabbath predates Israel. Furthermore, the three annual festivals commemorate national historical events, and so would not exist if not for the Exodus from Egypt.

All this explains why the Sanctification of the Day for the festivals celebrates our being chosen, the election of Israel to a covenant establishing divine partnership. In contrast, the Sanctification of the Day for the Sabbath never mentions our having been chosen.

The original Sanctification of the Day for Shabbat was the same at each of the four Sabbath services. Various introductory paragraphs were added to give each service its own unique character. The key texts giving uniqueness to the various "Sanctification of the Day" blessings on Shabbat are:

Va-y'chu-lu	(Genesis 2:1–3)	used in Shabbat *Ma-ariv*	Friday evening	(Creation)
V'sha-m'ru	(Exodus 31:16–17)	used in Shabbat *Shacharit*	Saturday morning	(Revelation)
A-tah E-chad		used in Shabbat *Mincha*	Saturday afternoon	(Redemption)
Yis-m'chu		used in Shabbat *Musaf* (the Additional Service)		

These texts explain various aspects of the relationship between Jews and Shabbat. *Va-y'chu-lu* speaks of the Sabbath as a commemoration of creation. *V'sha-m'ru* speaks of the Sabbath as an eternal sign of the covenant between God and the Jewish people. *Atah Echad* speaks of the Sabbath rest as a loving gracious gift, like a foretaste of the utopian world-to-come.[29] Thus *Ma-ariv, Shacharit,* and *Mincha* are aligned with the themes of creation, revelation, and redemption, respectively. The same themes appear in the same order in the *Sh'ma* Section of the service, and are discussed in detail later (on page 148).

Yis-m'chu speaks of the Sabbath as a delightful rejoicing in the everpresent Kingship of Heaven. The Shabbat *Musaf Amidah* also emphasizes the yearning for a return to Zion in very moving terms. It uses the theme of the resumption of the *Musaf* (Additional) sacrifice as a metaphoric touchstone of the fulfillment of national longing. "May it be thy will . . . to bring us in joy back to our land and to plant us within our borders."[30]

R'TSEI VIM-NU-CHA-TEI-NU

The original Sanctification of the Day for the Sabbath was called *R'tsei Vim-nu-cha-tei-nu*. It is now the common ending paragraph in the *K'dushat HaYom* of each of the four Sabbath "Amidahs." With this paragraph, one consecrates oneself to life's noblest purposes. One seeks to be a part of a transcendental plan, and strives to gain a pure heart so that one can understand the heritage of Israel. This endowment is secured by means of one's observance of the holiness and restfulness of the Sabbath day.[31]

In most traditional *siddurim*,[32] *R'tsei Vimnuchateinu* has three versions that differ only in one pronoun. "*Vah*" (female), "*vo*" (male), and "*vom*" (plural) are used to refer to Shabbat in the evening, morning,[33] and afternoon, respectively. They occur in the phrase, "may Israel rest thereon," referring to Shabbat. In Jewish metaphor, the Sabbath is often personified as the Sabbath Bride, and Israel is personified as the groom awaiting her arrival and eager to establish the relationship. The Sabbath Bride is a manifestation of the Divine Presence, and a commemoration of creation. She exists independently of the groom and arrives whether or not the groom shows up. Furthermore, the utopian world-to-come is often metaphorically described as an endless string of Sabbaths—like a perpetual wedding night between the material and the transcendental. Therefore when *R'tsei Vim-nu-cha-tei-nu* uses three different pronouns to say "may Israel rest thereon," it can refer to the female, male, and plural aspects of Shabbat: the Sabbath (as a commemoration of creation); this Sabbath day (as an expression by the groom of the covenantal relationship established by the revelation at Sinai); all Sabbaths (the infinite majority of which come after the future redemption). Thus these pronouns further serve to align the three Sabbath services with creation, revelation, and redemption.

The Talmud[34] considers *Vayichulu* and *R'tsei Vimnuchateinu* to be an essential part of every Shabbat *Ma-ariv* (Friday evening) service. We shall see liturgical ramifications of this later.[35]

The first phrases of *R'tsei Vimnuchateinu* speak of sanctification, satisfaction, and deliverance. This reminds us of the spiritual, physical, and national needs that comprise the central petitions of the weekday *Shemoneh Esreh*, replaced on Shabbat by *R'tsei Vimnuchateinu*.

Therefore *"Amidah"* is a better name than *"Shemoneh Esreh,"* because the "Eighteen Benedictions" actually don't have eighteen benedictions on Sabbaths and festivals. There are only seven benedictions on Sabbaths and festivals. Even on weekdays, there are nineteen benedictions, but the weekday *Amidah* is still often called *Shemoneh Esreh*.

This leads to a peculiar oddity of modern times. While it has always been the case that many Jews did not attend synagogue services every single weekday, it is only in modern times that many no longer pray thrice daily when alone. Those who never pray the daily service get a distorted view of Jewish worship, due to praying only the Sabbath and festival liturgy. On these occasions the central part of the Service of the Heart is replaced; the heart of the service is removed. Thus their experience of prayer is devoid of petition and (as we'll see later) confession, and the utopia-building program of our sages is excluded.

PRAYER AS AN UNNATURAL ACT

The Talmudic sages constructed the service with an awareness of prayer as a reflexive activity. This was not a novel idea. The ancient Hebrew word for prayer is *t'fi-lah*. Whereas the

Latin root[36] of the English word "pray" means "to beg," the Hebrew root[37] for "*t'filah*" means "to judge [oneself]." Thus prayer is understood to be a reflexive act of introspection. The sages designed this activity to take the worshipper through a specific succession of transformational states. The debates of the sages display a concern with the mental and emotional state of the worshipper. Although couched in anthropomorphic terms, they never suggested that God needed us to talk to Him in order for Him to know our needs and our feelings, or that He needed our prayer. What is needed is the improvement of people. The sages focused on the worshipper.

The ancient sages realized that talking, as a strategy for establishing intimacy with the transcendental, can feel ridiculous. Prayer is often an unnatural act, particularly on the occasions of fixed congregational prayer. They sought to promote the reasonableness of prayer.

One result of this is that the central petitions of the *Amidah* are preceded by three benedictions that are designed to promote the idea that prayer is reasonable in the mind of each individual. The first benediction is a reminder that, in attempting to pray, the worshipper is merely continuing in an ongoing activity of the worshipper's parents and ancestors and community; working jointly at an effort that so many have deemed important for so long. Therefore participation is probably reasonable even if one does not yet see how.

The second and third benedictions suggest that prayer is reasonable by asserting that two key prerequisites for its effectiveness are already met. The second benediction focuses on the immanence of the source of blessings, and the third benediction on the transcendence of the source of all good. Both immanence and transcendence are required for prayer to be effective. We must feel that our personal mundane needs are important, that our lives are entwined with that which is eternal. And we must have a power that helps us effect transformations when we manage to articulate our deeply-felt needs. So prayer should be undertaken because it is reasonable to expect it to effect transformations. In anthropomorphic terms, God has to be close enough to care, but different enough to be able to help.

THE FIRST THREE BLESSINGS

Now let's examine the first three benedictions as independent units, and then look at the last three benedictions. These six are older than the intermediate benedictions. The first three contain elements of praise.[38] They are:

1 Avot: Spiritual ancestors

Avot means "fathers" or "ancestors." "The Avot" are the Patriarchs. Abraham, Isaac, and Jacob are thought of here as people of the highest spiritual character, who put aside their own desires and wholeheartedly served the greater cause.[39] Their personalities have been idealized in Midrash (extra-biblical narrative) and folklore over the millennia. They are also thought of as the people who began divine service and bequeathed it to us, their spiritual descendants.[40] They are the spiritual "fathers" of the Jewish people.

The Patriarchs are cited in this benediction because they are also thought of as the instituters of prayer. A *midrash*[41] suggests that Abraham instituted the habit of morning prayer, Isaac afternoon prayer, and Jacob evening prayer.[42] The popular word for praying, *davening*, is widely regarded as stemming from the Aramaic word for "of our fathers."[43] Thus they are thought of as having brought the presence of the divine to the Earth.[44] For this reason they are sometimes called "God's chariot" in ancient Midrash.[45]

Abraham is credited with the invention of monotheism. Although all three Patriarchs are cited in this prayer, only Abraham is cited in the *chatima* (climactic conclusion) of the benediction, which is: *"Baruch Atah Adonai,* Shield of

Abraham."[46] The phrase "Shield of Abraham" comes from Genesis 15:1.[47]

Jews are proud of the merit of the Patriarchs, and the memory of the merit of the Patriarchs is still thought to animate behavior.[48]

Recitation of *Avot* evokes recognition that we are connected to the individuals of the past. We are part of an eternal corporate entity. Thus we are the link between our ancestors and their ideals. We determine their future. "May their memory be for a blessing."

In addition to our responsibility for our own actions, our responsibility to their memory creates a Jewish societal responsibility for the behavior of all Jews. "All Jews are responsible for each other."[49]

This connection to the past is spiritual rather than genetic. A Jew-by-choice and a born-Jew recite all prayers identically, including common phrases like "God of our Fathers" and "Abraham our Father," and *Avot*.

Avot can also be experienced as an appreciation of kindness. Merit is rewarded with kindness. In part, it says: ". . . and although He is Master of Everything, He still remembers the kind deeds. . . ."

Body English and Shuckling

In traditional congregations, you will see people bend their knees on the word *"Baruch"* and then bow slightly on the word *"Atah."* This becomes one smooth two-part motion. This occurs once at the beginning of *Avot* and again near its end.

In fact, much of the *Amidah* looks "choreographed." Worshippers sway forward and back, with a body language that becomes a personal form of expression.[50] This is called "shuckling."[51] (Men have a higher center of gravity than women. A high center of gravity makes it harder to balance in an unstable position. Swaying, in a controlled way, about such a position is much easier than trying to freeze in the balanced position. A man's center of gravity is in his chest. Therefore swaying is a natural spontaneous and unconscious behavior for most men. Women have a lower center of gravity, about the waist, and usually do not shuckle much.) For some individuals this personal expression goes beyond mild swaying:

> It has been taught that R. Judah said: "This was the habit of R. Akiva: When he said the *Amidah* . . . , left in one corner, he would be found in another corner."
>
> Talmud, Tractate *Berachot*, folio 31a.

2 Gi-vu-rot: Mighty Deeds

The second benediction is called *Givurot*.[52] *Givurot* means "mighty deeds." It begins: "You are mighty universally, eternally, boundlessly . . ." *Givurot* recounts the greatest manifestations of divine power. One might have expected such a list to describe the flood, the parting of the sea, the ten plagues, or the creation of the sun, moon, and stars. But in Jewish tradition the epitome of "mighty deeds" is God's intimate, nurturing involvement in human lives. *Givurot* cites "sustaining the living with kindness, . . . supporting the fallen, healing the sick, loosening the bound, and remaining faithful to those that sleep in the dust." The last expression is a reference to the dead, resurrection being the climactic example of the divine quality that *Givurot* celebrates.

Thus *Givurot* can be used to evoke appreciation for the performance of deeds animated by love, without hope for or possibility of reward. For none are less able to repay a kindness than the dead. *Givurot* can also be recited as an appreciation of all forms of deliverance. This prayer aligns Jewish tradition with the side of the weak. And *Givurot* recounts the omnipotence of that which animates all kindness.

Thus *Givurot* also evokes the idea that, no matter how bad a desperate situation may be, one should never give up hope.[53] As with all prayers, there are many other messages that can be extracted and made central.

Givurot: Enlivening the Dead

Judaism in pre-exilic times (i.e., before 576 B.C.E.) did not have any concept of "immortal souls" or "resurrection." Death was final, but one's name might live forever. The new foreign ideas were debated during the Hellenistic period (333 B.C.E. to 70 C.E.). Rabbinic Judaism firmly established the ideas of the immortality of the soul and resurrection. But the exact nature of these concepts has been debated and reinterpreted ever since.[54]

This is not the place to develop a systematic philosophy. However, it is interesting to note how some modern interpretations have come full circle, and correspond to the original Biblical conceptions, but are expressed in the post-biblical terminology. For example, "name" can be equated to "lasting effect of personality," which corresponds to "immortality of soul" in later terminology.

In any case, Judaism is not preoccupied with the details of eschatalogical speculation. There is no agreement among the sages of our tradition, and deliberate amibiguities are often found. So any detailed philosophy in this area is personal.

> "There will be no difference between this world and the Days of the Messiah except an end to subjugation to empires."
> R. Shmuel ben Abba Ha-Kohen (*Yar-chi-na-ah*)
> Talmud, tractate *Sanhedrin*, folio 99a.

Givurot: In Praise of Rain

"He makes the wind to blow and and the rain to fall" is inserted in *Givurot* during the winter months (i.e., between

Sukkot and Passover).[55] This is the rainy season in *Eretz Yisroel* (The Land of Israel). *Givurot* associates rain (power), life (kindness), and death (mercy, compassion). The association of rain with omnipotence is natural in Jewish thought.

In ancient times, the amount of rain made the difference between survival and starvation.[56] Rain prevented drought and famine. Rain is an instantiation of the general idea of revival and rebirth in nature. Rain also came in violent storms, associated with flood, destruction, and death.

So rain represents and unifies two opposite extremes in Jewish thought.[57] Rain represents the most powerful instance of life-nurturing power, and the most powerful instance of death-dealing power. Thus it was appropriate to link thoughts of rain with reflections on resurrection and omnipotence. The Talmud[58] considers rain to be as great a manifestation of divine power as the resurrection of the dead.[59]

3. K'dushat HaShem: Sanctification of the Name

The theme of the third benediction is holiness. Translated into English, this very brief prayer says:

> You are holy, and your Name is holy,
> and holy beings praise you daily.
> *Baruch Atah Adonai . . . the Holy God.*

The second line refers to us, the Jewish people (c.f., Leviticus 19:2).

But what is holiness? Generally all agree that it is a feature of God, and that we should be capable of emulating it.[60] But which feature? Goodness, mercy, and love have all been suggested. But primarily it refers to alone-ness, which is what actuates all the others.

Human holiness is the art of remaining apart, separate from outside influence. It is the art of being all alone inside in order to be free. This enables one to design a personality by determining to absorb the influences that make us better, and reject the influences which diminish nearness to our ideals. This art enables one to be true to oneself, refusing to betray one's integrity. Without this art, one lives a life adopted from others, having assumed external values, but void inside.[61]

The challenge of holy living is to be thoroughly involved with everyone, while maintaining separation from the mundane; to attach all actions to one's highest principles. Judaism frowns on practices that isolate one from full communal and individual relationships, such as monasticism or celibacy. One function of Jewish rituals is to transform all required mundane acts (like eating) into holy acts as reminders of fundamental values.

Attaining human holiness is the art of living. This art demands involvement, not retreat. The art of living requires education, cultivation, hard work, a system, discipline, communion with fellow artists, and constant focus, just like any other art. Jewish tradition develops this art. Our simultaneous alone-ness and involvement mirrors the simultaneous transcendence and immanence we attribute to God, implied by the juxtaposition of *Givurot* (immanence) with *K'dushat Ha-Shem* (transcendence).

Judaism interprets our role as a holy people to mean that all actions by Jews constitute public testimony. We cannot regard any of our decisions as personal. All our actions constitute "Sanctification of the Name" (*Kiddush HaShem*) or the reverse (*Chillul HaShem*, Desecration of the Name). Because of the association between Jews and God, our behavior will enhance or weaken the divine reputation's power to transform the world. This is an important concept that places a great personal and communal responsibility on every Jew. The third blessing could be recited as a joyful acceptance of this burden.

The Lord Our God (Deuteronomy 6:4): Having already said **the Lord is One**, why does Scripture say also **our God? Our**

God, however, serves to teach us that His name rests in greater measure upon us. A similar case is the verse, **Three times in the year shall all thy males appear before the Lord God, the God of Israel** (Exodus 34:23): having said **the Lord God,** why does Scripture go on to say **the God of Israel?** To indicate that His name rests in greater measure upon Israel. Another example is the verse, **Thus saith the Lord of hosts, the God of Israel** (Jeremiah 32:14): having said further on, **Behold I am the Lord, the God of all flesh, is there anything too hard for me?** (Jeremiah 32:14), Scripture nevertheless adds here **the God of Israel,** to indicate that His name rests in greater measure upon Israel.

> *Sifre* to Deuteronomy (Piska 31),
> (the earliest extant commentary on Deuteronomy.)
> translated by Reuven Hammer,
> published 1986, by Yale University Press.

The K'dushah

During the repetition of the *Amidah*, the short third blessing (*K'dushat HaShem*) becomes a longer prayer on the theme of holiness. This is done by inserting an introductory meditation, called the *K'dushah* (Sanctification). Although it now introduces the third benediction, it was once a separate liturgical unit. The entire result is also often called "the *K'dushah.*"

The *K'dushah* is a mystical text. Its authors were preoccupied with attempts to experience the divine through altered forms of consciousness. This was accomplished by meditation on intense words of praise arranged in patterns thought to facilitate ascent, accompanied by appropriate body language. Motivated by the intensity of the angels' exclamations in the first and third chapters of Ezekiel and the sixth chapter of Isaiah, they combined these texts and added others to provoke ecstasy. The effect does not survive translation:

We sanctify your name in the world
even as they sanctify it in the highest heaven,
as it is written by the hand of your prophet:
"They [the Serafim] keep calling to one another:

> 'Holy! Holy! Holy! The LORD of Hosts!
> The whole earth is full of his glory.'"   Isaiah 6:3

Those [in a second choir] opposite them offer praise saying:
  "Blessed be the glory of the LORD from his place."
                                                   Ezekiel 3:12

And in your holy scriptures it is written:

> "The LORD shall reign forever,
> Your God, O Zion, through all generations.
> Praise the LORD."   Psalm 156:10

The *K'dushah* is sung antiphonally, alternating between the reader and the congregation. The three key phrases (i.e., those indented in the quote above) are sung by the congregation. The second choir in the prophetic vision consisted of Seraphim, but in the context of prayer the reference could be applied to the congregation. Thus the congregation aspires to act as a human choir in unison with the heavenly hosts of prophetic vision, and to experience the proclamation of the holiness of the source of being with similar intensity.[62] The last quote can be thought of as facilitating a return to earth (by referencing Kingship) after being mentally aloft.

Traditionally, one stands erect, feet together to resemble the angels of Ezekiel's vision,[63] and raises one's heels high off the ground three times as one says "*kadosh, kadosh, kadosh*" (meaning "holy, holy, holy"). This is done either to emulate the fluttering of the angels in Isaiah's vision,[64] or to draw nearer to them. Either way this expresses a desire for unity with divine forces.

The congregation sits down after completing the *K'dushah*. (The congregation has been standing since the repetition of the *Amidah* began, and perhaps since the beginning of the silent *Amidah*.) The rest of the repetition is said seated. The *K'dushah* is one of only three places in the service where all present are expected to stand, even if not participating.

K'dushah Variations and Migrations

The *K'dushah* is an expansion to the structure of the *Amidah* Section that breaks the symmetry of the section. The *K'dushah* has many forms. The text shown above is used in Ashkenazic rite on weekday mornings, weekday afternoons, and Saturday afternoons.[65] There are different versions of the *K'dushah* for both Shabbat *Shacharit* (Saturday morning) and Shabbat *Musaf*.[66,67]

In Ashkenazic rite,[68] the *K'dushah* does not lead into the normal third benediction. The benediction is replaced by an alternately worded version, beginning "*L'dor va-dor . . .* " ("Through all generations . . . "). This is a good example of the common Hebrew poetic technique of beginning a paragraph with the last words of the previous one. Here it shows that this benediction was designed as a response to the inserted *K'dushah*. The contents of the alternate benediction indicate that we respond to the prospect of everlasting kingship with everlasting song.[69]

In addition to these permutations, other versions of the *K'dushah* are inserted into several other parts of the Jewish services, sometimes in Hebrew and sometimes in Aramaic translation.[70] All this deviation from simplicity is strange, and becomes understandable only by tracing the history of this prayer. (See note 71 for details.)

The Loud K'dushah (*Heiche Kedushah*)

Mincha (the afternoon service) must be completed by sundown. But sometimes a congregation starts late for want of a *minyan*, and runs out of time. So an emergency procedure was devised for such occasions. The procedure enables the congregation to recite the *K'dushah* even though it eliminates the repetition to save time. Hence this special type of *Amidah* is called the *heiche k'dushah* (The loud *K'dushah*) in Yiddish.

First, the reader chants the first two benedictions (*Avot* and *Givurot*) aloud, so that the congregation can then say the *K'dushah* with the reader's third benediction. The congregation does not say *"a-mein"* to the first two benedictions but remains silent until the *K'dushah*. After the *K'dushah*, the reader continues silently, while the congregation recites the entire *Amidah* silently from the beginning. There is no repetition.

In modern times, some less traditional congregations have adopted this practice even when time is available, and at services other than *Mincha*. They also tend to sing along with the reader's first two benedictions, rather than saying them silently later.

THE LAST THREE BLESSINGS OF THE AMIDAH

The first three blessings expressed praise. The last three are considered expressions of thanks, although only the middle one is explicitly structured as such. The other two are structured as requests, just like the thirteen intermediate petitions. This is rationalized as indicating that the most sincere thanks includes recognition of our continuing needs.

The three final benedictions come from liturgy used in the Temple in connection with the sacrificial service. When the *Amidah* replaced sacrifice, these texts were incorporated into it.

17 Avodah (*worship = work = service*)

This prayer is an expression of our desire to be more in touch with our values; for our lives to be informed by those values more effectively than at present. We desire an improved form of communication between our conscious thoughts and the source of our values. (Something even more effective than the *Amidah*.) *Avodah* is not a benediction asking that prayer be "heard" (i.e., be effective).[72] It is a benediction asking for a more effective way than prayer itself to approach the divine.

Avodah was originally a prayer for the acceptance of the sacrificial offering. As noted earlier, the Temple process was experienced as an introspective act leading to a restoration of wholeness and intimacy. The prayer was adapted after the destruction of the Temple to become a request for the restoration of the Temple service. The Temple processes were a much more intense, immediate, and dramatic experience of divine nearness than prayer. The *chatima* (climactic conclusion) of the benediction is "*Baruch atah Adonai* . . . who restores the *Shechina* (Divine Presence) to Zion.*" This demonstrates that it is the loss of divine intimacy that is the paramount consideration.

Although the prayer was moved into the *Amidah*, it still includes the original petition for acceptance of the "offerings of Israel." The Talmud[73] says that this mention of "offerings" should be recited as a reference to the "souls of the righteous of Israel," rather than to Temple sacrifices. This benediction suggests that our acts of human self-sacrifice throughout history, including martyrdom, approximate the Temple service in their effect. Hence, most Jews understand these offerings to be selfless human acts in general. These bring us, collectively and individually, nearer to the *Shechina* than does prayer.

This benediction reminds us that the *Amidah* was originally invented as the replacement for sacrificial procedures that had been unwillingly discontinued when the first Temple was destroyed by the Babylonians. Conservative prayerbooks have deleted two words from *Avodah* to make the sacrificial nature of the original Temple service less evident. Reform prayerbooks have gone further, obscuring any relationship between the Temple and the *Shechina*.

Many people think of animal sacrificers as barbarians. This sense of superiority is not useful. People aren't that different. Only by understanding the noble psychological processes that inform sacrifices can we extract the intent behind the words of this prayer. Fundamentally, the Temple sacrifice was a mechanism to restore intimacy between the individual and the individual's God-concept. Since this function is now fulfilled by prayer and Torah study, we often use the restoration of the Temple as a symbol of the future redemption, the achievement of utopia. A good example of this is in the *K'dushat Ha-Yom* (Sanctification of the Day) of the *Musaf Amidah*, discussed earlier. But here in *Avodah*, we do not cite the Temple as a symbol of longing for the future utopia. We cite its service as an example of a mechanism capable of drawing us near to the divine more effectively than talking (i.e., praying).

This has nothing to do with actually expecting or wanting a resumption of animal sacrifices. The eschatological question of whether sacrifices actually will resume in the future is moot. They cannot be restored under Jewish law until after the coming of the Messianic Age. Even then it would require a restoration of prophesy to clarify several humanly insurmountable halachic problems.[74] Obviously, no present debate could be well enough informed about such future conditions to be meaningful.

The two Temple metaphors may be related, since the utopian future ought to include a constant nearness exceeding what we can experience through prayer.

It is interesting to note that "*Avodah*" also means "work." So the concepts of divine service and earthly work are metaphorically one in Jewish thought.

18 Modim (Thanks = Acknowledgement)

This is a straightforward thanksgiving prayer. It is based on Psalms 79:13 and 55:18. In nontheistic philosophical terms, it is an expression of our conviction that everything that is going significantly right with the world can be attributed to veneration of the transcendental values that we believe in.

In traditional congregations, you may notice people bowing slightly on the word *"Modim"* ("We acknowledge Thee") and arising at the divine Name near the beginning of *Modim*. And at the *chatima* they will bend their knees on *"Baruch"* and bow on *"atah,"* just as was done during *Avot* (the first benediction).

There are two different forms of *Modim*. The standard form is said silently by the congregation during the *Amidah*, and later sung aloud by the reader during the repetition of the *Amidah*. The other form is called *Modim d'Rabannan* (Scholar's *Modim*). It is said in an undertone by the congregation during the reader's repetition of the primary form. This is another example of the how the rabbis unified divergent traditions in an inclusive way.[75]

Generally, the congregation's use of "body english" is confined to the silent *Amidah*. But since the repetition is the first time congregants recite *Modim d'Rabannan*, some will bow on the word *"Modim"* from their seated position. Others may stand during the repetition of Modim in order to bow.

19 Shalom (Peace)

It is important to note that the Jewish notion of peace differs from the usual Western conception. The English word "peace" comes from the Latin word *"pax."* *"Pax"* literally means quiet. The Hebrew word *"shalom"* comes from the root *"shalem,"* which means "complete" or "whole." While one of the meanings of *"shalom"* is translated as "peace," the vision expressed in the Hebrew is not the same. *"Shalom"* means "wholeness," "completeness" or "fulfilledness"; well-being. This is a dynamic conception of "peace."[76] In many contexts, *shalom* can be taken as a reference to the utopian future, the completed creation.

The Priestly Blessing

> [Aaron and his sons shall] say to them:
> [May] *HaShem* bless you and keep you.
> [May] *HaShem* make his face shine on you and be gracious to you.
> [May] *HaShem* lift his countenance upon you and grant you Peace.
> . . . and I shall bless them.
>
> *BaMidbar* (Numbers) 6:23–27

In the ancient Temple,[77] the final element of the service was the Priestly Blessing over the assembled people.[78] This is called "*Birchat Kohanim*" in Hebrew. The climactic final thought in the Temple was for "peace." In essence, the people were "dismissed" with the words of Numbers 6:24–26.

In the morning *Amidah*, the last prayer is *Sim Shalom*, which is an elaboration and expansion of the original Priestly Blessing.[79] *Sim Shalom* recasts it into the formal structure of a fixed benediction, thereby rendering it appropriate for an individual or reader in the absence of an active priesthood.

During the reader's repetition, the Priestly Blessing is inserted after *Modim* and before *Sim Shalom*, as a preface to Sim Shalom.[80] The full ritual[81] is still performed by *Kohanim* (the descendants of Aaron) with the assistance of the Levites, and is popularly called "*duchening*" (as though there were an English verb "to *duchen*"). It includes ritual handwashing of the *Kohanim* by the Levites, a benediction by the *Kohanim* before they perform the mitzvah, the blessing itself (accompanied by the *kohanic* handsign, popularized by the Star Trek TV show), and meditations after. The congregation responds to each phrase of the blessing with "*A-mein.*"

But in Ashkenazic rite, *duchening* only occurs on special holidays. The rest of the time, the reader simply recalls briefly the text of the blessing that the priests would say. The congregation does not say "*a-mein.*" Intead, it answers each phrase of the blessing with "*Kein y'hi ra-tson*," meaning "Yes, may it be Thy will." (The Priestly Blessing is also lovingly recited by parents to their children as part of the Friday night home Sabbath ritual.)

Reform congregations are an exception. They generally do not recite the Priestly Blessing.

In the ancient Temple, priests could not perform their functions after consuming alchohol. To avoid shameful investigation of qualifications, the Priestly Blessing was not recited at *Mincha* (the afternoon service). This is still the case.[82] Note that on important fast days the Priestly Blessing does appear at *Mincha*, since drinking would be unthinkable. No question arose with regard to *Shacharit* because it happens early in the morning, and one does not eat (except perhaps very lightly) before morning prayers.

In some synagogues, the rabbi may ask for a blessing on the congregation (in English or in Hebrew) at the end of the entire service, using the formula of the Priestly Blessing. This is not in the liturgy. (There is no function for a rabbi in the liturgy at all.) It's just something a rabbi might do. In any case, no human being (priest, reader, or rabbi) can bestow a blessing. They can only request one.

Scripture states "*and I [i.e., God] will bless them*" (Numbers 6:27). [The stress is on the "I," so] that the Israelites should not say that the blessing that is coming to us depends on the gift of the priests, and so that the priests should not say "We shall bestow the blessing on Israel."

excerpt from "*Sifre* to Numbers," XLIII:II
(the earliest extant commentary on Numbers)
translated by Jacob Neusner;
Brown University Judaic Studies #118,
published by Scholars Press, 1986.

When the sacrifice was first replaced with the *Amidah*, the end of the *Amidah* was the end of the whole service. So *Sim Shalom* was the end of the service. This climactic regard for peace is typical. As we shall see later, the kaddish and the Torah-Reading Section of the service build to a similar conclusion. (So does the Grace After Meals.)

The last benediction has two forms, *"Sim Shalom"* (grant peace) and *"Shalom Rav"* (great peace). *Sim Shalom* is used in *Shacharit* and *Musaf*. *Shalom Rav* is used for *Mincha* and *Ma-ariv*. This is another example of rabbinic compromise. (Some Sephardic communities have never adopted *Shalom Rav*.)

Since many Jews only go to synagogue on Friday night (*Ma-ariv*, when the *Amidah* is not repeated aloud) and Saturday morning (*Shacharit* and *Musaf*), they only hear *Sim Shalom*. The exceptions are Reform Jews, who have a very lovely modern melody for *Shalom Rav* that is often sung aloud on Friday nights.

BRACKETING THE AMIDAH

Many Jews take three steps forward at the beginning of the *Amidah* and three steps backward when concluding.[83] If there is no room, tiny symbolic steps are taken. The receding steps are preceded by bows, first to the left, then the right, and then straight ahead. Taking leave of someone was accompanied by much ceremony in Talmudic times,[84] so it is not surprising to find ceremony here. These motions emulate the way people used to take leave of authorities. This is an instance of applying an earthly king metaphor to the Jewish God-concept.

In third century Palestine, an opening line and a closing line were added to the *Amidah*.[85] The opening line is Psalm 51:17, "Lord, open my lips, that my mouth may declare your praise." The closing line is Psalm 19:15, "May the words of my mouth and the meditations of my heart be pleasing before you." Since the closing line also appears in *Elohai N'tsor* (described below), many Jews say it only there.

ELOHAI N'TSOR (MEDITATION
AFTER THE AMIDAH)

It is deemed meritorious for everyone to insert silent personal prayers at the conclusion of the silent *Amidah*. These will differ on every occasion. The idea is that devotion might stagnate if prayer becomes a fixed task.[86] "One ought . . . not to be like one who carries a load, unloads it, and departs."[87] Many such personal prayers are recorded in the Talmud.[88] These spontaneous silent individual prayers are referred to in the Talmud as "supplications" and "falling on one's face."

Since most people can't compose moving liturgical poetry themselves, they may prefer to select a text that expresses their feelings and recite that. Therefore the personal prayers of various rabbis have migrated from the Talmud to the siddur over time. A siddur may include several different examples.

There is one particular meditation, called *"E-lo-hai N'tsor"* ("O God, guard my tongue from speaking evil, my lips from speaking guile . . ."), that has become a fairly universal addition to the *Amidah*. In some congregations, it is also read aloud in English after the repetition. It is taken (with slight modifications and later insertions) from the personal prayer of Mar ben Ravina, reported in the Talmud.[89] It is thought to have been in use in some form since the Second Temple. It is in the singular, which is unusual for prayers in the siddur. This reflects its origin as a private personal prayer.

TACHANUN (SUPPLICATION)

On weekday mornings and afternoons (*Shacharit* and *Mincha*), there is a moving section called *Tachanun*. This is an example of spontaneous *Amidah* prayers becoming a standardized addendum to the repetition. *Tachanun* contains horribly anguished pleas for relief, and confessions of inadequacy. It may have been written during the persecutions of the seventh century, although tradition ascribes it to the destruction of the Second Temple in 70 c.e. Naturally, it is not said on Shabbat or festivals, nor in the afternoon service, if the Sabbath or festival evening service will follow immediately. (There are also other dates and conditions under which *Tachanun* is omitted.)

VA-Y'CHULU AND R'TSEI VIM'NU-CHA-TEI-NU

As noted earlier,[90] the Talmud considers *Va-y'chulu* and *R'tsei Vim-nu-cha-tei-nu*, to be an essential part of every Shabbat *Ma-ariv* (Friday evening) service. *Va-y'chulu* and *R'tsei Vim-nu-cha-tei-nu* are included in the "Sanctification of the Day" for Shabbat *Ma-ariv* (the middle blessing of the Sabbath *Amidah*, replacing the thirteen weekday petitions).

But when a festival happens to fall on Shabbat, the "Sanctification of the Day" for the festival will be recited in place of the one for Shabbat. This does not include *Va-y'chulu*, nor *R'tsei Vim-nu-cha-tei-nu*. Therefore since *Va-y'chulu* and *R'tsei Vim-nu-cha-tei-nu* are essential to welcoming Shabbat, they would have to be recited after the festival *Amidah*. Because of this, it has become the rule[91] to include *Va-y'chulu* and *R'tsei Vim-nu-cha-tei-nu* after the *Amidah* on all Friday nights. That means that on most Friday nights they occur twice, once as part of the silent *Amidah*, and once aloud thereafter.

MAGEIN AVOT

Magein Avot contains paraphrases of the seven blessings of the Shabbat *Amidah*. It was added after the Friday night *Amidah* in order to prolong the service. It is inserted between *Va-y'chu-lu* and *R'tsei Vim'nu-cha-tei-nu*. These three together sit where a reader's repetition of the *Amidah* would be, if it were not an evening service.

In ancient times, as now, more people came to synagogue on Shabbat than the rest of the week. Those who came only on Shabbat would be the least familiar with the service and would take more time, and there were always some people that would arrive late. By prolonging the Friday night service, they were given an opportunity to finish their prayers with the rest of the congregation, so everyone could leave together. Synagogues were often located outside the precincts of the city, since the rulers did not tolerate Jewish worship within the confines of their municipalities,[92] and as it was dangerous to walk home alone at night outside city walls, leaving at the same time as other worshippers promoted physical safety.

THE DIAGRAM OF THE SERVICE

The structure of our service can be represented by the following diagram. As before, each trip to the synagogue is represented by a column, with liturgical events listed in order from top to bottom. The left side shows the services for weekdays, the right side for Sabbaths. I have used the term *Shemoneh Esreh* on the left side and *Amidah* on the right, just to remind us of the differences between the nineteen weekday benedictions and the seven Sabbath benedictions. In synagogue life, the two terms are used interchangeably.

Weekday Services:

	Morning	Afternoon	Evening
Amidah	Shacharit Shemoneh Esreh: - avot, givurot - k'dushat hashem - 13 benedictions - Avodah, Modim - Sim Shalom Meditation Repetition: - avot, givurot - k'dushah - 13 benedictions - Avodah - Modim/Modim - Sim Shalom Tachanun	Mincha Shemoneh Esreh: - avot, givurot - k'dushat hashem - 13 benedictions - Avodah, Modim - Shalom Rav Meditation Repetition: - avot, givurot - k'dushah - 13 benedictions - Avodah - Modim/Modim - Shalom Rav Tachanun	Ma-ariv Shemoneh Esreh: - avot, givurot - k'dushat hashem - 13 benedictions - Avodah, Modim - Shalom Rav Meditation
Amidah			

Shabbat Services:

Friday Evening	Saturday Morning	Saturday Afternoon
Ma-ariv Amidah:	Shacharit Amidah:	Mincha Amidah
- avot,givurot - k'dushat hashem - K Hayom-Vayichulu - Avodah, Modim - Shalom Rav	- avot, givurot - k'dushat hashem - K Hayom-Vishamru - Avodah, Modim - Sim Shalom	- avot, givurot - k'dushat hashem - K Hayom-Ata Echad - Avodah, Modim - Shalom Rav
Meditation	Meditation	Meditation
	Repetition: - avot, givurot - k'dushah - shabbat - K.Ha-yom-Vishamru - Avodah - Modim/Modim - Sim Shalom	Repetition: - avot, givurot - k'dushah - K.Hayom-Ata Echad - Avodah - Modim/Modim - Shalom Rav
Vayichulu Magein Avot R'tsei Vimnuchateinu		
	Musaf Amidah: - avot, givurot - k'dushat hashem - K Ha-yom (Yismechu) - Avodah, Modim - Sim Shalom	
	Meditation	
	Repetition: - avot, givurot - k'dushah-musaf - K HaYom (Yismechu) - Avodah - Modim / Modim - Sim Shalom	

Notes

1. c.f., Talmud Berachot 26b; and Rambam's *Mishneh Torah* Laws of Prayer 1:5.

2. This sentence taken from a note in Birnbaum's siddur.

3. c.f., Talmud Berachot 28b.

4. c.f., I Samuel 1:13; Daniel 6:12; Talmud Sotah 32b; Talmud Berachot 31a; Responsa Radbaz IV, 94.

5. Although Ramban (Nachmanides) understood Numbers 10:9 to be the source for the obligation to pray. C.f., his commentary to Rambam's Book of Commandments, positive commandment #5.

6. now appended as part of the weekday *Hashkiveinu*, described later.

7. c.f., Talmud Berachot 27b; Yerushalmi Berachot 4:1, 7c–d.

8. Although reciting *Shacharit* without delay first thing in the morning is traditionally thought to be ideal.

9. c.f., Talmud Berachot 26a; Rambam Mishneh Torah Ahavah 3:6; Shulchan Aruch Orach Chayim 89:1, 108:1–2, 286:8.

10. c.f., Ben Sira 51; Talmud Megillah 17b; Berachot 12a, 33a, and 40b.

11. Mishneh Torah, Laws of Prayer 1:4.

12. Although Rambam's historical analysis may be inaccurate, his point is valid.

13. This paragraph adapted from the notes of Birnbaum in his siddur.

14. In recent times, some prayerbook editors have provided titles, often with unfortunate results. For an example of the sad effects of neglecting this tradition, see the usually excellent *Art Scroll Siddur*, which gives the twelfth benediction the title: The Suppression of Heresy.

15. Sifre on Deuteronomy, Piska 306.

16. This insight is taken from a class taught by Rabbi Naphtali Bier of the Boston *Kollel*.

17. c.f., Berachot 28b; Y. Berachot 7d–8a; Tosefta 3:25.

18. Vayera 1.

19. In emulation of the prayer practices of Moses, David, and Solomon. C.f., Sifre Deuteronomy Piska 343.

20. c.f., Talmud Megilla 17b.

21. c.f., Mishnah Berachot 2:5 (16a); T. Berachot 34b, and Tosafot to 17b; Eruvin 65a; Shulchan Aruch, Orach Chayim 101:1; Rambam, M.T., Laws of Prayer 4:15 and 10:1.

22. This paragraph is my adaptation of an observation of the Rambam as presented by Birnbaum in a note in his siddur.

23. The twelfth benediction is the one that has undergone the most frequent censorship and the most numerous changes. The Talmud reports that the benediction was composed in about 90 c.e. (twenty years after the Romans destroyed the second Temple) by Samuel the Lesser under the direction of Rabban Gamliel, head of the Sanhedrin (Jewish Supreme Court) at Yavneh. (c.f., Talmud Berachot 28b.)

This benediction is actually structured as a curse! This is the one about "slanderers and enemies of the people." It originally cited "Nazarenes and sectarians." The goal of the composition was to exclude proto-Christians from the congregation. Proto-Christians were presumed to be Roman informers.

Longstanding Jewish dissatisfaction with Roman domination had turned to open rebelliousness beginning about 6 c.e. By 90 c.e. the might of Rome had repeatedly squashed all Judean attempts to implement the normative Jewish concept of an Anointed as a prophetically ordained earthly warrior king—another David— who would overthrow Rome as Cyrus had overthrown Babylon. In the severe persecutions after the revolt that began in Nero's reign, Judaism's continued existence appeared doubtful.

The proto-Christians maintained a strategy of distancing themselves from other Jews, and mitigating the circumstances of Rome's involvement in Judea—the former to insulate themselves from Roman wrath, the latter to curry favor. (The Christian Testaments exhibit this policy, with disastrous results for much of later Jewish history.)

Anyone refusing to recite the twelfth benediction when leading the congregation, or refusing to say "*A-mein*" to the benediction, would be exposed as a proto-Christian, presumed to be there as a Roman informer.

The only other liturgical curse I can think of is in the Passover Haggadah, where it is directed against the Romans themselves: "Pour out Your wrath upon the nations that do not know You, and on the governments that do not call Your Name . . ." In both cases, these benedictions/curses reflect the Jewish rejection of all totalitarian governments, all absolute forms of earthly authority, as a necessary step in the arrival of a universal utopian society.

In the wake of modern (mostly Christian) history, it is easy to miss the point of these curses. It is important to recognize that these curses are not focused on supression of heresy but toward relief from oppression. In most times and places it has been reasonable for Jews to regard "the nations that do not know You" as ill-willed. As always with Judaism, it is behavior not theology that matters. This is clear from the continuation of the curse: ". . . for they have devoured Jacob and laid waste his dwelling place. . . . They have left Your servants' corpses as food for the fowl of heaven, the flesh of Your faithful for wild beasts" (translation taken from *"The Passover Haggadah,"* published by The Rabbinical Assembly).

The Jewish opposition to Roman tyranny did not end until the second century, during Hadrian's reign, when the glorious but disastrous revolt led by Simon bar Kochba, "The Son of a Star," ended organized Jewish opposition in *Eretz Yisroel* (The Land of Israel) for 1,700 years. This calamity began the slow eastward shift of the center of gravity of Jewish civilization.

This benediction's wording has been modified by Jews (and by Christian censors) on several occasions. But it is always related to opposing forces of external oppression.

24. By the fourth century c.e., the entire Jewish world looked to the heads of the Babylonian academies, and to the Exilarch, who was a descendent of the House of David, for spiritual leadership. The prayer for the return of the House of David was a natural follow-on to the prayer for the restoration of Jerusalem (the fourteenth benediction). This addition spread from the Babylonian academies to all of world Jewry.

25. c.f., Talmud Berachot 28b.

26. c.f., Talmud Avodah Zara 7b-8a; Berachot 31a.

27. Pirke Avot 2:18.

28. Berachot 29b.

29. Atah Echad is inspired by Zachariah 14:9 and I Chronicles 17:21.

30. It begins with a reverse alphabetical acrostic (starting with *Tikanta Shabbat*).

31. This paragraph is parahrased from the liner notes, written by Dr. Sidney B. Hoenig, to an old record of Sabbath litugical music by Cantor Sholem Katz with a choir directed by Seymour Silbermintz. (I could find no number or other mark on the product that could further identify it.)

32. except for Birnbaum's

33. including *Musaf*

34. c.f., Shabbat 119b.

35. on page 133.

36. *precare*

37. *hitpalal*

38. c.f., Talmud Rosh Hashana 32a, which finds support for the first three blessings in Psalm 29.

39. c.f., Sifre Deuteronomy Piska 336.

40. c.f., Sifre Deuteronomy Piska 59.

41. c.f., Talmud Berachot 26b.

See also Yerushalmi Berachot 4:1 for a naturalistic explanation of why they selected those times.

Another tradition finds the personal character of each Patriarch reflected in their choice of time for prayer. (C.f., Avraham Weiss, *Women at Prayer*, page 20 published by KTAV (1990).)

42. Another tradition says that the Patriarchs wrote the first three benedictions of the *Amidah*. Abraham instituted *Avot*, Isaac instituted *Givurot*, and Jacob instituted *K'dushat HaShem*.

43. But another theory suggests that Rashi took it from Old French, so it has the same root as the English word "devotion."

44. c.f., Sifre Deuteronomy Piska 313.

45. Some less traditional congregations have recently begun inserting a reference to the Matriarchs (Sarah, Rebeccah, Rachel and Leah) after the reference to the Patriarchs, although it was Hannah who taught our sages how we are to pray. If the subject of *Avot* is the reasonableness of prayer, its originators, and its most effective practitioners, then Hannah (and not the Matriarchs) is an appropriate citation.

46. This is in fulfillment of Genesis 12:2, which says: ". . . I will make your name great, and you shall be a [standard by which] blessing [is invoked]."

47. *Avot* also contains phrases from Exodus 3:15, Deuteronomy 10:17, and Genesis 14:19.

48. c.f., Sifre Deuteronomy Piska 184.

49. c.f., Rambam, Sefer ha-Mitzvot 205.

50. c.f., Psalms 35:10; Talmud Berachot 31a and 34a.

51. In prayer as well as engineering, controlled oscillation is the natural solution to the problem of maintaining position about a point of meta-stable equilibrium.

52. The text of *Givurot* includes phrases from Psalms 145:14 and 146:7, Daniel 12:2, and I Samuel 2:6.

53. c.f., Talmud Berachot 10a.

54. Givurot may have been modified or inserted as part of an effort to exclude Non-pharisees from synagogue. Resurrection was a Pharisaic doctrine.

55. c.f., Mishnah Berachot 5:2, and Ta-anit 1:1 2a.

56. c.f., Mishna Ta-anit 2:1.

57. c.f., Rashi on Job 37:11, relating rain to both 'anger' and 'health.'

58. c.f., Talmud Sotah 49a.

59. Some later Jewish mystics regarded the body and the person as not being in harmony during life. This friction results in death, at which point they separate, and each undergoes rehabilitation. The personality is purified and fortified against mundane influence. The body is planted in the soil like a seed. Flesh and seeds were both thought to rot and disintegrate prior to germination. In the end time, the seed germinates into something that conforms perfectly to every desire of the perfected personality. They are integrated as one blissful unit. Rain is psychologically associated with this process. Rain causes seeds to rot and disintegrate, and then germinate and grow. Rain supplies the food and water from which human bodies are formed. So rain is like a restorative downpour of human life.

(This paragraph is a paraphrase from "*Shemoneh Esreh*" by Abraham Feuer.)

60. c.f., Sifra Leviticus (Kedoshim 195) CXCV:I:2–3.

61. This paragraph is a rearrangement and paraphrase of ideas taken from "*Shemoneh Esreh*" by Abraham Feuer.

62. c.f., Sifre Deuteronomy Piska 306 last paragraph.

63. c.f., Ezekiel 1:7. (These angels have one foot.)

64. c.f., Isaiah 6:2.

65. The Sephardic rite on those occasions differs only in having a slightly different introduction to the first biblical quote.

66. In both Ashkenazic and Sephardic rites.

67. On Saturday mornings, the last quote is introduced by a longer paragraph (different for *Shacharit* and *Musaf*) emphasizing Kingship. This paragraph begins with "From his place...," which is inspired by the ending of the prior paragraph. The *Musaf* version of this paragraph appends a representation of the Sh'ma, including its first and last lines. (The Sh'ma is discussed later in this book.)

The first paragraph of the *K'dushah* also changes in the *Musaf Amidah*. There are two versions of this. The more mystical version, found in non-Palestinian Sephardic communities, suggests that we and the angels are "crowning God" together by reciting the *K'dushah*.

68. and in weekday Sephardic rite

69. In Sephardic rite on Shabbat (*Shacharit*, *Musaf*, and *Mincha*), this replacement is not made. The normal third benediction (*K'dushat HaShem*) of the silent *Amidah* is retained after the inserted *K'dushah* in the repetition.

70. e.g., Yo-tseir (the first benediction of the Sh'ma Section), and *Uva L'tsion* (in the Praise Section of the Saturday afternoon service, and in the Closing Section of the weekday morning service).

71. The information that follows is taken, with some adaptation, from *"Jewish Worship"* by Abraham Milgrom:

The *K'dushah* began in Babylonia but was resisted elsewhere. Strangely enough, it was Christianity that promoted the now universal acceptance of the *K'dushah*. It did so in two ways. First, it persecuted and decimated Palestinian Jewry, so that Palestinian authority over world Jewry eventually yielded to that of the Babylonian academies (which the Church could not reach). Second, the Church forbade most forms of Jewish worship on penalty of death, with the notable exception of the *K'dushah*. So even the Palestinian communities started accepting the Babylonian practice, since it was their only safe form of congregational religious expression.

As Christians and Roman culture assimilated into each other, the Church intensified its intolerance of Palestinian Jewry. When the Roman machinery of state became Christian in 312, more serious waves of persecution immediately followed. The worst arrived with the reign of Justinian. Over time, the authority of the healthy Babylonian Jewish community grew as the Palestinian community was being decimated. This prompted other (non-Palestinian) Jewish communities to adopt Babylonian practices, including the K'dushah.

More direct support for the K'dushah was given when the Church forbade reciting the *Amidah*, because of the anti-Nazarene benediction. They also forbade reciting the Sh'ma (which was the only other component of the Jewish service at that time) because it was incompatible with the Trinity. They permitted Jews to continue to gather for Bible-reading with the exception of reciting the Sh'ma (which is a biblical excerpt). But no rabbinic teaching was permitted to accompany it. Censors were posted in synagogues, and the penalty for violating any of these rules was death.

But the Church permitted the K'dushah because they mistook "*kadosh, kadosh, kadosh*" as an indication of the Trinity! The Jews took advantage of this by clandestinely appending key lines from the Sh'ma to the K'dushah. In this way, the K'dushah even came to be accepted by Palestinian Jewry. The Sh'ma excerpts are still in the *Musaf K'dushah* today.

But the Palestinians never accepted the mystical first paragraph, which suggests that we and the angels are crowning God together by reciting the K'dushah. Thus, in a strange reversal of the usual associations, Ashkenazic Jews now follow the Palestinian practice, while non-Palestinian Sephardic Jews follow the Babylonian practice!

Eventually the Church figured out that Jews did not say the K'dushah as an affirmation of the Trinity, but as a defiant affirmation of Unity. So the K'dushah was also banned. The Jews then circumvented this ban by incorporating parts of the K'dushah into other prayers that occurred when the congregation reassembled for homilies prior to the Saturday afternoon service (when censors were not expected to be present). The Jews even inserted an Aramaic translation of the K'dushah. (Aramaic was the vernacular of the day.) This non-literal translation explicitly made the *K'dushah* an affirmation of Unity: "Holy in the highest heaven . . . Holy upon the Earth . . . Holy to all eternity . . . is the LORD of Hosts!"

This period of persecutions finally ended in 636 c.e., when the Arabs conquered the area. The banned parts of the service were restored. But the additions and modifications resulting from the emergency measures have been retained to this day.

Some scholarly opinions differ from *Milgrom*. They hold that the Sh'ma excerpts were added to the *K'dushah* during Zoroastrian persecutions in middle of the sixth century in Babylonia under the Persian ruler Yezdigird II. (See the Morning Supplications in the Preliminary Morning Service, discussed later, for additional liturgical effects of this persecution.) When Moslems conquered the area, ending the persecutions, the Sh'ma was reinstated. The Sh'ma excerpts in the *K'dushah* were then moved to *Musaf* (or retained in *Musaf*) in gratitude.

The various theories are not mutually exclusive. It is possible that many persecutions in different places and times resulted in somewhat similar survival strategies. Censors could leave after the time for reciting the Sh'ma had passed, permitting it to be hidden in the repetition of the *Shacharit Amidah*, or in the *Musaf* service, or even in independent occasions for the *K'dushah*.

Furthermore, if different communities adopted different strategies, later attempts to unify the service might require including everything present in several different rites.

72. This is the function of *R'tsei*, the sixteenth benediction of the weekday *Amidah*.

73. Menachot 110a.

74. e.g., Who is a true Ko-hein? Where is the altar site? How can vestments requiring extinct resources be constructed?

75. c.f., Talmud Sotah 40a.

76. This paragraph has been taken from a private letter, but is believed to originate in a published source that I have been unable to identify. I'd welcome any information that would enable proper attribution in the future.

77. c.f., Sifre Numbers XXXIX:I to XLIII:II.

78. c.f., Numbers 6:23 and 27; Mishnah Tamid 5:1 and 7:2.

79. c.f., Sifre Deuteronomy Piska 62.

80. On Sabbaths in Israel, and on festivals and High Holy Days in the United States, the priests (i.e., the descendants of Aaron) still perform this recitation. (These individuals will be described in more detail in the description of the Torah-Reading Section of the service.) Normally, the reader chants it.

81. c.f., Leviticus 9:22.

82. c.f., Betzah 21.

83. c.f., Genesis 18:23 and I Kings 18:36.

84. c.f., Talmud Berachot 31a and 64a; Yoma 53a; and Genesis Rabbah to 15:16.

85. c.f., Talmud Berachot 4b.

86. c.f., Mishnah Berachot 4:4; Yerushalmi Berachot 8a; Bavli Berachot 29b.

87. Rambam, Laws of Prayer 4:16.

88. c.f., Talmud Berachot 16b–17a.

89. c.f., Berachot 17a.

90. in the section beginnning on page 108.

91. c.f., Tosafot, Pesachim 106a.

92. Even in twentieth century America, local political processes have sometimes been used to the same effect.

The Sh'ma Section
(K'riyat Sh'ma)

THE SH'MA

The *Sh'ma* is the keynote of Judaism. In many homes it is the first words Jewish mothers teach their children, and is the prayer Jewish children say at bedtime every night as they go to sleep. It may be briefly called to mind every time we enter a room or leave. It is the last words Jews, especially martyrs, say when they die.

The *Sh'ma* may be perceived as an assertion that there is one permanent standard of the highest ethics, and as a statement of dedication to it. Through this dedication to a transcendent standard of good, our lives are given purpose and our temporary existence is given significance in relation to something eternal.

The *Sh'ma* is the oldest prayer in the siddur—older than the *Amidah*. It was the primary prayer before there was ever a need for the *Amidah*. It was an important part of the service in the Second Temple. By the first century C.E. it was already considered ancient.[1] Tradition ascribes it to Moses.

The *Sh'ma* consists of three biblical paragraphs strung together.[2] There is no benediction within it. It is recited as a declaration of love, dedication, and faith in Jewish principles.

THE FIRST LINE OF THE SH'MA

The first line of the *Sh'ma* is a major signpost. It is always said aloud.[3] Some Jews cover their eyes when they say it, in order to concentrate better.[4] There is one melody commonly used. It is readily recognized and learned.

"*Sh'ma Yisraeil, Adonai Eloheinu, Adonai Echad*"

Deuteronomy 6:4

"Hear O Israel! The Lord Our God, The Lord is One!"[5]

This proclaims the oneness of God. Judaism doesn't prescribe a single definition of God. Every Jew can formulate a personal philosophy. But the *Sh'ma* defines God's most important attribute, and thereby limits some God-concepts from being Jewish ones.

In Judaism (unlike Christianity) oneness is not a mathematical concept. It does not mean that we eliminate all the other gods until just one is left. It refers to an internal unity. Oneness means that whatever your personal God-concept is, it must, by its very definition, preclude the possibility that there could be more than one of them—or a fraction of one. It should not be possible for anyone to share your concept but believe in two of them—or in only a part of your one.

Nothing in human experience has this oneness. Everything material can be subdivided into parts or else multiplied. In all religions there is always a tension between viewing God as transcendental (utterly outside the material world) and viewing God as immanent (a part of the material world). The Jewish assertion of oneness limits Jewish God-concepts to the transcendental end of the spectrum. A valid Jewish God-concept has no material parts. Pagan God-concepts were completely immanent in the material world. Christian God-concepts are half material and half transcendental, or one third material and two thirds transcendental, depending on denomination. Neither view can be reconciled with the *Sh'ma*.

The central concept of the Shema's opening line is built into the *tallis* (prayer shawl). As noted earlier, the fringes on a *tallis* are tied in a precise way. There are five knots and eight threads in each fringe. One of the threads is wound around the others to create a spiral-edged spacing between the knots. The number of windings between knots forms the sequence 7-8-11-13. This sequence represents the thought that "God is One." The first two numbers add up to the numerical value of the first two letters in the Tetragrammaton, the four-letter Name. Eleven is the numerical value of the remaining two letters. The Hebrew word for "one" is *echad*. *Echad* is numerically equivalent to thirteen. (Its letters, when regarded as symbols used to represent numbers, add up to thirteen.) The unification of the Name is another view of the mystical model of the process Jews use to perfect creation.

The animating principle evident in the action of time, and the source of transcendental standards, is a unity. We work in alliance with that unity.[6]

Some traditional congregants will elongate the word *echad* (one), and pronounce the final "D" distinctly, to emphasize the word "one." Some *siddurim* enlarge the last letters of the first and last words in the *Sh'ma*'s first line (i.e., *shemA* & *echaD*).[7] This spells *ad* (witness). This acrostic evokes the idea that we function as witnesses to the unity of the transcendent by reciting the *Sh'ma*.[8]

Another perspective: By associating the divine name
A-do-nai (signifying mercy and love) with the divine name
E-lo-hei (signifying infinite power) the Sh'ma's first line de-
clares the unity of immanence and transcendence.

Usually, the rest of the Shema is read silently. Often, the
rest of the first paragraph is sung aloud. Some congregations
also recite the second paragraph aloud; I've been to one
congregation that read the second paragraph silently but
then the third paragraph aloud.

Halacha (Jewish law) specifies that the *Sh'ma* is to be
recited while seated.[9] But some Reform congregations stand
up for it.

THE THEMES OF THE SH'MA

The first paragraph (Deuteronomy 6:4–9) emphasizes the
theme of loving God. Expressing this love is linked to
educating our children, and to studying Torah under all
circumstances.

In ancient anatomical metaphor, the heart was the seat
of intellect, not emotion. Hence, the beginning of this paragraph could be understood as: "You shall love *HaShem* your
God with all your mind, with all your being, and with all
your strength," referring to the commitment of all one's intellectual, emotional, and material resources.

The second paragraph (Deuteronomy 11:13–21) proclaims that human actions lead to inevitable consequences.
An unjust social order and a morally corrupt people cannot
reach a lasting prosperity. Only personal character and social justice can create enduring human happiness.[10]

The third paragraph (Numbers 15:37–41) stresses the
importance of ritual observance, and clearly indicates that
ritual is a means to an end. The goal of ritual is to facilitate
adherence to good conduct; that is, conduct in harmony with
our most cherished values.

Thus the themes of the *Sh'ma* are the unity of any valid God-concept, devotion to it and to its progress toward utopia, educating ourselves and our children to be a part of the process, the inevitability of consequences,[11] and the importance of ritual to maintain peak performance. That's Judaism in three short paragraphs! The *Sh'ma* is Judaism's most important prayer. It defines the means by which we have become a holy nation.

The order of the three paragraphs is also significant. By loving the divine unity and serving it (P#1), human society will enjoy blessings in this material world (P#2), and this service is accomplished by setting oneself apart (emulating holiness, God's essential nature of separateness) through the performance of the commandments (P#3).

The first paragraph is in the second person singular, while the others are in the plural. The individual's study of Torah (P#1), enables communal observance of Torah (P#2), which results in the holiness of Israel (P#3).[12]

WHEN AND WHERE TO FIND THE SH'MA

The *Sh'ma* is a self-referential statement. It contains Deuteronomy 6:7, which is a commandment incumbent upon Jews, that we fulfill by reciting the *Sh'ma*. We are reciting Deuteronomy 6:7 in fulfillment of Deuteronomy 6:7. (The next two biblical lines contain commandments that are the basis for *t'fillin* and *mezzuzot*, both of which contain a parchment of the *Sh'ma*.)

Since one recites the *Sh'ma* in fulfillment of the self-referential biblical commandment to "speak of [these words] when you lie down and when you rise up," the *Sh'ma* is included in *Shacharit* (the daily morning service) and *Maariv* (the daily evening service), but not *Mincha* (the daily afternoon service).[13]

K'riyat Sh'ma (recitation of the *Sh'ma*) refers to the commandment to recite the *Sh'ma,* or to its performance. This is qualitatively different from *Talmud Torah* (performing the commandment to study Torah, in which the same text could be encountered), and from general Bible-reading activity (in which the same text could also be encountered). What one is in fact doing when reading the text of the *Sh'ma* depends on one's *kavannah* (inner intent).

Recalling that Jewish days begin at sundown, our services now schematically look like this:[14]

Weekday:			*Shabbat:*		
Shacharit (A.M.)	Mincha (P.M.)	Ma-ariv (Evening)	Saturday Morning	Saturday Afternoon	Friday Evening
K'riyat Sh'ma	——	K'riyat Sh'ma	K'riyat Sh'ma	——	K'riyat Sh'ma
Shemonah Esreh repetition	Shemonah Esreh repetition	Shemonah Esreh ——	Amidah repetition	Amidah repetition	Amidah ——
			Musaf Amidah repetition		

PRAYERS ATTENDANT UPON THE SH'MA: CREATION, REVELATION, AND REDEMPTION

The central theme of the *Sh'ma* is our love of God. In the liturgy, the *Sh'ma* is attended by three other prayers; two before and one after. The first of these recalls creation, the second recalls the giving of the Torah. The last recalls redemption from slavery in Egypt. While these subjects are mentioned frequently in the siddur, they are depicted in a unique way here. They are thought of here as acts of love. This is most explicit in the second prayer. Thus the *Sh'ma* is sandwiched in prayers that talk about evidences of God's love for us, and the relationship is thought of as reciprocal.[15]

The two prayers before the *Sh'ma* cite the great events of the Jewish past. The third prayer looks to the future redemption by analogy with the past.

The morning and evening versions of these prayers are different. In the morning, the *Sh'ma* section looks like this:

1. *Yo-tseir Or*   creation (as Time-Development Operator)
2. *Ahavah Rabbah*   revelation (as act of great love)

The Sh'ma

3. *Ga-al Yisraeil*   [A.M. version] Redeemer of Israel

In the evening, the *Sh'ma* section looks like this:

1. *Ma-ariv Aravim*   creation (as Time-Development Operator)
2. *Ahavat Olam*   revelation (as act of everlasting love)

The Sh'ma

3. *Ga-al Yisraeil*   [P.M. version] Redeemer of Israel

1. Yotseir Or and Ma-ariv Aravim

The Jewish concept of creation is philosophically aligned with the concept of time-development (as opposed to thinking of creation as a one-time event). Creation is ongoing; it is the consistent experience of a material reality.

Yotseir Or's treatment of the theme of creation focuses on the recurrence of the daily sunrise. This is appropriate to the timing of the morning service.

> Blessed are you, LORD our God, King of the Universe,
> who forms light[16] and creates darkness,[17]
> who makes peace and creates all things . . .
> In mercy you give light to the earth and to those who dwell
>   on it,
> In your goodness you renew the work of creation every day,
>   constantly . . .
> Blessed are you, LORD, creator of the luminaries.

In the evening service, *Yotseir Or* is replaced by *Maariv Aravim*, which focuses on the recurrence of evenings, and evokes a sense of security in the face of impending darkness.

> Blessed are you, LORD our God, King of the Universe,
> who at your word brings on the evening twilight.
> With wisdom you open the gates of the heavens,
> with understanding you order time in cycles, and vary seasons
>   in alternation,
> setting stars in their courses in the sky according to your will.
> You create day and night,
> rolling away the light before the darkness, and the darkness
>   before the light . . .
> Blessed are you, LORD, who makes evenings [become]
>   evenings.

There are several poems that have been inserted into *Yotseir Or* over time. A variant form of the *K'dushah*, called the "Sitting *Kedushah*" has also been inserted. The included poems differ on different occasions. The result of all this is that *Yotseir Or* is now very long. One of the poems inserted on the Sabbath is called *Eil Adon* and is usually sung aloud by the congregation. Information about the inserted poems and the Sitting *Kedushah* may be found in note 18.

2. Ahavah Rabbah and Ahavat Olam

The second prayer has two versions. The morning version is called *Ahavah Rabbah* (Great Love). The evening version is called *Ahavat Olam*[19] (Eternal Love), and is a shorter version. This is another example of the sages reconciling divergent traditions by incorporating both. They are thought to have been written between 444 and 300 B.C.E.[20] and are both very beautiful.

It is appropriate that these benedictions, which express gratitude for the Torah, immediately precede reciting the *Sh'ma*, which is a Torah excerpt.[21, 22]

The *chatima* (closing formula) of *Ahavah Rabbah* is: "*Baruch atah Adonai*, who has graciously chosen your people Israel in love." The closing of *Ahavat Olam* is: "*Baruch atah Adonai*, who loves your people Israel."[23] They lead directly to the first line of the *Sh'ma*, begun by the congregation aloud, which declares, "God is *echad*." The numerical value of *ahavah* (love) is thirteen, which is the same as that of *echad* (One). The Shema then continues, "You shall love [God] . . ."

3. Ga-al Yis-ra-eil

The benediction following the *Sh'ma* is called "*Ga-al Yis-ra-eil*" which means "Redeemer of Israel." It recalls the Exodus. It is said in fulfillment of *Ze-chi-ra* (the halachic requirement to remember the Exodus every day).[24] It is also a bridge from the *Sh'ma* to the *Amidah* that follows, as it relates past kindnesses to the requests about to be made, and affirms the requisite power to make the *Amidah* effective.

As the congregation silently reads the latter part of the *Sh'ma*, they continue without interruption through the first word of *Ga-al Yis-ra-eil*, which is "*Emet*" ("true"). Then they stop and wait.[25] After the reader marks the completion of the *Sh'ma*, the Congregation continues reciting *Ga-al Yisraeil* beginning with the second word, which is *"v'ya-tsiv"* ("and certain") in the morning, and *"v'e-mu-nah"* ("and faithful") in the evening.

The reader marks the completion of the *Sh'ma* by singing:

Adonai E-lo-hei-chem Emet.

This phrase is formed out of the last two words of the *Sh'ma* and the first word of *Ga-al Yisraeil*. And it is a meaningful sentence ("The Lord Your God is True"). The purpose of this practice is to emulate the prophet Jeremiah who made a similar declaration (c.f., Jeremiah 10:10).[26] (Other wordplay and number harmonies related to the end of the *Sh'ma* are described in note 27.)

There are two different versions of *Ga-al Yisraeil*, one for morning and one for evening. The morning version emphasizes our experience of kindness, while the evening version stresses our experience of faithfulness. This is in accordance with Psalm 92:3: "to proclaim your kindness at daybreak, your faithfulness each night." Our experience of kindness and trustworthiness justifies our faith in the inevitability of utopia.

The morning version of *Ga-al Yisraeil* begins with a mystical chant[28] of sixteen synonyms for "true"—one to affirm each sentence of the *Sh'ma*'s first two paragraphs.[29] This is abbreviated in the evening version.

There are three key phrases in *Ga-al Yisraeil* that the congregation, rather than the reader, recites:

1. *MI CHAMOCHA* (Exodus 15:11)

Mi cha-mo-cha ba-ei-lim Adoshem	Who is like you among the mighty, LORD?
Mi ka-mo-ka ne-'dar ba-ko-desh	Who is like you, glorious in holiness,
No-rah t'hi-lot o-sei fe-leh.	awe-inspiring in praises, doing wonders?

This is one of the most familiar and stirring passages in Jewish tradition. Racing desperately before Pharaoh and his army, we sang this song as we plunged into the sea—*before* it split! (Notice the unusual variation of the word *cha-mo-cha* appearing in the second line, and compare it to the first line.)

> Moses was engrossed in prayer when God chastised him, exclaiming, "My beloved are drowning in the sea and you stand there praying!?!?!" Moses replied, "But, Sovereign of the Universe, what can I do?" And God said, "Tell the Children of Israel to go forward! Lift up your rod and stretch out your hand."
>
> At the first *"Mi,"* we splashed into the water, ankle deep. At *"cha-mo-cha"* we were sloshing through water knee-deep. At *"ba-eilim"* we were plowing into the sea where the water was waist deep. By *"Ad-o-shem"* it was up to our chests. At the second *"Mi"* the water reached our necks! We strode on, and as our heads went completely under water, began to sing *"cha-mo-cha!"* Of course, mouths full of water can not make a "cha" sound, but produced "ka" instead. It was at that moment that God parted the sea.[30]
>
> Once safely on the farther shore, with Pharaoh and his army being destroyed by the waters as they came crashing back together, Miriam led the women in The Song at the Sea, beginning with *Mi Chamocha*. The angels also wished to sing songs of praise. But God silenced them, saying, "My children are drowning in the sea, and you want to sing songs!?!?!"

Mi Chamocha is usually sung to a very old melody. There are two variations, differing only in the presence (or absence) of a semitone rise in pitch between *"Ko-"* and *"-desh."* Subsequent melodic intervals are maintained but are all a semitone higher. So if you are new to a congregation, listen alertly at that point.

2. Exodus 15:8

Adonai yimloch l'olam va-ed   The LORD will reign for ever and ever!

3. *TSUR YISRAEIL*[31] [appears only in the morning version]

Tsur Yisraeil	Rock of Israel,
<u>Ku</u>-mah b'ez-rat Yisraeil	arise to the help of Israel,
Uf'dei ki-nu-<u>me</u>-cha	deliver, as promised,
Y'hu-da v'Yisraeil	Judah and Israel.
Go-a-<u>lei</u>-nu	Our Redeemer,
A-do-mai ts'va-ot sh'mo	LORD of Hosts your Name,
K'dosh Yisraeil.	Holy (One) of Israel.

The *chatima* (conclusion) is: "*Baruch atah Adonai*, redeemer of Israel."

USING THE TALLIS AND T'FILLIN DURING THE SH'MA SECTION

Some Jews actively use their *tallis* during the morning *Sh'ma* section, beginning with *Ahavah Rabbah*. *Ahavah Rabbah* recounts the giving of the *mitzvot* as an act of love. To indicate our acceptance and appreciation, we take the four *tsi-tsis* (which represent the 613 *mitzvot* through *gematria*) and gather them to us, by wrapping them around a finger.

Since the pattern of the knots represents that "God is One," this act of gathering the four corners together can also be an assertion of dedication to accelerating the coming unity of the divine Name. This is an appropriate bridge to the *Sh'ma*, which asserts the unity of the Divine itself.[32]

Tsi-tsis are mentioned three times in the last paragraph of the *Sh'ma*. Some Jews kiss their *tsi-tsis* each time. They are kissed a fourth time upon completing the *Sh'ma* (i.e., on the word "*E-<u>lo</u>-hei-<u>chem</u>*"). These four occurrences can also be thought of as corresponding to the four letters of the Name. For the same reason, some Jews kiss the *tsi-tsis* four times at each occurrence. Similarly, on weekdays, some Jews touch their *t'fillin* when they are mentioned in the *Sh'ma*.

The *tsi-tsis* can be held beyond the end of the *Sh'ma*, but must be given up prior to the part of *Ga-al Yisraeil* that recounts the drowning of the Egyptians (i.e., the paragraph that begins, "*Ez-rat A-vo-tei-nu . . .*"). It is inappropriate to keep the *tsi-tsit* together, representing utopia, when recounting evidence of our still divided world. (This is reminiscent of diminishing our wine, a symbol of joy, at the Passover *Seder* when recounting the destruction even of our enemies; and of the associated *midrash*: When God brought the Sea of Reeds crashing back together, the angels began singing songs of praise to the Almighty. But God rebuked them, saying "My children are drowning in the sea and you sing!?!?")

Bringing the four corners together may also be done as a reference to the ingathering from the Diaspora (i.e., dispersion), which is requested in *Ahavah Rabbah*.[33]

THE INSERTED WHISPERED LINE

There is a phrase between the first sentence of the *Sh'ma* and the rest of the first paragraph. It is often printed in a smaller font, or in parenthesis:

> *Ba-ruch sheim k'vod mal-chu-to l'olam va-ed.*

This is not in the biblical paragraph. It is a later insertion. This line is recited in an inaudible whisper (except on Yom Kippur).

In the ancient Temple, when the priests called out the first line of the *Sh'ma*, the people responded by answering with this phrase. This exclamation was recorded in the siddur. This line has been translated in different ways. Here are a few of the renderings found in modern prayerbooks:

> "Blessed be his Name, which is the glory of his kingdom for ever and ever."[34]
> "Blessed be the Name of him whose glorious kingdom is for ever and ever."
> "Blessed be the name of his glorious kingdom forever and ever."
> "Blessed be the name of his sovereign glory for ever and ever."
> "Praised be his glorious sovereign Name for ever and ever."

In any case, the key idea is the metaphor of earthly kingship applied to the Jewish God-concept. This reflects the view of the Mishnah (an authoritative repository of Jewish tradition, redacted circa 200 c.e.) that the purpose of reciting the first line of the *Sh'ma* was the acceptance of the "yoke of heaven."

Malchut HaShamayim means "The Kingship of Heaven." The "Kingship of Heaven" is an ever-present reality in Judaism. It is sometimes mistranslated as "Kingdom of God." Christianity tends to use this term to refer to an anticipated future condition. But to Jews, it has always implied an ever-present sovereignty that can be individually percieved and accepted (and thereby effected). Many elements of Jewish congregational liturgy have been used at different times as a "pledge of allegiance" to "the Kingship of Heaven."[35]

Why is the inserted line whispered? According to one view,[36] when the Roman emperors began to rule The Land of Israel as the Roman province of Judea, this congregational response was not seen as just an abstract theological statement, but also as a defiant political declaration advocating a return to theocracy. For fear of the Romans, the response was whispered (except on Yom Kippur). Another view[37] suggests that the whispering is just to indicate that it is not part of the biblical excerpt. A third view suggests that the whispering is a way to stress that we are keeping faith with our spiritual ancestors, by emulating the way Jacob recited that line of the *Sh'ma*.

Keeping Faith With The Past

There is an ancient *midrash*[38] concerning the origin of the first line of the *Sh'ma* and the whispered response:

After Jacob, on his deathbed, addressed his sons individually (Genesis 49:1–8), he summoned them all together again. He knew that just as Esau had abandoned his father Isaac's faith and as Ishmael had abandoned his father Abraham's faith, some of his own sons might have doubts about maintaining the tradition of their father. So he put the question to them, and they replied: "*Hear O Israel*, our father! Just as you have no doubts . . . so do we have no doubts. Rather, *The Lord, our God, the Lord is one.*" Jacob joyously responded as noted in Genesis 47:3: *And Israel bowed down* (i.e., gave thanks and praise to God) *upon the bed's head* (i.e., concerning his children, the issue of his bed[39]) that unworthy ones had not issued from him, exclaiming: *Blessed be the name of his glorious majesty for ever and ever.*

This *midrash* purports to describe the first *K'riyat Sh'ma*. Note that it splits the first line, which was originally recited antiphonally in the Temple. Because of this *midrash*, many Jews view reciting the *Sh'ma* as a way of keeping faith with their ancestors (both genetic and spiritual). The *Sh'ma* binds each new generation to its parents, like a chain back to Jacob.

This *midrash* is also cited as the reason why the second line of the *Sh'ma* is whispered. We are emulating Jacob in his weakened state.

HASH-KI-VEI-NU
(THE EVENING PRAYER)
AND V'SHA-M'RU (EXODUS 31:16–17)

Hash-ki-vei-nu is a key part of Jewish nightly bedtime prayers. (The Jewish analogue of "Now I lay me down to sleep . . ."; but with a very different attitude and message.) At *Ma-ariv* (evening services), *Hash-ki-vei-nu* is added to the end of the *Sh'ma* Section (i.e., after *Ga-al Yisraeil*). Thus *Hash-ki-vei-nu* was once at the very end of evening congregational prayer. (The *Amidah* at *Ma-ariv* was not yet established.) It is not clear which usage of *Hash-ki-vei-nu* came first.

According to the Talmud,[40] this addition to the *Sh'ma* Section was intended to bring the number of daily liturgical prayers to seven, in emulation of the author of Psalm 119: 164, who says, "Seven times a day I praise thee."

The conclusion of the benediction is *"Baruch atah Adonai . . . who guards your people Israel forever."* This clearly indicates that the events recounted in *Ga-al Yisraeil* are indicators of the future redemption. This reassurance has enabled us to survive two millennia of persecution, exile, humiliation, and religious coercion. On *Shabbat* (Friday night), the conclusion of *Hash-ki-vei-nu* becomes, *"Baruch atah Adonai . . . who spreads the shelter of peace over us and over all your people Israel and over Jerusalem."*

Hash-ki-vei-nu was later extended by passages of praise (*Baruch Adonai L'Olam*), containing eighteen references to the divine Name.[41] Later, another addition (*Yiru Ei-nei-nu*) was tacked on. On *Shabbat* (Friday night), *V'sha-m'ru* (Exodus 31:16–17) is appended to *Hash-ki-vei-nu* in lieu of the usual additional passages.[42] *V'sha-m'ru* was described above, as part of the Sanctification of the Day in the *Amidah* for *Shabbat Shacharit*.

MERGING THE SH'MA AND THE AMIDAH

The *Sh'ma* represents the original development of prayer as devotional text. The *Amidah* represents displaced sacrificial worship, by a liturgical form of worship. Together, they are the heart of every Jewish service. It was the sages of the first century c.e. that merged them into a single liturgy. They ruled that nothing could interrupt the flow from *Ga-al Yisraeil* to the *Amidah*.[43] It is still the rule that congregations do not take a break between the *Sh'ma* Section and the *Amidah* Section.

Since there was no evening *Amidah* at that time, this rule applied only to the morning service. Thus the historical core service consists of the *Amidah* in the afternoon and at the *Musaf* service, the *Sh'ma* at the evening service, and the combined *Sh'ma-Amidah* in the morning.

Since the obligation of the evening *Amidah* has been assumed by us for many centuries and is now binding, modern Jews often think of the evening *Sh'ma* and *Amidah* as a unit, and would not break the service between them. But the structure of the service makes it clear that the evening *Amidah* was introduced as a separate nonobligatory inserted section, and was not part of the historical core service. For although *Hash-ki-vei-nu* might be rationalized as an extension of the theme of redemption begun in *Ga-al Yisraeil*, and *V'sha-m'ru* (or *Baruch Adonai L'olam* on weekdays) might be rationalized as an extension of *Hash-ki-vei-nu*, the *Sh'ma* Section is still separated from the evening *Amidah* Section by a Half-Kaddish (discussed below).

BA-R'CHU (THE CALL TO ASSEMBLY)

Long ago the core service was the whole service. The *Sh'ma* Section was begun with The Call to Assembly; and the sacrificial service (now the *Amidah*) ended with the Priestly

Blessing. The Call to Assembly is named for its first word, *Ba-r'chu*. The entire congregation stands up for the *Ba-r'chu*. It is traditional to bow toward Jerusalem. (In America, this is toward the eastern wall of the synagogue, where the Ark generally is.) Here is the reader's call to assembly:

> *Ba-r'chu et Adonai ha-m'vorach*
> (Bless *HaShem* who is to be blessed.)

And the congregation responds:

> *Baruch Adonai ha-m'vo-rach l'olam va-ed*
> (Blessed is *HaShem* who is to be blessed for ever and ever!)

And then the reader repeats the congregational response. This exchange is a major signpost in the service. The congregation then sits for *Yotseir Or* (in the morning) or *Ma-ariv Aravim* (at night).

The *Ba-r'chu* requires a minyan. The *Ba-r'chu* is one of the three places in the liturgy where all present are expected to stand, even if not worshipping.

In Sephardic *shuls* on Friday night, which is the start of the Sabbath, the *Ba-r'chu* gains an introductory meditation known as *K'gav-nah D'i-nun*. This is a complex mystical passage from the *Zohar* (a classic mystical commentary on the Torah). *K'gav-nah D'i-nun* describes God in some of Her mystical attributes. Although other parts of the congregational liturgy may deal with God's feminine aspects, *K'gav-nah D'i-nun* is the only frequently-occurring part of congregational liturgy to address God as feminine. It is not translatable or intelligible without training in Kabbalah (Jewish mysticism). The basic idea is that the limitations imposed on us by material existence make it impossible to understand divine unity fully, but that the experience of the holiness of the Sabbath (which is felt as we start the Shabbat *Ma-ariv* service) will enable insights that are more nearly in unison with those apparent in the transcendental reality that is hidden from us.

Both the *Ba-r'chu* and the Priestly Benediction are still in the liturgy, but they no longer constitute the extremes of the service. A support structure developed around the *Sh'ma-Amidah* service, and expanded outward. Just as the *Sh'ma* picked up attendant blessings over time, the core service was eventually surrounded by attendant sections before and after.

The following diagram shows the structure of Jewish services with the Sh'ma Section added.

Weekday Services:

	Shacharit	Mincha	Ma'ariv
Shema Section	Barchu Yotseir (creation) - weekday version Ahavah Raba (revelation) Shema Ga'al Yisraeil - AM version		Barchu Ma'ariv Aravim (creation) Ahavat Olam (revelation) Shema Ga'al Yisraeil, for P.M. Hashkiveinu for weekday Baruch Hashem L'olam

Amidah Section	Shacharit Shemoneh
	  Esreh:
	- avot, givurot
	- k'dushat hashem
	- 13 benedictions
	- Avodah, Modim
	- Sim Shalom
	
	Meditation
	
	Repetition:
	- avot, givurot
	- k'dushah
	- 13 benedictions
	- Avodah
	- Modim/Modim
	- Sim Shalom
	
	Tachanun
		Mincha Shemoneh
		  Esreh:
		- avot, givurot
		- k'dushat hashem
		- 13 benedictions
		- Avodah, Modim
		- Shalom Rav
		
		Meditation
		
		Repetition:
		- avot, givurot
		- k'dushah
		- 13 benedictions
		- Avodah
		- Modim/Modim
		- Shalom Rav
		
		Tachanun
			Ma-ariv Shemoneh
			  Esreh:
			- avot, givurot
			- k'dushat hashem
			- 13 benedictions
			- Avodah, Modim
			- Shalom Rav
			
			Meditation

Amidah Section of Musaf Service			

Shabbat Services:

Saturday Morning	Saturday Afternoon	Friday Evening
Barchu Yotseir (creation) - Shabbat version Ahavah Raba(revelation) Shema Ga'al Yisraeil, for A.M.		Barchu Ma'ariv Aravim (creation) Ahavat Olam (revelation) Shema Ga'al Yisraeil, for P.M. Hashkiveinu, for Shabbat - with V'shamru
Shacharit Amidah: - avot, givurot - k'dushat hashem - K Hayom-Vishamru - Avodah, Modim - Sim Shalom Meditation Repetition: - avot, givurot - k'dushah - shabbat - K Ha-yom-Vishamru - Avodah - Modim/Modim - Sim Shalom	Mincha Amidah - avot, givurot - k'dushat hashem - K Hayom-Ata Echad - Avodah, Modim - Shalom Rav Meditation Repetition: - avot, givurot - k'dushah - K Hayom-Ata Echad - Avodah - Modim/Modim - Shalom Rav	Ma-ariv Amidah: - avot,givurot - k'dushat hashem - K Hayom-Vayichulu - Avodah, Modim - Shalom Rav Meditation Vayichulu Magein Avot R'tsei Vimnuchateinu
Musaf Amidah: - avot, givurot - k'dushat hashem - K Ha-yom (Yismechu) - Avodah, Modim - Sim Shalom Meditation Repetition: - avot, givurot - k'dushah-musaf - K HaYom (Yismechu) - Avodah - Modim / Modim - Sim Shalom		

Notes

1. c.f., Josephus Antiquities 4:8:13; Misnah Tamid 5:1; Talmud Berachot 11b-12a, Tamid 32b.

2. Deuteronomy 6:4–9, 11:13–21, and 15:37–41.

3. c.f., Sifre Deuteronomy Piska 31 "Hear O Israel . . ."

4. c.f., Talmud Berachot 13b.

5. Scholars of ancient Hebrew might point out that the original meaning could have been "Hear Israel! *Adonai* is our god! *Adonai* alone!" However we are not interested here in what the original orator intended, as much as in what Jews and the prayerbook (and perhaps even the biblical canonizers) mean by it.

6. Star Trek fans: This is the argument that Kirk uses on the bearded Spock in "Mirror Mirror" just before beaming to his own Enterprise.

7. The large "A" (*ayin*) at the end of the first word can also remind us to emphasize the final syllable, so that the word means "Hear!" to all present, rather than sounding like the word for "Perhaps"!

The large "D" (*dalet*), which is also the number four, can be thought of as an allusion to omnipresence, as a reference to the four corners or directions of the earth. *C.f.*, Rambam Mishneh Torah.

8. c.f., Abudarham.

9. Deuteronomy 4:7 originally prompted diversity of opinion on this subject (c.f., Mishnah Berachot 1:3; Yerushalmi Berachot on 1:3). In later times, the tradition had evolved so that Palestinians stood and Babylonians sat (c.f., *The Canonization of the Synagogue Service* by Lawrence A. Hoffman, pp. 46–49, University of Notre Dame Press, 1979). Jewish law adopted the Babylonian practice.

10. This paragraph and the one that follows are paraphrased from the note on page 378 of the Rabbinical Assembly of America's *Sabbath and Festival Prayer Book*.

11. That is, the bearded Spock's empire can't last. See note 6.

12. Some commentators associate the first paragraph with the theme of creation, the second with revelation, and the third with redemption. Or the first with immanence and the second with tran-

scendence. C.f., *Women At Prayer* by Avraham Weiss, pp.26–7, published by KTAV (1990).

13. c.f., Sifre Deuteronomy Piska 34.

14. You will also find fragments of the *Sh'ma* within other parts of the service: *Shabbat Musaf K'dushah*, removing the Torah from the Ark on Saturday morning, and the Morning Supplications of the daily Preliminary Morning Service.

15. This arrangement was established under Rabban Gamliel II around 100 C.E.

16. c.f., Isaiah 45:7 and Talmud Berachot 11b.

17. *Yotseir* contains: "who forms light and creates darkness." *Ma-ariv Aravim* contains a similar reference to both day and night. These lines may be explicitly designed to negate a dualistic Persian doctrine of separate divine sources of light and darkness, good and evil. In any case, by relating light to Torah, and darkness to "evil," we can use these prayers to express appreciation for the totality of reality and assert divine responsibility for it all.

18. There are several poems that have been inserted into *Yotseir Or* over time. On weekdays, *Eil Baruch* touts the creation of the luminaries. It maintains both rhythm and rhyme, while being a word-by-word acrostic on the alphabet. On Shabbat it is replaced by *HaKol Yo-du-cha*, which is a *midrash* on the opening lines of *Yotseir Or*.

On Shabbat, there are two more inserts: *Eil Adon* is an eighth century hymn of praise for the creation of celestial bodies. *Eil Adon* is a double acrostic. The first letters of each line form an acrostic on the alphabet, followed by an acrostic on the names of the planets. And the first words of each line form a completely independent prayer. This independent prayer was once a part of *Yotseir Or* until *Eil Adon* expanded on it. The second inserted Sabbath hymn, *La-eil Asher Shavat*, is based on a midrashic tradition that Adam and the Sabbath sang praises together at the conclusion of creation.

In addition, a variant form of the *K'dushah* has been inserted into *Yotseir* on both weekdays and Shabbat. This is called "*K'dushah d'Yeshiva*" (the Sitting *K'dushah*), or *K'dushah Yotseir*. This may have been put here by Babylonian mystics to allow all Jews, including those unable to join a congregation, to enjoy reciting this important text daily. Recall that, although everyone recites the service three times a day, the repetition of the *Amidah* (and hence the standard *K'dushah*) only happens in a congregational setting.

The result of all this is that *Yotseir Or* is now very long.

19. The phrase comes from Jeremiah 31:3.

20. c.f., Berachot 11b; Hoffman, pp. 30–39. Nusach Sfard follows the Rambam, using *Ahavat Olam* as the opening at all times. c.f., Orach Chaim 60:1.

21. Some form of these blessings are thought to have functioned as Torah-Reading blessings in ancient times.

22. That they follow *Yo-tseir Or* and *Ma-ariv Aravim* reminds us that the Torah is a greater light than the luminaries. The duty to reciprocate divine love by fulfilling the divine plan as perfectly as possible necessitates making the study of the Torah, which is the greatest gift of grace, central to our lives. This is emphasized in *Ahavah Raba* when it recounts eight aspects of growing strong in Torah. The covenant is symbolized by eight, as it is the number of days to circumcision.

23. **Insertions From the Babylonian Diaspora**

In the gaonic period (c. 600 to 1100 C.E.), many additions to the liturgy became established, and divergent liturgical traditions were reconciled in accordance with systematic principles. Several of the practices codified at this time may reflect the desire of Diaspora Jewry to restore the Davidic line (represented by the Babylonian exilarch) to Jerusalem. This was seen as a touchstone of a general resuscitation of Jewish life. (The exilarchs were the dynastic leaders of the Jewish community while in exile. They were recognized as such by the non-Jewish authorities. Later, the exilarch's authority was assumed by the academies.)

In *Yotseir*, the following sentence (known as *Or Chadash*) was inserted before the concluding *chatima*: "Cause a new light to shine upon Zion and may all of us soon be worthy to enjoy its brightness." [This could also be interpreted in an eschatological sense, associated with either Isaiah 40:1 (messianic) or Psalms 136:7 and Isaiah 60:1 (the light stored away for the righteous). Either way, the ideas are wholly unrelated to the main subject of the prayer.]

In *Ahavah Raba*, they added: "Bring us home in peace from the four corners of the earth, and make us walk upright to our land."

Technically, petitions should not be a part of the Sh'ma Section. These insertions violate a basic Jewish idea, by combining two of the five different Jewish modes of worship. Joyous praise, dignified petition, statement of affirmation, abject supplication, and Torah study are not ordinarily mixed. These insertions mixed praise for the past with petition for the future, but were too popular for the Gaonim to eradicate.

24. c.f., Mishnah Berurah to Orach Chayim 70:2.

25. c.f., Talmud Berachot 14a-b; and Hoffman, pp. 39–46.

26. c.f., Talmud Berachot 12a.

27. **Wordplay and Number Harmonies in the Sh'ma**
There are 245 words in the *Sh'ma*. When the reader sings the above sentence aloud (which repeats the last two words that had been said silently), that brings the total to 248, corresponding to the 248 parts of the human frame. (Presumably one is putting them all at the service of one's God-concept.)

When reciting the *Sh'ma* alone (i.e., without a minyan), one first says: "*Eil Me-lech Ne-e-man.*" These three words mean "God is a faithful King." But they are also an acrostic (*A-M-N*) for the word "*a-mein.*" They are added to maintain the number of words at 248.

If "*emet*" is viewed as a part of the *Sh'ma*, then the morning version of *Ga-al Yisraeil* begins with 15 synonyms for "true," corresponding to the 15 words in the last sentence of the *Sh'ma*.

28. *Merkevah* (Chariot) mysticism flourished in the first century c.e. and produced mantras of praise. Examples are scattered throughout the service. This is one of them.

29. *Etz Yosef* draws parallels between each synonym and its corresponding verse.

30. C.f., Talmud Sotah 36b.

31. c.f., Isaiah 30:29.

32. c.f., the climax of the Aleinu prayer, described later.

33. c.f., earlier footnote concerning Babylonian Insertions.

34. c.f., Talmud Ta-anit 16b.

35. The biblical passages at Exodus 20:2–14 and Deuteronomy 5:6–18 are popularly, but innaccurately called "The Ten Commandments." According to some traditional Jewish commentaries, the plain meaning of the text contains only nine command-

ments. Other traditional Jewish commentaries demonstrate (via complex textual analysis) that these passages can be understood as a "shorthand" notation containing all six hundred thirteen commandments.

The Hebrew term for these passages is "*Aseret HaDibrot.*" This can be translated as "The Ten Utterances" or "The Ten Things" (or more idomatically as "The Ten Statements"). Thus the best English word for them is The Decalogue, which comes from Greek for "Ten Utterances."

In any case, the traditional Jewish view is that the whole Torah was divinely revealed to Moses at Sinai. Therefore every commandment, word, and even letter, of Torah is of infinite, hence equal, importance. Thus the Decalogue is not more important than any other part of Torah.

The most ancient form of *K'riyat Sh'ma* (Recitation of the *Sh'ma*) stood on its own as a separate liturgical event. Two thousand years ago, this liturgy consisted of the Decalogue and the *Sh'ma* together; with a blessing before and after. (c.f., Josephus, Antiquities 4:8:13; Mishnah Tamid 5:1)

At that time, the focus of the *Sh'ma* was love for divine service. Reciting the Decalogue was the primary daily ceremony of covenental renewal. So *t'fillin* (c.f., page 45) may have functioned as early prayer-books. The presence of the Decalogue is also hinted at by a line in *Ahavat Rabbah* (c.f., page 151), which may have been the blessing preceding the Decalogue/Sh'ma pair at that time.

By late Tannaitic times (i.e., the third century c.e.), the Decalogue had been removed from the liturgy. (c.f, Yerushalmi Berachot 1:5 [venice 3c, vilna 9a] and 1:8 [3c, 9b]; Bavli Berachot 12a; and Bavli Tamid 35a.)

This may have been done to support the authority of the entire Torah against claims from some non-pharasaic sects that only the Decalogue had come from Sinai; and/or to challenge the later claims of the Church, which sought to invalidate all of the Torah except for the Decalogue. The traditional Jewish view is that every commandment, word, and even letter, of Torah is of infinite, hence equal, importance.

Many Protestant Christian denominations still believe that the Torah is no longer valid, except for "The Ten Commandments." This belief is what the Catholic Church calls the "Doctrine of

Supercessionalism." The current Catholic view, which is relatively new, rejects this doctrine, and recognizes it as a primary cause of antisemitism. According to the Catholic view, Torah is not needed by faithful Christians because Christians enjoy an ability to fulfill God's will in a new and surprising way: a covenant based on their faith, as transmitted to and interpreted by Christians. But according to the new Catholic theology, the original covenant between God and Jews is also a loving gift of divine grace and remains effective. So the Torah, as transmitted to and interpreted by Jews, still represents a viable way for Jews to fulfill God's will. With this declaration, Catholicism has quietly taken a giant leap forward for humankind.

The struggle to maintain the authority of the Torah as opposed to just the Decalogue may also have affected the *Amidah* Section. On Sabbath morning, the Sanctification of the Day (the benediction that replaces the thirteen intermediate petitions of the weekday *Amidah*) extolls Sabbath observance as a sign of the covenant. The introduction begins:

Moses rejoiced at the lot assigned . . .
a faithful servant . . .
He brought down the two tablets of stone
on which was written the observance of the Sabbath,
as it says in your Torah: . . .

The most logical biblical prooftext might seem to be to quote the Decalogue: "Remember the Sabbath day to keep it holy." But *V'sha-m'ru* (c.f., page 110–113) was chosen instead. This careful demotion of the Decalogue seems deliberate.

Without the Decalogue, the *Sh'ma* section was reoriented over time. (c.f., Mishnah Berachot 2:2; Yerushalmi Berachot 1.8.3c.) The attendant blessings gained insertions related to accepting the yoke of heaven. For example:

Ga-al Yisraeil (c.f., page 151) acquired The Song at the Sea, reenacting ancient Israel's acceptance. (c.f., Tosefta Berachot 2, 1; Tosefta Berachot 1,10; Yerushalmi Berachot 1.9.3; Bavli Berachot 14b)
Yo-tseir Or (c.f., page 149) gained a modified *K'dushah*, reenacting the angelic acceptance.

And reciting the first line of the *Sh'ma* publicly represented contemporary Israel's acceptance. (c.f., page 155)

As a result of this transformation, reciting the *Sh'ma* in a congregational service is often referred to as "accepting the yoke/kingship of heaven" in ancient literature, and is still thought of that way. (c.f., Shulchan Aruch, Orach Chayim 70:1)

Generally, the places in the *Sh'ma* Section where the reader and congregation break silence and chant antiphonally are exactly those passages that affirm allegiance (c.f., Philo, Contemplative Life 88; Tosefta Sotah 6, 2–3; Bavli Chullin 91b; Deuteronomy Rabbah 2, 31; Tosefta Pesachim 2, 19).

(For a detailed description of the excision of the Decalogue from the service, see *The Shema and its Blessings: The Realization of God's Kingship*, by Reuven Kimmelman, an essay contained in *The Synagogue in Late Antiquity*, edited by Lee I. Levine, a centenniel publication of the Jewish Theological Seminary of America.)

36. taken from *Ayn Keloheinu*, by Noah Golinkin, Shengold Publishers.

37. cited by Rabbi Hayim Donin in *To Pray as a Jew*.

38. Sifre Deuteronomy Piska 31; see also Pesachim 56a, Targum Yerushalmi at Genesis 49:1 and Deuteronomy 6:4, Targum Jonathan at Deuteronomy 6:4; and Rambam Mishneh Torah 1:1.

39. This interpretation of the Hebrew word for bed is also found in Leviticus Rabbah 36:5.

40. c.f., Talmud Berachot 11b.

41. This probably began in a time and place when the *Shemoneh Esreh* was not yet established at *Ma-ariv* (evening services), but was retained when the *Amidah* was added to the evening service.

42. The variation between the weekday version and the Shabbat version has been related to mystical considerations. Certain passages had come to be regarded as symbolically referring to the dead. The weekday passages were thought to comfort tormented souls. The modified last line (and *Vishamru*) calls to mind that, under the covenant, those souls would be given rest each Shabbat and would not need our mitigation.

43. Talmud Berachot 4b.

The Kaddish

The kaddish is a short mystical prayer that may be recited many times in the course of a single service. It functions like a curtain that is lowered and raised to delimit sections of the service. There are several different melodies, so it will not sound exactly the same each time. The kaddish requires a minyan. There are five different forms of kaddish. All but one occur regularly during services.

THE LITURGICAL USES OF KADDISH

The Half-Kaddish (*Chatzi Kaddish*) is recited by the reader between the major sections of the service. The term "Half-Kaddish" is a misnomer, for it is actually the complete original kaddish. All the other forms consist of the "Half-Kaddish" with some petitions appended. The congregation stands for the Half-Kaddish.

The *Amidah* must be immediately preceded by a Half-Kaddish, except at *Shacharit* (the daily morning service) when the inseparable *Sh'ma-Amidah* pair must be immediately preceded by a Half-Kaddish. This rule is unbreakable, good for any service on any special occasion.

The Full Kaddish (*Kaddish Sha-leim*) is recited by the reader at the end of the service. It appends three requests: for the efficacy of prayer, for peace (in Aramaic), and for peace (in Hebrew). The last petition is just a Hebrew paraphrase of the Aramaic petition that precedes it. The request for the efficacy of prayer is unique to this form of kaddish. It begins with the word "*Tit-ka-beil.*" As a result, this form of kaddish is also called *Kaddish Tit-ka-beil. Kaddish Sha-leim* is the minimum content for the Closing Section of any service.[1] The congregation stands for the Full Kaddish.

Kaddish D'Rabbanan (Scholar's Kaddish) inserts a prayer for scholars in place of the request for the efficacy of prayer. It is said after studying passages of Talmud. This occurs both within and outside the context of synagogue services. At synagogue services, mourners, rather than the reader, usually rise and recite the *Kaddish d'Rabbanan*. Be alert, as local customs vary. In some congregations, all will stand with the mourners. In a few, all will recite.

The Mourner's Kaddish (*Kaddish Yatom*) is said after the recitation of certain Psalms and hymns. It appends to the 'Half-Kaddish' only the two requests for peace. Upon the death of a parent, individual congregants recite the Mourner's Kaddish for eleven (Jewish calendar) months minus one day (i.e., thirty days less than a year). The Mourner's Kaddish is also recited for thirty days after the death of a child, sibling, or spouse; and by those observing a *yahrzeit* (the anniversary of a death of a parent). Tradition regards reciting kaddish under these circumstances as obligatory.

Optionally, an individual may rise and recite the Mourner's Kaddish for close friends, scholars, righteous non-Jews, and Jews who die for the sanctification of the Name (such as many of those murdered in the Holocaust)—but only after losing a parent. If both parents are alive, one does not recite the Mourner's Kaddish.

The mourners rise and recite the Mourner's Kaddish, while all others remain seated if seated, standing if standing. (The reader does not recite it, unless the reader is also a mourner.)

The last form of kaddish is the Expanded Mourner's Kaddish. It is said at the cemetery after a burial, and does not occur in synagogue services.

In Reform synagogues, only the Half-Kaddish and Mourner's Kaddish are used; there is no Full Kaddish nor Scholar's Kaddish.

As in the *Amidah*, and in the Torah-Reading Section (described later), the climactic thought of all the petitions appended to Kaddish is for peace. (Peace is also the final thought of the grace after meals.)

Types of Kaddish

	Petition appended for efficacy of prayer?	Prayer appended for scholars?	Two final petitions appended for *Shalom*?	Who recites?	Who stands?
Half-Kaddish (*Chatzi Kaddish*)	No	No	No	Reader	Congregation (except Sephardim)
Mourner's Kaddish (*Kaddish Yatom*)	No	No	Yes	Mourners	Mourners, and those already standing
Full Kaddish (*Kaddish Shaleim*) (*Kaddish Tit-ka-beil*)	Yes	No	Yes	Reader	Congregation (except Sephardim)
Kaddish D'Rabbanan (Scholar's Kaddish)	No	Yes	Yes	Usually just Mourners	Local custom: Mourners only, or everyone.

THE HISTORICAL DEVELOPMENT
OF THE KADDISH

Scholars speculate that in the First Temple when the priests mentioned the divine Name, the congregation chanted a response similar to Daniel 2:20.[2] By the end of the Second Temple, the response was probably this:

Y'hei sh'mei ra-ba m'va-rach l'a-lam,	May his great name be blessed forever,
L'al-mei u-l'al-mai-ya yit-ba-rach.[3]	Ever and to all eternity be blessed.

Aramaic was the spoken language of Jews for about 1,000 years after the Babylonian captivity (586 B.C.E.). This response is in Aramaic. In Mishnaic times (200 B.C.E. to 200 C.E.), this Aramaic phrase was exclaimed by the congregation at the close of sermons and Torah study. (Sermons and Torah study were not then part of the services.) Sermons were delivered in Aramaic, and religious discourses were held in Aramaic. Hence the kaddish is in Aramaic.

The words *"m'va-rach"* and *"yit-ba-rach"* are different grammatical forms of *"baruch."* Earlier we noted that this root can connote the imperative "to magnify," rather than a descriptive "blessed be."

The kaddish developed around this congregational response,[4] which (with a minor modification) is still the essential part of kaddish.

As biblical passages and Talmudic passages were added to the liturgy, the kaddish was introduced into the liturgy to mark the conclusion of those readings. The evidence (by omission) of the Talmud suggests that kaddish, although very old, was incorporated into the daily liturgy quite late.[5]

KADDISH AS A MOURNER'S PRAYER

Torah study was an activity traditionally engaged in while people were sitting *shiva* for a deceased scholar. (Sitting *shiva* is a mourning process, usually one week long, in which the community gathers in the mourner's home.) To avoid shaming others through such distinctions, it became the norm in the homes of all mourners. As a result, kaddish was recited in the homes of mourners.

There is firm evidence that kaddish was in use as a mourner's prayer by 1208 C.E. Kaddish contains no reference to the dead, but it makes statements that, in the wake of bereavement, are poetic. The kaddish praises the greatness and holiness of the Name. Amidst feelings of disruption, disorientation, and guilt, the mourner affirms life, holiness, and the inevitability of *shalom* (fulfillment, peace).

Reciting kaddish is an important mechanism for preserving the memory of one's deceased parents and incorporating the best of their values in one's life. Reciting kaddish testifies to the merit of one's parents, since this behavior does them credit. The mourner is now the parent's Name, the parent's influence, in this world. Reciting kaddish is an important filial duty[6] and a mechanism for expressing and healing grief. In addition, the requirement for a minyan brings mourners and the community together, ensuring that the bereaved will not be alone.

Every human death diminishes our perception of holiness. Kaddish not only praises the greatness of the divine Name, but reciting kaddish makes the Name greater.[7] The idea that the divine Name is diminished, and divine sanctity lessened, by each human death; and that the mourners can strengthen the divine by reciting kaddish to compensate; is itself a comfort to mourners.

Originally, only one mourner said each Mourner's Kaddish. The multiple occurrences of Mourner's Kaddish at services accommodated attendance by multiple mourners. There is a well–worked-out order of priority for deciding cases of conflict. In many communities, additional opportunities were created by giving the *Kaddish d'Rabbanan* to mourners. Many congregations still follow these practices, but in most congregations, all mourners say kaddish in unison each time it occurs. When no mourners are present, all instances of the Mourner's Kaddish are omitted except the Kaddish after the *Aleinu* prayer, discussed later.

During Mourner's Kaddish, the mourners stand. The rest of the congregation remains seated. If you are already standing for some other reason (e.g., if the prior prayer required all to stand) remain standing as a sign of respect; but do not recite the Mourner's Kaddish unless you are a mourner.

In some less-traditional congregations everyone stands with the mourners, and in some Reform congregations everyone recites the Mourner's Kaddish. The reason sometimes given is that this is done for the victims of the *Shoah* (Holocaust) who might not otherwise have anyone to perform this remembrance for them. In any case, be alert to local custom.

THE CONTENTS OF THE KADDISH

The kaddish begins with a hypnotic introduction, established by the second century c.e., based on Ezekiel 8:23. The opening line is an exhortation to "Magnify and sanctify the great Name in the world he created as he willed."

The key line of the kaddish is the congregational response at its center:

Y'hei sh'mei ra-ba m'va-rach,   May his great name be blessed
L'o-lam u-l'al-mei al-mai-ya.   for ever and to all eternity.

This has seven words and contains twenty-eight letters. This is the same as the first verse of the Torah:

B'rei-shit ba-ra E-lo-him   In the beginning of the creating by God
eit ha-Sha-ma-yim v'eit ha-Aretz   of the heavens and of the land . . .

This numerical correspondence evokes the idea that by reciting kaddish one becomes a partner in the ongoing creation.

The exhortation at the beginning of the kaddish continues with "May He give reign to his kingship, in your lives, in your days." When the congregation takes this opportunity to "rise and sanctify God's Name" by public declaration, it is another example of a congregational response functioning as a "pledge of allegiance" to the "Kingship of Heaven"; another way to make the divine manifest in the world.

The Hebrew word for "strength" is "*ko-ach.*" *Ko-ach* has a numerical value of twenty-eight. The introductory paragraph of the kaddish, along with the congregational response, contains twenty-eight words.[8] The congregational response is followed by a mystical closing paragraph, and together they also have twenty-eight words.[9] Thus the kaddish consists of two twenty-eight word passages whose climactic intersection has twenty-eight letters. Thus the structural form of the kaddish is a mantra on *Ko-ach.* This expresses the idea that we are actually giving strength to the divine Name by reciting kaddish; we empower the divine.

The closing paragraph that follows the central congregational response begins with the word "*Yit-ba-rach*" ("be blessed," or "be magnified"). The congregation frequently includes this word in their response, emulating the practice of ancient times, as noted above.

The closing paragraph then continues with a mystical mantra, consisting of seven synonyms for "*Yit-ba-rach*" before arriving at "*Sh'mei d'Ku-d'shah B'rich Hu*" (the Name of the Holy One, blessed be He). This is like a sevenfold amplification of the Name. The chanting of seven synonyms is a Merkavah technique. Merkevah mysticism was an ancient stream of Jewish thought that shaped several key prayers. The mystics had assimilated from Hellenistic culture the idea of seven heavens. They tried to experience a Heavenly Throne through a process of successive ascent, through mantras of praise accompanied by appropriate body language.

In such prayers, the meanings of words (and their order) may not be important. The mystical idea was to transform the mind from normal cognitive functioning to an altered state of perception, by mantra-like use of words and body language. These long passages of synonyms generally don't translate well, but they work in the original Hebrew or Aramaic. Thus the words of the kaddish are not intended to stimulate thinking. They have the power to help us experience holiness. We have already seen the Merkevah influence in the *K'dushah*, and sporadically in the prayers attendant on the *Sh'ma* (e.g., the beginning of the morning version of *Ga-al Yisraeil*). You will encounter more of this elsewhere.[10]

Recall that the opening of the kaddish calls for "magnification" of the Name; and recall that the congregation responds "May his great Name be blessed," which can also connote "magnified." Recall also that the Name, sometimes called the Tetragrammaton, consists of four letters. Magnifying four letters seven times yields twenty-eight letters. The twenty-eight letters of the congregational response can be thought of as constituting that sevenfold magnification called for in the introduction. Thus on many levels, the structure of the kaddish links the Name with *Koach* through our own declaration of participation in a process of ascent.

INTRODUCTION TO MYSTICISM

Judaism has sometimes been described as "normative mysticism," because recognition of the unknowability of reality pervades the tradition and is expressed constantly in mundane ways throughout daily life. This recognition is embedded throughout law, custom, and ritual.

We have no definition of God. We have many metaphors and epithets, but all are presumed to be inadequate and inaccurate. Everyone has a unique awareness of the transcendental, and a relationship with it, but does not have a lot of details. The mystic in Judaism is not a qualitatively different or gifted person, but is a thoughtful explorer of experience.

The self-created model of perception, which we call "material reality" is necessarily illusory. It depends wholly on us. What it means to *be* is fundamentally unknowable. I may model my awareness as though it were the result of *existence* through *time* of a *self* within a materiality that is *outside*. But "within" and "without" and "time-development" are artificial conceptual parts of my model of self-perception. Reality is what you make it.

Yet we have a faith in the existence of a true reality which is independent of us. It is transcendental and hidden. It is fundamentally unknowable because it is totally other than us. There is a correspondence between the elements of our model (material reality) and the structure of hidden reality. The behavior of our illusory material reality is animated by this correspondence rather than by any internal dynamics of its own. We interact with the true hidden reality, which reacts according to its own dynamics, and the changes in its condition are then reflected in our own illusory reality.

Because of this correspondence, we can contemplate some aspects of hidden reality though it is ultimately unknowable. Mysticism is the probing of this hidden reality and has two facets. One is the philosophical analysis of the hidden reality. What is the structure of the hidden reality and what are its dynamics? This is an intellectual effort in which speculations are logically examined and theories formally developed.

The other facet is the practical attempt to directly experience the hidden reality. Techniques are developed to commune with it, to gain a more direct knowledge of the source of "beingness." To escape the self-created illusory reality, one must transform the mind from normal cognitive functioning to an altered state of perception. Mystics have used

mantras, fasting, sudden inversions of body postures, meditation, and mind-altering substances. Jewish mysticism has
used all but the last of these.

Jewish mystical philosophy is called Kabbalah. In
Kabbalah, the illusory material reality is called the "lower
world," or the world of "separation." The hidden transcendental reality is called the "upper world," or world of "truth."
This hidden divine reality is modeled as *Ein Sof* plus ten
sefirot. *Ein Sof* is the unknowable root of what it means to
be. It is not even contemplatable; we cannot apprehend it.
It is the wellspring of reality. The *sefirot* are humanly
contemplatable aspects of the divine, called "emanations"
from *Ein Sof*, or "garments" or "colors" of *Ein Sof*. They are
all intrinsic to the divine. The divine is represented by a
carefully worked out pattern of structural connections between the *sefirot*, and the characteristics of each of the *sefirot*.
The dynamic interactions between *sefirot*, and the correspondences between each of the *sefirot* and elements of the lower
world, are elaborately examined.

Human conduct influences the upper world, affecting
sefirotic relationships. Even small deeds below can have
large ramifications above. The current condition of the divine structure is badly damaged by human misdeed. Every
moment is an opportunity for repair. The Torah prescribes
a lifestyle in which one consciously and constantly partici-
pates in mending the world. Each *mitzvah* is an act of repair
and an opportunity to mystically experience the *Shechina*
(The Divine Presence; the surface of contact between the
material and the transcendent). *Tikkun Olam* (mending the
world) is the essence of being a Jew, a divine partner.

The process of *Tikkun Olam* is sometimes depicted as
elevating, or releasing, sparks. Sparks are divine light trapped
within all elements of the lower world. Restoring them to the
upper world of harmony corrects imbalances in the *sefirotic*
structure, uniting male and female *sefirot*. Our individual and

communal task is to elevate all elements of material reality to reveal their hidden potential for divine service. This we do by performing *mitzvot*.

"God's job is to make the spiritual material. A Jew's job is to make the material spiritual."

In recent years, it has become possible to read books, and even take courses, on kabbalah. These are lessons *about* kabbalah rather than lessons *in* kabbalah. One cannot take lessons *in* kabbalah until forty years old. One can then learn Kabbalah through a personal relationship with a master. Many of the greatest sages throughout our history, who today are remembered for their political leadership, their Bible commentaries, their legal rulings, or their poetry, were practiced in kabbalah as well. As a result, kabbalistic concepts and images affect the ideas of all Jews, even those that think of themselves as antimystical.

The following diagram shows the structure of Jewish services developed so far, including the Half-Kaddish and the Closing Kaddish. All the occurrences of the Mourner's Kaddish and Scholar's Kaddish are attached to elements of the service not yet on our chart. They will appear later.

Weekday Services:

	Shacharit (morning)	Mincha (afternoon)	Ma'ariv (evening)
Shema Section	Barchu Yotseir (creation), for weekdays Ahavah Raba (revelation) Shema Ga-al Yisraeil - A.M. version		Barchu Ma-ariv Aravim (creation) Ahavat Olam (revelation) Shema Ga-al Yisraeil - P.M. version Hashkiveinu, for weekdays - with Baruch Adonai L'olam
		Half-Kaddish	Half-Kaddish
Daily Amidah Section	Shacharit Shemoneh Esreh: - avot, givurot - k'dushat hashem - 13 benedictions - Avodah, Modim - Sim Shalom Meditation Repetition: - avot, givurot - k'dushah - 13 benedictions - Avodah - Modim/Modim - Sim Shalom Tachanun	Mincha Shemoneh Esreh: - avot, givurot - k'dushat hashem - 13 benedictions - Avodah, Modim - Shalom Rav Meditation Repetition: - avot, givurot - k'dushah - 13 benedictions - Avodah - Modim/Modim - Shalom Rav Tachanun	Ma-ariv Shemoneh Esreh: - avot, givurot - k'dushat hashem - 13 benedictions - Avodah, Modim - Shalom Rav Meditation
Daily Closing Section	Full-Kaddish	Full-Kaddish	Full-Kaddish
Musaf Amidah Section			
Musaf Closing Section			

Shabbat Services:

Saturday Morning	Mincha (Saturday afternoon)	Ma'ariv (Friday night)
Barchu		Barchu
Yotseir (creation), for Shabbat Ahavah Raba (revelation) Shema Ga-al Yisraeil - A.M. version		Ma-ariv Aravim (creation) Ahavat Olam (revelation) Shema Ga-al Yisraeil - P.M. version Hashkiveinu, for Shabbat - with Vishamru
	Half-Kaddish	**Half-Kaddish**
Shacharit Amidah: - avot, givurot - k'dushat hashem - K Hayom-Vishamru - Avodah, Modim - Sim Shalom Meditation Repetition: - avot, givurot - k'dushah - shabbat - K Ha-yom-Vishamru - Avodah - Modim/Modim - Sim Shalom	Mincha Amidah: - avot, givurot - k'dushat hashem - K Hayom-Ata Echad - Avodah, Modim - Shalom Rav Meditation Repetition: - avot, givurot - k'dushah - K Hayom-Ata Echad - Avodah - Modim/Modim - Shalom Rav	Ma-ariv Amidah: - avot, givurot - k'dushat hashem - K Hayom-Vayichulu - Avodah, Modim - Shalom Rav Meditation Vayichulu Magein Avot R'tsei Vimnuchateinu
Full-Kaddish	**Full-Kaddish**	**Full-Kaddish**
Musaf Amidah: - avot, givurot - k'dushat hashem - K Ha-yom (Yismechu) - Avodah, Modim - Sim Shalom Meditation Repetition: - avot, givurot - k'dushah - musaf - K Ha-yom (Yismechu) - Avodah - Modim/Modim - Sim Shalom		
Full-Kaddish		

Notes

1. A mourner leaves out the *titkabal* request. Therefore it is also omitted on *Tisha B'Av*.

2. c.f., Targum Yerushalmi at Deuteronomy 6:4. See also Targum Y. ben Uziel to Genesis 49:1 which attributes the response to Jacob.

3. c.f., Hoffman, p. 57.

4. c.f., Berachot 3a.

5. Parts of the Kaddish appear to be the basis for the opening of the *Pater Noster* (Our Father, The Lord's Prayer) and for the *Magnificat* of the Catholic Church.

6. For some time, kaddish was recited for the full year of mourning. Later on, Jewish mystics ascribed special significance to kaddish. Saying kaddish assisted the souls of the departed in rising to a blissful state (*Gan-Eden*), from a tormented condition (*Gehinnom*) that is the Jewish analogue of hell. They believed that the wicked must spend twelve months in *Gehinnom* so they began to recite kaddish for only eleven months, so as not to count their parents among the wicked. Despite the opposition of many rabbis and philosophers who considered this to be superstition, this became the custom. Furthermore, there is a tradition (originating in Germany) of saying Mourner's Kaddish on the anniversary of death (called by the German word "Jahrzeit," pronounced "*Yartsait*," and sometimes spelled *Yahrzeit* in non-German Jewish sources), to continue the further elevation of the departed soul.

7. c.f., Aruch Ha-Shulchan, Orach Chaim 55:1, Yalkut Shimoni Isaiah 296, Levush Hilchot Berachot 56:1.

8. This is true only of the Ashkenazic version. The Sephardic version inserts an extra four-word phrase in the introduction.

9. This number is achieved by writing "*min chawl bir-cha-tah*" as one trope, using the *makof* (the Hebrew equivalent of a hyphen). Some modern prayerbook editors fail to do this.

10. E.g., *Ha-Aderet v'ha-Emunah* and *Baruch Sheamar* and *Yishtabach, Ana B'Koach*.

The Praise Section

Each service is preceded by an introductory section whose main theme is praise. This is intended to get us into the proper mood for what follows.[1] It helps bridge the wide psychological gap between the active working world and the introspective world of prayer. The main ingredient in these sections are Psalms of praise.

Although the *Musaf* (Additional) Service for Shabbat is almost always performed on Saturday mornings without a break, it is technically a separate event from the daily *Shacharit* (morning) Service, so it has its own praise section.

ASHREI (PSALM 145) AT MINCHA AND MUSAF

At *Mincha* (the daily afternoon service) and at *Shabbat Musaf* (the extra service for Sabbath), the praise section consists of *Ashrei. Ashrei* consists of Psalm 145, prefaced by Psalm 84:5 and 144:15, and followed by Psalm 115:18. "*Ashrei*" means "happiness" or "good fortune." The first two sentences contain the word "*ashrei*" three times:

> Oh the happiness of those that dwell in your house!
>   May they always praise you, *selah!*
> The happiness of the nation for whom this is so!
> The happiness of the nation whose god is *HaShem!*

The first sentence calls to mind the value of prayer and meditation to our psychological and spiritual well-being, while the second tempers the desire to spend one's life absorbed in contemplation, by hinting that progress toward real utopia requires taking what one learns in contemplation, and applying it to the daily trials of communal life.

The main theme of the remainder of *Ashrei* (which is Psalm 145) is that the needs of human society and of every living thing will then be taken care of. *Ashrei* is optimistic, inspiring social justice by citing areas where we can imitate the metaphoric behavior of God as described in the Psalm.

Ashrei is an acrostic on the Hebrew alphabet (i.e., Each sentence starts with the next letter of the alphabet). Many prayers, Psalms, and hymns are structured this way. The use of every letter commmunicates a sense of completeness. In some contexts it is an indication that everything created— from A to Z—is good. In others it indicates that every human faculty is to be employed in divine service. In some cases such acrostic designs are just intended to facilitate memorization. But in *Ashrei*, the letter *"nun"* (corresponds to N) is missing, implying incompleteness. There is a traditional association between the letter *"nun"* and the destruction of the Temple, which gives meaning to the omission here as well as in other alphabetic acrostics.[2]

Ashrei is often sung responsively (i.e., reader and congregation take turns singing alternate lines). The usual music is quite repetitive.[3]

The Talmud[4] deems it meritorious for each individual to recite *Ashrei* three times a day. So *Ashrei* is recited twice every morning and once every afternoon. The *Mincha* Praise Section accounts for one daily afternoon occurrence. On Saturday only, the *Musaf* Praise Section provides one of the two daily morning occurrences. We will encounter the other occurrences of *Ashrei* later.[5]

SHABBAT MA-ARIV

At Shabbat *Ma-ariv* (Friday night), the Praise Section consists of Psalms 92 and 93, followed by a Mourner's Kaddish.

Psalm 92 contrasts righteousness and wickedness. It begins by depicting the wicked as grass, a short-lived seasonal plant. Although begun silently, the congregation often joins in singing the very beautiful ending, called *"Tsadik Katamar,"* which translates as:

> The righteous shall flourish like the date palm,
>> like a cedar of Lebanon grow tall.
> Planted in the House of the LORD,
>> in the courts of our God they shall flourish.
> Still fruitful in old age,
>> full of sap, and green.
> Attesting that the LORD is just,
>> My Rock, no unrighteousness within.

Psalm 92 attests that wickedness is ephemeral while righteousness endures. How many of us remember the names John F. Kennedy, Martin Luther King, John Lennon, and Abraham Lincoln? How many of us remember the names of their murderers? Most Americans will know quite a bit about the first group but be unsure of even the names of the second. Even when we still can remember the killers' names, most of us consider them only as potential answers to a good *trivia* question. Their names are becoming trivia! And the difference between the remembrance of good and evil becomes greater over time, attesting to the transcendence of the good. The faults of net contributors fade with time; their memory is a blessing that empowers others. The net detractors fade away; their influence dissipated.

Psalm 92 was the Psalm of the Day used on Shabbat mornings in the ancient Temple. Psalm 92 depicts the world at rest, confident, and happy. In the *Midrash*, Psalm 92 is the song that Adam and the Sabbath sang together on the first night. (This is referred to in *Yo-tseir Or*, the first benediction of the *Sh'ma* section.) In Jewish tradition, Psalm 92, like each Sabbath itself, is considered a foretaste of the world to come.

Psalm 93 was the Psalm of the Day used on Friday mornings in the ancient Temple. Traditionally, the power and majesty described in Psalm 93 is thought of as evidencing the security of the moral order in the world. Mourner's Kaddish follows.

In Ashkenazic Orthodox *shuls*, this recitation of the Mourner's Kaddish will be followed[6] by excerpts from the Talmud, dealing with the rules for lighting Shabbat candles, and with the responsibility of scholars to bring peace. This is called *Ba-meh Mad-li-kin*, which are its opening words. Then a *Kaddish d'Rabbanan* (Scholar's Kaddish, recited only by mourners in most *shuls*) completes the Talmud study and ends the Praise Section. Sephardic *shuls* defer the Talmud study until the Closing Section, or omit it entirely.

Conservative synagogues generally omit the Talmud study. Reform synagogues replace it with a candle-lighting ceremony. (Conservative and Orthodox Jews light candles at home before sundown. This marks the beginning of their Sabbath observance. In Reform synagogues, candles are often lit by an individual as part of the service.[7])

OTHER EVENINGS

At *Ma-ariv* for the conclusion of Shabbat (i.e., on Saturday nights), the Praise Section consists of Psalms 144 and 67. They express the joy resulting from work.

At *Ma-ariv* (the evening service) on weekdays, the Praise Section consists of Psalm 134, followed by three phrases:

Psalms 46:8, 84:13, and 20:10. But if weekday *Ma-ariv* is said immediately following *Mincha* (which is the usual arrangement), then the Praise Section is omitted from *Ma-ariv*, since we are already in the proper frame of mind.

THE VERSES OF PRAISE (P'SU-KEI D'ZIM-RAH)

At *Shacharit* (the morning service) the Praise Section is quite long. Psalms 145 through 150 form the heart of it.[8] This is a symbolic finishing of the entire book of 150 Psalms, reflecting a desire to have recited the whole collection. The custom of some pious individuals to arrive early in the morning to chant Psalms goes back at least to the second century.[9] The morning Praise Section is framed by benedictions that function as a prologue (*Ba-ruch She-a-mar*) and epilogue (*Nishmat/ Yishtabach*). Between the prologue and epilogue, but outside the central psalms, are a variety of biblical texts that are prominent passages of praise. This whole liturgical structure is called *P'sukei D'zimrah* ("Verses of Praise" or "Verses of Song"). The current selection and arrangement of texts was sanctioned by the *Gaonim* (the heads of the ninth century Babylonian academies; "*Gaon*" means "Excellency").

In Ashkenazic rite, the structure looks like this:

The Verses of Praise for Weekday Mornings (Ashkenazic Rite):
Prologue: *Ba-ruch She-a-mar*
  Biblical Song: David's song of praise, on bringing the Ark to Jerusalem (I Chronicles 16:8–36)
  Biblical passages of praise: *Ro-m'-mu Adonai*
    Psalm 100 (*Mizmor L'Todah*) and *Y'hi Ch'vod*
    Psalms 145 through 150
  Biblical passages of praise: (I Chronicles 29:10–13; Nehemiah 9:6–11)
  Biblical Song: The Song at the Sea (Exodus 14:30–15:18)
Epilogue: *Yishtabach*

THE PROLOGUE (BA-RUCH SHE-A-MAR) AND OTHER CONTENTS OF THE VERSES OF PRAISE

The original prologue was a formal benediction, traditionally ascribed to the Men of the Great Assembly during the Persian period (circa 450–325 B.C.E.). A mystical introduction (beginning *Ba-ruch She-a-mar* . . .) was added in gaonic times to give the prologue a total of eighty-seven words. This word count is a deliberate reference to The Song of Songs 5:11, which says: "His opening words were finest gold." The numeric value of "finest gold" is eighty-seven. Therefore one could have translated the biblical passage as: "His opening words were eighty-seven [in number]." Since we wish our words to be like the finest gold, and wish our song to be as effective as King Solomon's, our prologue to the Verses of Song uses eighty-seven words.

The first group of biblical passages begins with King David's song upon bringing the Ark to Jerusalem (I Chronicles 16:8–36; *Hodu Ladonai* . . .), which is based in part on Psalm 105. This is followed by *Ro-m'mu Adonai*, which is a collage of biblical verses.[10] Then come the Psalms, which form the heart of the Verses of Praise. Afterwards come more biblical texts, beginning with the last words of David (I Chronicles 29:10–13), followed by the last praise in scripture (Nehemiah 9:6–11), and finishing with the "Song at the Sea" (Exodus 14:30 to 15:18).[11]

Yish-ta-bach is the epilogue to the Verses of Praise. An acrostic message at the beginning of *Yish-ta-bach* says "Praised be Solomon the King," which has encouraged a tradition ascribing *Yish-ta-bach* to King Solomon or his court. *Yish-ta-bach* includes a chant of fifteen synonyms of praise in the Merkevah mantra style. Each word is traditionally associated with one of the fifteen Psalms known as "Songs of Ascents," Psalms 120 to 134. After this climactic chant of praise, *Yishtabach* concludes with a benediction to complete the Verses of Praise: "*Baruch atah Adonai*. . . . extolled with praises . . . creator of all breath . . . who makes choice of song and psalm . . . the life of all worlds."

PSALM 100 (MIZMOR L'TODAH) AND Y'HI CH'VOD

On weekdays, Psalms 145 to 150 are preceded by Psalm 100 followed by *Y'hi Ch'vod*. *Y'hi Ch'vod* is a collection of eighteen biblical verses (taken from Psalms, Chronicles and Proverbs), mentioning the divine Name eighteen times.

Psalm 100 is also known by its opening words, *Mizmor L'Todah* ("A Song of Thanks"). In the ancient Temple, Psalm 100 was sung in association with thanks-offerings. Thanks-offerings were personal offerings brought after surviving a threatening situation. Today, when we recognize a major reason to give thanks, we generally do so with a special blessing, called *Ha-go-meil*, said during the Torah-Reading Section of the service (c.f., page 222).

Today, Psalm 100 is included in the weekday Verses of Praise as an expression of appreciation for all the tiny, unrecognized, daily redemptive miracles that comprise continued existence.[12] The congregation stands while reciting Psalm 100.

THY MIRACLES DAILY WITH US

There is no Hebrew word corresponding to the English word, "miracle," in the limited sense of a suspension of natural physical laws. The closest Hebrew word, *nes*, means "wonder." The physical laws themselves produce wonders and were thought of as a divine medium of expression. The sages saw a wondrous deed in every benefit that came from material reality. Each tree, flower, and drop of rain was a miracle and a worthy reason to spend time in appreciation of a miracle. In *Modim*, the explicit prayer of thanksgiving that is the eighteenth benediction of the *Amidah*, we cite (among other things) "Thy miracles [that are] daily with us."

The wonders of the Bible, such as the nourishing manna that fell from heaven,[13] the mouth of Balaam's talking ass,[14] Noah's rainbow after the flood,[15] the staff that performed the miracles in Egypt and that parted the Sea of Reeds,[16] and the mouth of the earth that swallowed Korach and his followers[17] were regarded by the ancient rabbinic sages as having been "constructed at creation" in divine anticipation of the kinds of occasions when they might be needed. Therefore, although such phenomena have occurred so infrequently as to appear unique, they are nonetheless built-in features of the world rather than supernatural events.[18]

Miracles in Judaism are never theological proofs. They occur in scripture and folklore as exclamation points in the narrative, producing a dramatic effect. But they are never offered to buttress an argument. Miracles must never frighten one into abrogating one's responsibility for rational discussion and decision.

The Rambam said, "He who believes because of miracles still has doubts."

It is not in Heaven

The Rabbis are debating a fine point of law—the kashrut of an oven—in the academy at Yavnah. Eliezer, the greatest authority of all, is present. But Eliezar is failing to convince his colleagues.

He says: "If the Law be as I say, let yon carob tree prove it!" Immediately, a nearby carob tree uproots itself, flies 100 yards into the air—maybe even 400—and then crashes to the ground! "What does a carob tree know of the Law?" reply the other sages. But Eliezar knows he is right, and says: "If the Law be as I say, let yon stream prove it!" Immediately, the nearby stream churns, throws up rocks, and reverses direction! "What does a stream know about ovens?" replies the unperturbed assembly of sages. Eliezar continues: "If the Law be as I say, let the very walls of this academy prove it!" And indeed the walls begin to fall inward. But Rabbi Joshua leaps forward and addresses the walls: "Stop! When great scholars debate the Law, what right have walls to interfere?" And the walls did not fall—out of respect for Rabbi Joshua. But neither did they straighten—out of respect for Rabbi Eliezar. And they remain leaning to this very day! Now Eliezar is frustrated, and exclaims: "If the Law be as I say, let Heaven itself prove it!" BIG THEOPHANY OCCURS, and a voice from everywhere says, "Why do you contend with Rabbi Eliezar when you know the Law is always as he says?" Their calm response: "It is not in heaven."

Some time later, one of the sages encountered the Prophet Elijah and asked what had gone on in the heavenly court on the day of that famous debate. Elijah reports that God laughed and laughed with happiness, laughed till tears came, saying: "My children have defeated me. My children have defeated me."

The point of their response, "It is not in heaven," is that prophesy cannot alter Torah, and Study (of Torah) is now the instrument of revelation. The covenant established at Sinai was binding on both parties and is the complete contract, and nothing unilateral is valid. Halacha follows the majority of authorized sages, as prescribed in the eternal Torah itself.

adapted from the Talmud, tractate *Bava Metzia*, folio 59b.

THE VERSES OF PRAISE ON THE SABBATH AND FESTIVALS

In the Temple, thanks-offerings were not made on Shabbat and festivals. So Psalm 100 is not included in the Verses of Praise at those times.

Instead, Psalms 145 to 150 are preceded by another collection of Psalms. The particular Psalms were selected to help us reflect on three themes: the creation, the exodus (and its consequences), and the idea of Shabbat as a foretaste of *Olam Ha-Ba* (the utopian world to come). They are Psalms 19, 34, 90, 91, 135, 136, 33, 92, and 93.

A second difference on the Sabbath and festivals is that the Verses of Praise conclude with an elaborate hymn of praise, called *Nish-mat*. *Yish-ta-bach* (the epilogue on weekdays) is actually just the last paragraph of *Nish-mat*.

The Verses of Praise on Saturday Morning (Ashkenazic Rite)

Prologue: *Baruch She-amar*
> Biblical Song: David's Song of Praise, on bringing the Ark to Jerusalem (I Chronicles 16:8–36)
>> Biblical passages of praise: *Ro-m'-mu Adonai*
>>> **Psalms 19, 34, 90, 91, 135, 136, 33, 92, and 93.**
>>> Psalms 145 through 150.
>> Biblical passages of praise: (I Chronicles 29:10–13; Nehemiah 9:6–11)
> Biblical Song: The Song at the Sea (Exodus 14:30–15:18)

Epilogue: **Nishmat**/*Yishtabach*

Whenever Psalm 91 is used in prayer, its last line is repeated and is printed twice in the siddur. This is a symbolic repetition of the whole Psalm, which increases the total number of words from 124 to 248, which is the number of positive comandments and also traditionally the number of parts of the human frame.

THE GREAT PRAISE (PSALM 136)
"KI L'O-LAM CHAS-DO"

One of the extra Psalms included on Shabbat and festivals is Psalm 136, traditionally known as "The Great Praise" (*Halleil Ha-Gadol*).[19] Psalm 136 has twenty-six verses. Each verse recounts a powerful divine deed and then characterizes it as a kindness.

The verses list specific divine acts of might that were involved in the creation, the exodus, and in giving the Land of Israel to us. The recurring refrain is *"Ki l'o-lam chas-do,"* meaning "For His kindness is everywhere," or "For His kindness is forever," or even "For His kindness is for the world." Thus the refrain could celebrate providential care, or it could indicate the enduring nature of each of the acts, or it could celebrate selflessness.

The climactic last example is different from the others. The other verses cite dramatic exhibitions of power, but the last verse is: "He gives bread to all flesh, *Ki l'olam chasdo.*" This expresses the idea that the divine care evident in providing for all is equal to all the wondrous deeds cited in the previous verses.

The structure of the Psalm also alludes to kindness. The twenty-six verses correspond to the twenty-six generations that lived before the giving of the Torah. These generations were sustained by kindness, without an ability to keep *mitzvot.*

Twenty-six is also the numerical value of the divine Name. For this reason, many congregations stand when reciting Psalm 136.

NISHMAT

Nishmat, the conclusion of the Verses of Praise on Shabbat and festivals, is an elaborate hymn of praise. It is built out of numerous Biblical quotations and allusions. Its contents, and their order, were fixed long before the Verses of Praise became fixed.[20] *Nishmat* begins with:

The breath of all life shall praise your Name . . .

This is a reference to the end of Psalm 150 (". . . Let all that breathes praise *HaShem.*"), which once may have been recited just before *Nishmat*. *Nishmat* continues the themes of The Song at the Sea, which it now follows, and echoes its phrases and imagery.

Many literary devices are exploited in *Nishmat*, resulting in soaring poetry. This is apparent even in translation. Here is an excerpt:

Were our mouth[s as] full of song as [the] sea [is of water],
and our tongue[s as filled with] joy as the number of its waves;
Our lips [as wide] with praise as the width of the firmament,
and our eyes [as] enlightening as [the] sun and moon;
[Were] our hands [as] outspread as eagles of the sky, and our
    feet light as deer,
We could never sufficiently thank you, *HaShem*, Our God and
    God of our Ancestors,
and bless your Name for even one of the thousands
of billions
of trillions of goodnessess
which you did for our ancestors
and for us . . .

Nishmat includes many biblical verses. Here is its treatment
of Psalm 35, verse 10:

Therefore the limbs you have apportioned us,
and the spirit and breath you have breathed into our nostrils,
and the tongue that you have set in our mouth[s],
shall all   thank,   [Seven step ascent, mantra to the Throne
                bless,   of Glory]
                praise,
                glorify,
                exalt,
                revere,
                hallow,
and make sovereign your Name, Our King.
                        [Using Isaiah 45:3, similar to *Aleinu*]
For every mouth to you will give thanks,
        and every tongue to you will swear,
Every knee to you will bend,
        and every frame prostrate itself before you,
All hearts shall revere you,
        and all innards and kidneys sing unto your Name,

As it is written:

> *"All my bones will say, HaShem, who is like unto you?"*
> [Psalms 35:10].

In the ancient anatomical metaphors quoted above, the heart is the seat of intellect and personality, not of emotion. The modern equivalent would be "brain" or "mind." The bowels are the seat of deep emotions. The modern metaphor for this is the heart. And the kidneys are the seat of conscience and innermost thoughts. (The liver, not mentioned in the quote above, was the seat of anger, the cause of losing one's temper.)

Nishmat includes *midrashic* exegesis (explanatory expansion) of biblical passages:

> Who is like unto you? Who is equal to you? And who can be compared to you?
> *"The God, The Great, The Mighty, and The Awesome"*
> [Deuteronomy 10:17]
> *The God*—in your strength's power
> *The Great*—in your name's honor
> *The Mighty*—for ever
> *and The Awesome*—through your awesome doings.

Nishmat also includes acrostics. The last four of the verses below have been broken into columns to call attention to an acrostic. This is also done in many *siddurim*. In Hebrew, each of these verses has only three words. (The English words "you shall be" are conveyed by the grammar of the last Hebrew word in each verse.) The first Hebrew letters of the central words ("upright," "righteous," "loving," and "holy"), spell *"Yitz-chak"* ("Isaac"). In the Sephardic version of *Nishmat*, the four last words of the verses ("praised," "blessed," "exalted," and "hallowed") are reordered so that their first letters spell *"Riv-kah"* ("Rebecca"), making a rather sophisticated double acrostic.

He who inhabits eternity, exalted and holy is his name;
and it is written:
"Express joy, [you] righteous [ones], in *HaShem*;
            For the upright, fitting is praise." [Psalm 33:1]

By the mouth[s]	[Y]	of the upright	you shall be	praised
by the lips	[Tz]	of the righteous	you shall be	blessed
by the tongue[s]	[Ch]	of the loving	you shall be	exalted
and in the midst	[K]	of the holy	you shall be	hallowed.

Nishmat culminates in a concluding benediction that parallels its opening: "*Baruch atah Adonai* . . . extolled with praises . . . (creator of all breath . . .) who makes choice of song and psalm . . . the life of all worlds."

On weekdays, *Nishmat* is abbreviated. Only its final paragraph (*Yishtabach*) is recited.

THE BEGINNING OF THE MORNING SERVICE: PSALM 30

There is an addition at the beginning of the morning service. It consists of Psalm 30 (followed by a Mourner's Kaddish).

Although the Psalm's original meaning may have related to surviving an illness, the text of this Psalm can be used to reflect gratitude for having awakened from the night's sleep (rather than having died). So it is an appropriate first prayer of the day.

Furthermore, tradition holds that this Psalm was used by Solomon to inaugurate the First Temple, and by the Maccabees to rededicate the Second Temple. Thus it is also an appropriate beginning for our synagogue service.[21]

SINGING PSALMS SILENTLY

Usually, the Psalms of the Praise Section are recited quietly and independently. Some congregants read fast while others read slow. Some people have swaying body motions that indicate their progress. This results in an exciting drone; an unchanging sonic envelope animated within.

The reader sings the last few lines of each Psalm and the first line of the next. This is done elaborately and takes up time, so that everyone is together as the congregation moves silently from one Psalm to the next. This is also an art form. The reader has total freedom to improvise beautiful recitatives at length. (Recitative is an operatic term, denoting unstructured musical emulation of speech.) Ideally, the reader would begin singing the last line just as the fastest congregant finished the Psalm, and would complete the last line just as the slowest congregant finished.

Less traditional congregations may excerpt Psalms from this section and sing (and study) them aloud together.

KABBALAT SHABBAT AND L'CHA DODI

On Friday night, there is a preliminary service called *Kabbalat* Shabbat. In English we call it "Welcoming the Sabbath." The metaphor of Sabbath as a guest in our homes is deeply impressed in Jewish thought. This service was introduced by Jewish mystics in Safed (in Galilee) in the sixteenth century. It makes the Friday evening service very different and very beautiful. *Kabbalat Shabbat* is omitted when Shabbat coincides with a festival.

Kabbalat Shabbat begins with six psalms, representing the six working days of the week. They are 95, 96, 97, 98, 99, and 29 (*Havu L'Adonai*). These were selected by Rabbi Moses Cordovero.[22] This section of the *Kabbalat Shabbat* is called "*L'chu N'ra-n'na*," which are the first words of Psalm 95. As we proceed through each psalm, congregants have an opportunity to recall the events of the corresponding day of the week now ending, and to let go of them.

In all Jewish services, the cantor gets to improvise melodies in familiar Jewish modes (musical scales other than major and minor). In traditional synagogues, there is a certain musical mode peculiar to *Kabbalat Shabbat*.

The six "working days of the week" (i.e., the Psalms) are followed by the wonderful poem, *L'cha Dodi*. *L'cha Dodi* is constructed out of a mosaic of biblical phrases, yet it is seamless. Each stanza has four phrases; the first three rhyme, and the last ends in a common rhyme throughout the entire poem. The poem is also an acrostic; the first letters of each stanza spell out the author's name. It was written by Rabbi Solomon Alkabets, the brother-in-law of Rabbi Cordovero, in the middle of the sixteenth century. (The acrostic spells "*Sh'lo-mo Ha-Lei-vi*," i.e., Solomon the Levite.)

L'cha Dodi depicts the incoming Sabbath as a beloved bride; and the community is the groom honoring and welcoming her. (This is similar to the metaphorical sexual relationship between God and Israel, established in Jeremiah 2:2, and applied to the Song of Songs.) Like Shabbat itself, *L'cha Dodi* is much beloved, and thousands of melodies have been written for it. On the last verse the congregation rises and faces the door to welcome the Sabbath Bride. The original Safed mystics went to meet her and escorted her in from the edge of town, all of them dressed in white and singing.

L'cha Dodi is easy to learn. In many congregations the cantor sings all the verses, and the congregation sings the recurring refrain[23]:

L'cha Do-di lik'rat ka-la
p'nei Shabbat n'ka-b'la

Come, my friend, to meet the Bride!
The face of Shabbat let us welcome!

In the last verse, as the poem reaches its climax, "Come! O Bride! Come! O Bride!" the congregation bows three times as it turns back to facing the front, as though it were following the progress of the Bride as she walks from the door to the front.

L'cha Dodi is the end of the preliminary *Kabbalat Shabbat* service. It will be followed by the regular Friday night Praise Section (i.e., Psalm 92 and Psalm 93 followed by a Mourner's Kaddish). Since mourning customs are suspended on Shabbat, Friday evening is the first time mourners attend synagogue after a death. (During the week, congregants will make a minyan at mourners' homes.) In most synagogues there is a custom that the mourners, in their first week of mourning, wait by the door until this point.[24] Or they may seat themselves for *Kabbalat Shabbat*, but get up and leave just before *L'cha Dodi*. When there are mourners waiting at the door, the congregation does not turn back to the front during *L'cha Dodi*. Instead, now that it has faced the door and "noticed" them, it says words of comfort to them in unison:

Ha-ma-kum y'na-cheim et'chem b'toch sh'ar a-vei-lei tsi-on viy-ru-sha-lay-im.

May The Omnipresent comfort you among the other mourners for Zion and Jerusalem.

The mourners then enter and seat themselves. Note that the phrase, "the other mourners," refers to ourselves, the entire congregation. The community is in mourning for the loss of the Temple, hence we empathize rather than sympathize.

When festivals coincide with Shabbat, the *Kabbalat Shabbat* service is omitted. The service begins with the praise section of the *Ma-ariv* service.

Our diagram of Jewish worship, now revised to include the Praise Section of each service, follows:

Weekday Services:

	Shacharit (morning)	Mincha (afternoon)	Ma'ariv (evening)
Preliminary Service			
Praise Section	Psalm 30 / Mourner's Kaddish prologue: Baruch Sheamar - texts - Psalms 100 - Psalms145 (Ashrei) thru 150 - texts epilogue: Yishtabach Half-Kaddish	Ashrei (Psalm 145) Half-Kaddish	Psalm 144 (Sat. only) Psalm 67 (Sat. only) Psalm 134 (if no Mincha) Half-Kaddish (if no Mincha)
Shema Section	Barchu Yotseir (creation), for weekdays Ahavah Raba (revelation) Shema Ga-al Yisraeil - A.M. version		Barchu Ma'ariv Aravim (creation) Ahavat Olam (revelation) Shema Ga-al Yisraeil - P.M. version Hashkiveinu, for weekdays - with Baruch Adonai L'olam Half-Kaddish

Shabbat Services:

	Shacharit & Musaf (Saturday Morning)	Mincha (Saturday Afternoon)	Ma'ariv (Friday Evening)

Preliminary Service			**Kabbalat Shabbat:**
			- Psalm 95
			  (L'chu N'ran'na)
			- Psalm 96 & 97
			- Psalm 98 & 99
			- Havu L'adonai
			  (Psalm 29)
			- L'cha Dodi
			greeting mourners

Praise Section	Psalm 30 / Mourner's
	  Kaddish
	prologue:Baruch Sheamar
	- texts
	- Psalms: 19, 34, 90-1,
	  135-6, 33, 92-3,
	- and Psalms145 (Ashrei)
	  thru 150
	- texts
	epilogue: Nishmat-
	  Yishtabach
	Half-Kaddish
		Ashrei (Psalm 145)
		Uva L'Tsion
		
		Half-Kaddish
			- Psalm 92
			- Psalm 93
			- Mourner's Kaddish
			
			- Torah Study,
			  on candles
			- Kaddish D'Rabbanan

Shema Section	Barchu
	
	Yotseir (creation),
	  for Shabbat
	Ahavah Raba (revelation)
	  (revelation)
	Shema
	Ga-al Yisraeil -
	  A.M. version
			Barchu
			
			Ma-ariv Aravim
			  (creation)
			Ahavat Olam
			
			Shema
			Ga-al Yisraeil -
			  P.M. version
			Hashkiveinu, for
			  Shabbat
			- with Vishamru
			
			Half-Kaddish

Continued on next page

Amidah Section	Shacharit Shemoneh Esreh: - avot, givurot - k'dushat hashem - 13 benedictions - Avodah, Modim - Sim Shalom Meditation Repetition: - avot, givurot - k'dushah - 13 benedictions - Avodah - Modim/Modim - Sim Shalom Tachanun	Mincha Shemoneh Esreh: - avot, givurot - k'dushat hashem - 13 benedictions - Avodah, Modim - Shalom Rav Meditation Repetition: - avot, givurot - k'dushah - 13 benedictions - Avodah - Modim/Modim - Shalom Rav Tachanun	Ma-ariv Shemoneh Esreh: - avot, givurot - k'dushat hashem - 13 benedictions - Avodah, Modim - Shalom Rav Meditation
Closing Section	Full-Kaddish	Full-Kaddish	Full-Kaddish
Musaf Praise Section			
Musaf Amidah			
Musaf Closing Section			

Amidah Section	Shacharit Amidah:	Mincha Amidah	Ma-ariv Amidah:	
	- avot, givurot - k'dushat hashem - K Hayom-Vishamru - Avodah, Modim - Sim Shalom	- avot, givurot - k'dushat hashem - K Hayom-Ata Echad - Avodah, Modim - Shalom Rav	- avot, givurot - k'dushat hashem - K Hayom-Vayichulu - Avodah, Modim - Shalom Rav	
	Meditation	Meditation	Meditation	
	Repetition: - avot, givurot - k'dushah - shabbat - K Ha-yom-Vishamru - Avodah - Modim/Modim - Sim Shalom	Repetition: - avot, givurot - k'dushah - K Hayom-Ata Echad - Avodah - Modim/Modim - Shalom Rav	Vayichulu Magein Avot R'tsei Vimnuchateinu	
Closing Section	Full-Kaddish	Full-Kaddish	Full-Kaddish	
Musaf Praise Section	Ashrei (Psalm 145) Half-Kaddish			
Musaf Amidah	Musaf Amidah: - avot, givurot - k'dushat hashem - K Ha-yom (Yismechu) - Avodah, Modim - Sim Shalom			
	Meditation			
	Repetition: - avot, givurot - k'dushah - musaf - K Ha-yom (Yismechu) - Avodah - Modim/Modim - Sim Shalom			
Musaf Closing Section	Full-Kaddish			

Notes

1. c.f., Mishnah 5:1, Talmud Berachot 32a.
2. The version found in the Dead Sea scrolls includes the missing line!
3. It can also be sung to the tune of *Anim Z'mirot*.
4. c.f., Berachot 4b.
5. They are: the Verses of Praise in the daily *Shacharit* Praise Section, and *Uva L'Tsion* in the weekday Closing Section.
6. on nonfestival Friday nights.
7. Sabbath candle-lighting was a pharasaic innovation, begun in hellenistic times. But the associated blessing was only adopted in the eleventh century. It was an adaptation of the Chanuka candle-lighting blessing.
8. c.f. Talmud Shabbat 118b.
9. c.f., Psalms 119:147–8; and Talmud Berachot 9b.
10. It is constructed of Psalm 99:5, 99:9, 78:38, 40:12, 25:6, 68:35–6, 94:1–2, 3:9, 46:8, 84:13, 20:10, 28:9, 33:20–22, 85:8, 44:27, 81:11, 144:15, and 13:6.
11. Tradition holds that the "Song of the Sea" was sung in the Temple during afternoon sacrifices. After the destruction of the Temple, the remaining Jews sang it as the ending of their Morning Praise Section (before *Yishtabach* took that spot). This custom spread to Italy, and eventually throughout the world. It was introduced in Germany in the eleventh century.
12. The thanks-offering was a personal offering, hence it was not brought on Sabbaths and festivals, and so Psalm 100 is only said on weekdays. The thanks-offering had to be eaten by midnight on the day it was donated, and so Psalm 100 is excluded on the day before Yom Kippur. The offering included bread, so Psalm 100 is excluded on *erev* and *chol hamoed Pesach*.
13. Exodus 16:1–35.
14. Numbers 23:2–33.
15. Genesis 9:13.
16. Exodus 4:2–5, 7:9–21, 8:1, 8:12, 9:23, 10:13, 10:21, 14:16–28, Numbers 18:17–25, 20:7–12, etc.
17. Numbers 16:1–35.

18. c.f., Talmud Pesachim 54a; Mishnah Avot 5:9; Genesis Rabbah 5.5; Rambam *Guide to the Perplexed* 2.29 and 3.24.

19. Talmud Pesachim 118a.

20. c.f., Mishnah Pesachim 10:7, Talmud Bavli Berachot 59b, Pesachim 118a.

21. In Sephardic rite, David's Song of Praise and *Ro-m'-mu Adonai* are placed in front of Psalm 30 at the head of the Praise Section.

22. The first letters of the six Psalms have the numerical value of 430 which equals that of *"nefesh"* (soul).

These are dramatic "nature psalms," featuring forces unleashed. They form a sequence. First, all creation joyously proclaims divine transcendence. Ancient sages saw a progression from this to recounting divine love for humanity, reflected in immanence, and culminating in the giving of the Torah at the climax of Psalm 29. They regarded Torah as synonymous with "strength" (and through biblical parallelism, "peace") in Psalm 29. (In addition, Psalm 29 features the phrase "The Voice of the Lord" seven times, which is another reason why it may have been selected.)

23. The refrain is based on Talmud Shabbat 199a.

24. In Jewish tradition, mourning is suspended during Shabbat. During weekdays, visitors make a minyan at the homes of mourners.

The Torah-Reading Section (K'riy-at HaTorah)

WHAT IS TORAH?

Like many of the important words in Judaism, 'Torah' can not be properly translated in a single English word. It is a set of related concepts that are metaphorically one in traditional Jewish thought. (Other examples of single Jewish concepts that translate to separate concepts in Western thought include: commandments and good deeds; worship and work;[1] justice and alms-giving;[2] "to do" and "to rectify."[3])

Torah can be translated as "Teaching," "Law," or "Way." In its most limited sense, Torah refers to The Five Books of Moses, also called the Pentateuch (Greek for "five books"). This is the oldest and most authoritative part of the *Tanach* (Jewish Scriptures).[4]

Traditionally, the Torah is thought of as the blueprint for building a utopian society, and as the revelation of divine will. *Mattan Torah* (the giving of the Torah) at Sinai is regarded as an incredible act of divine lovingkindness,[5] and as the central transforming event in human history.

The Torah functions as the national constitution of the Jewish people, and is also viewed as an early history of the nation. The Torah evidences the "election" of Israel by God. It is thought of as a negotiated, mutually agreed-upon contract establishing a mutually-dependent partnership between Jews and God, binding on both parties. The contract is commonly called "The Covenant."

The Torah is also viewed as a legal code that is the basis for evolving practical law. The Torah contains 613 commandments, from which the details of the legal system are derived.[6] (Observant Jewish communities maintain a *Bet Din*, a Jewish court, which hears all sorts of cases.) Viewed this way, the Torah includes an explanation of the origins of the law, plus examples of the results of adherence and nonadherence.

The Torah is thought of as a delight and a precious gift. The Torah is thought of as the "Tree of Life" that enables humans to harness their evil inclinations to the service of their good inclinations, so as to fulfill the intent of creation.[7] Note that the fifth benediction of the weekday *Amidah* presumes that Torah-study is the utopian means of achieving moral inspiration and repentance. The Torah facilitates atonement. Good conduct and devotion to Torah are the same thing.

TORAH AS ONGOING REVELATION

Humans have to be given information in a form that they can assimilate. Although tradition declares the text to be divine revelation, concessions to human modes of thought and communication had to be made to accommodate this requirement. Not all of the intended message has yet been recognized. As a result of this attitude, a new understanding of Torah or new insight about it can be understood by Jewish tradition to be part of the revelation at Sinai—a previously unrecognized (but intended) element of the divine communication. The revelation at Sinai is ongoing.

Therefore "Torah" also refers to the process by which Jewish tradition lives. We all stand at Sinai and participate in an ongoing revelation.[8] The climax of the blessing said before Torah-Reading may be translated: "*Baruch atah Adonai* . . . giver of the Torah.*"* Note the ambiguity of tense in ancient Hebrew grammar that permits this interpretation.

Torah continues to be applied and developed. When arguments are "for the sake of heaven" and in keeping with Jewish tradition, it can be said of two logically conflicting conclusions: "this is Torah, and that too is Torah." Torah has many faces. Jewish practice then follows the majority of sage opinion.[9]

As a result, "Torah" can also refer to the totality of Jewish tradition, including all of the Tanach, plus the Mishnah, Talmud, Midrash, and the works of later sages up to the present day. If someone invites you to "study Torah," chances are you will be reading the *Talmud* together and talking over the issues that arise. If someone invites you to "hear some words of Torah," you will be listening to a sermon. (Both activities are traditionally popular delights for those who can afford the luxury of study.)

"Torah" can denote a single law, verse, or idea from any element of Jewish tradition. "Torah" can also be a description of an idea or a behavior in relation to Jewish tradition. For example: "This is (or is not) Torah" means that some statement, behavior, or condition is (or is not) consistent with traditional Jewish ideals, culture, values, ethics, or law. Torah is the totality of Jewish civilization.

"He who loves Torah is never satisfied with Torah."

D'varim Rabbah 2:23

MIDRASH, PESHAT, AND D'RASH

Midrash is the study of Bible texts to resolve questions, solve textual problems, and explain meaning. The conclusions reached often take the form of a brief supplemental narrative, and serve a homiletical purpose. Each of these is called a "midrash." There are several ancient collections of *midrashim* (plural of midrash), often collectively called "The Midrash," that define traditional midrashic methodology. Midrash is a beautifully humble art form. One claims neither authority nor authorship as one introduces a newly recognized truth to the world. Reading a midrash often brings a warm smile.

The simplest analytical approach to extracting meaning from a text aims to resolve ambiguities and to determine the plain sense. This is called called *"p'shat"* in Hebrew. But because Jewish tradition treats the Torah (the original in Hebrew, not any translation) as divine revelation, every phrase, word, and letter of the Torah is as significant as any other. If the text is divine in origin, then the shape of any given letter could be as significant as the plain meaning of the Decalogue. This has enabled all kinds of complex exegesis, called *"d'rash"* in Hebrew. *D'rash* could be based on wordplay, number harmonies, small details of form, ambiguities of the text, comparisons of widely separated pieces of scripture, and the lifting of texts out of context. All exegesis (*peshat* and *d'rash*) actually modifies the practical application of the written Torah over time. The letter of the law is reshaped to maintain what we take to be the spirit of it, but always with the authority of the letter of the law.[10,11]

This is not the same as the classical Christian theory of "pious fraud." Even the most farfetched (by the standards of plain textual semantics) Jewish interpretations (if ultimately accepted by a majority) are thought of as having been intended. Since every bit of written Torah is divine, then the new revelation was intended for eventual communication.

> Even the words of a student [when consistent with the Tradition and for the sake of heaven] that his teacher has not heard before—were revealed to Moses at Sinai.
>
> Talmud Yerushalmi, *Peah* 2:4

The revelation at Sinai is ongoing. "Torah" includes all that is implied by the Pentateuch when consistent with prior Jewish interpretation, now and in the future. Fundamentally, the people of the Book are not fundamentalists.

A Bowl of Flax and Sheaves

Once upon a time, a king had to go on a long voyage. He had two trusted courtiers, one wise and one foolish. He divided his flax and his sheaves into two equal parts. Then he called for the courtiers and said, "Here, I give each of you a bowl of flax and sheaves. Hold them for me until I return." While the king was gone, the wise man spun the flax into thread. Then he bleached the thread. Then he wove the white thread into a beautiful tablecloth. When the wise man had done this, he then beat the sheaves so that the grain fell out. He took the resulting grain to the mill and had it ground into fine flour. Then he used the flour to bake a lovely loaf of bread. When the king returned, he called for the two courtiers. The wise man brought forth the beautiful tablecloth and spread it over the table before the king. Then he brought forth the lovely loaf of bread and set it in the center of the tablecloth. The foolish man carried in a bowl of flax and sheaves.

an ancient parable about the Torah[12]

TALMUD TORAH (TORAH STUDY)

In Jewish law, every Jew has an obligation to study Torah daily, and every scholar has an obligation to teach at every opportunity.[13] Thus teaching and learning are universal preoccupations. In Jewish tradition, study itself is a form of reverence and worship.

This is why Jewish law analyzes and debates moot issues and impossible scenarios with all the vigor of practical issues. Truth, rather than relevance, is paramount. The rules for living in a utopia must be determined even if there is no practical way to apply them yet. In some striking cases, technology renders these rulings relevant only after millennia. (Examples include: rights of surrogate mothers, hereditary rights after artificial insemination, etc.)

The Jewish tradition of adult scholarship is unique among western cultures.[14,15] An aged scholar is "as holy as the Ark."[16] Parents are exhorted to follow the commandments "so that their children should become scholars." "A man should always sell everything he has in order to marry the daughter of scholars [so his children will be scholars even if he himself dies prematurely]. A man should sell everything he has in order to have his daughter marry a scholar."[17] "All the Prophets prophesied only so that a person should marry his daughter to a Torah scholar." The leaders of the community are the teachers (rabbi means teacher). The most widely respected Jewish heroes are the ones who were learned (not just good). Jewish saints (a designation of the most righteous people in history—not conceived as indicating transcendental consciousness) are scholars.[18] All manner of questions, civil disputes, and legal decisions were referred to the scholars. Even the families in the poorest ghetto communities took turns housing and feeding local and transient scholars and students, as an honor and privilege and moral obligation. There is a *b'racha* (a fixed blessing) that one recites, whenever one sees an outstanding scholar.[19]

The processes of learning are sacred, and study is a holy pursuit. There is a moral obligation to attempt understanding, and a carefully worked out morality appropriate to scholarship, including an obligation to stand by the truth as one sees it against anything, including God Himself if He personally takes the other side! (Some of my favorite stories concern occasions for such impudence.)

The Mishnah records that Hillel originated the saying: "An ignorant man cannot be pious."[20]

TORAH AS THE ART OF LIVING

Scholarship is not only a matter of knowing facts. According to Jewish tradition, true scholarship must be associated with an exemplary lifestyle.[21] The former is expected to lead to the latter.[22] Therefore behavior is the touchstone of scholarship. And the scholar's behavior is a primary mechanism for instructing others. The lives of scholars are expected to teach us by example, and their habits are scrutinized as carefully as their words and writings. Without this, one is not a true scholar.

The Talmud scathingly refers to fact-rich but ethics-poor authorities as "asses laden with books."

In a famous story from the Talmud, a student hides beneath his rabbi's bed in order to study the rabbi's relations with his wife. Although he was reprimanded for inappropriate behavior, his diligence in the study of proper behavior was considered meritorious. Being learned entails tremendous responsibility for setting an example.

In Jewish law, unlike American law, legal precedents do not consist only of prior court rulings. The personal behavior of sages can be cited to establish the law. To appreciate this fully, imagine if the personal behavior of America's leaders defined what was legal and what was not.

Thus the word "Torah" can be used to describe a condition of being. A person can be described as "living Torah," "doing Torah," or "being Torah."[23] Our lives are expected to be demonstrations of the Torah's ability to produce utopian behavior, thereby "sanctifying God's Name" in the world.

It is natural to expect that symbolic or actual study should show up at several places in the liturgy. The Torah-Reading Section is the most elaborate of these places. Study as a form of worship appears most explicitly in the *Korbanot* section of the Preliminary Morning Service, discussed later (on page 298). The early Moslems called Jews "the People of the Book," because every Jew had acquaintance with scriptures and learning. This was a direct result of incorporating Torah study into the liturgy. Torah paradigms and passages are still the lens through which Jews view the world, even for those that don't believe in Torah as Divine revelation.[24]

TORAH AS A SCROLL

"Torah" is also a convenient way to refer to a *"Seifer Torah"* (Torah scroll). This is a parchment scroll, on which the written Torah has been handwritten by a *"sofer"* (scribe).[25] The parchment is very long, and is comprised of rectangular pieces sewn together side by side. The parchment is attached to two wooden rollers, one at each end. So the scroll can be rolled shut at any point in the parchment. *Sifrei Torah* (Torah scrolls) are stored in the Ark at the front of the synagoue. Everything about the preparation of a Torah is special, from the traditional materials and processes used, to the intention of the scribe. The parchment is handmade from animal skins, the special ink is handmade from nuts, and the letters are formed with a feather quill. The result is beautiful, costly, and cannot be produced any other way. One goal is such high contrast between the black words of the Torah and the light parchment that, subjectively, the words take on an independent existence. It can take years to make a Torah scroll, and the result must be perfect.

A synagogue needs to have a Torah, and it is desirable to have more than one, to save time on occasions when readings from different places in the scroll will be made. Three separate passages are the most read on any occasion. It is desirable to have extra *Sifrei Torah* (the plural of *Sefer Torah*) on hand, since the letters occasionally break and need repair. In most cases, the discovery of a flaw in a Torah instantly disqualifies it from use.

THE HISTORICAL BACKGROUND
OF TORAH-READING

In the ancient world, laws and rites were secrets controlled by divinely authorized rulers and/or priestly clans. The Jewish idea of universal education as a divine mandate was revolutionary. It was another aspect of being "a kingdom of priests."[26]

The Torah itself espouses a democratic ideal of universal education, saying that all parents are responsible for teaching their children,[27] and that once every seven years, on the Festival of Sukkot, the entire people would gather for a public reading of the entire Torah.[28]

Upon returning from Babylonian exile, Ezra[29] established the Second Commonwealth (in 444 B.C.E.) and instituted the current schedule of three readings each week.[30] These public readings were an entirely separate social function from worship. He chose Sabbath afternoons and the market days (Mondays and Thursdays) because everyone would be coming into town. When Mondays and Thursdays were no longer market days, Jewish tradition cited a new reason for the practice: that three days would not go by without instruction in the Torah.

Under Ezra, each phrase would be read, and then the scribe (an imperfect but traditional translation of the title, *meturgeman*) would explain its significance in at least one way, sometimes through a Midrash.[31]

According to tradition, Ezra read in a cycle that took three years to complete. But in early Mishnaic times, only a few special Sabbaths actually had assigned portions. The rest were selected by the reader or the preacher.[32]

In the second century C.E., Torah-reading began to be cyclical.[33] Reading flowed continuously from Saturday, to Monday, to Thursday, to Saturday. Only later did a Sabbath-based cycle emerge. Since the passages for special days were fixed before cyclic reading was adopted, the ordered portions of the Sabbath cycle fit in between the fixed portions of the special Sabbaths.[34]

In Palestine, they divided the Torah into 154 or 172 portions, called "*sidra*," that took about 3 years to complete.[35] The readings were accompanied by line-by-line translation and interpretation.[36]

In Babylon, they divided the Torah into fifty-four portions, called "*parashah*." This is the number of weeks in a Jewish leap year. By reading more than one of these on certain weeks, an annual cycle was achieved. Because this lengthened the service, the practice of line-by-line translation was dropped, and the current practice of preparing for Sabbath during the preceding week was instituted. Everyone studied the weekly portion in advance. Even then, many congregants required a translation and commentary in order to study the weekly portion. The *Targum Onkelos* was an Aramaic interpretive translation of the Torah, adopted in Babylon for this purpose.

With the decimation of Palestinian Jewry and the rise of the Babylonian academies, the Babylonian practice came to dominate. But it took many centuries for the Babylonian procedure to become universal. Today we often use the terms *sidra* and *parashah* interchangeably. ("*Sidra*" comes from the same root as "siddur," meaning "order." "*Parashah*" means "portion.")

CURRENT TORAH-READING PRACTICES

The Torah is still read on Saturday, Monday, and Thursday. What was once a separate social function has been integrated into the liturgy of the Sabbath morning services. This becomes the climactic centerpiece of the service. This section of the service is rich in ritual and pageantry. The attitude is, "At other times in the service, we pray to God. In the Torah reading, we listen to God." A rule of thumb regarding synagogue ritual: When you can see the Torah, stand.

Most editions of the Tanach note the starting point of each weekly *parashah* in some way. See for example Exodus 30:11, which is the beginning of a *parashah*. There may also be a summary table of the entire cycle. Each *parashah* has a name, usually formed from its first distinctive word.

So central is Torah to Jewish life, that each week of the year has its own unique character, determined by the contents of its *parashah*. Dates are often cited by reference to the upcoming Sabbath's *parashah*. For example: I am writing this sentence on *Yom Shi-shi Korach 5752* (day six of Korach 5752). That is, the Friday before *Korach* (Numbers 16:1–18:32) is read, year 5752. That date happens to correspond to the second day of the Jewish month of *Tammuz* 5752, and also to July 3rd, 1992 in the Gregorian calendar.

The weekday readings cover just a subset of the coming Sabbath's *parashah*. (They do not cover any different ground.)

Torah-Reading was a separate activity in ancient times, occurring after the morning service (or sacrifice). Eventually it was incorporated into the liturgy after the *Shacharit Amidah*, at the end of the daily morning service. On Shabbat, the *Musaf* service, also once a separate event, comes after the Torah-Reading.

In later times, the sages added a nonobligatory fourth weekly Torah-Reading on Saturday afternoons. According to some opinions, this was added for the benefit of those who could not attend synagogue on Monday and Thursday mornings.[37] Others suggest it was added to productively occupy the time of those who would stay at the synagogue all day but be idle between the services. They inserted the new Torah Reading before the *Mincha* service so that latecomers and people not interested in the new Torah Reading could return to the synagogue for just *Mincha*. Like the weekday readings, this reading covers the start of the next Sabbath's *parashah*.

In recent years, some less traditional congregations have adopted a new three year cycle. This bears no resemblence to the original Palestinian cycle. Instead of reading the whole Torah sequentially over three years, the new practice reads the first third of each *parashah* in year one, the middle third of each *parashah* in year two, and the last third of each *parashah* in year three. The purpose of the new three year cycle is to shorten the service. Line by line interpretation and commentary, as per the original three year cycle, is generally not present (which would certainly eliminate any time-savings).

THE CHUMASH

On occasions when the Torah is read, you will need to pick up a *Chumash* in addition to a siddur. The *Chumash* contains the Torah (the first five books of the Tanach). But the *Chumash* differs from a Torah in several ways:

It is vocalized. Written Hebrew does not ordinarily have vowels. Words are often distinguished by context. Adding vowels to a text is called vocalizing a text. This not only shows how to pronounce words, but may remove intended or accidental ambiguities.

It includes musical notation for chanting the Torah. You will not be able to recognize this fact without special training. This nonwestern system of musical notation is called "trope." The trope is imbedded in the Hebrew text. (The musical phrasing indicated by the trope also defines syntax in passages where ancient Hebrew is otherwise ambiguous.)

It further subdivides each weekly *parashah*. Eight places are noted in each *parashah*. Seven of these mark seven sections, the eighth marks a spot within the last section.

It has portions of *Nevi-im* (the Prophets) inserted after each week's *parashah*. Each of the 54 weekly Torah portions is associated with a different fixed prophetic reading.

It usually has a translation, and always has commentary.

The need for each of these features will be explained later.

ALIYOT

The *Chumash* notes seven subdivisions of each *parashah*. For each subdivision, someone in the congregation will be honored to "go up." The act of going up is called "*aliya*" (plural is *aliyot*). The subdivision to be read is also called an *aliya*. An *aliya* to the Torah is the supreme honor. The honoree talks of "getting an *aliya*." (Emigrating to The Land of Israel is called "*making aliya*".) The honoree is called an *oleh* in Hebrew.

In a large congregation, where *aliyot* are scarce, a person needs a special reason to get an *aliya*, such as the birth of a child, the Bar or Bat Mitzvah of a child, one's wedding, a child's wedding, the first return to synagogue after sitting *shiva* for a parent or spouse, surviving a dangerous experience, the anniversary of a parent's death, graduation or other achievement in studies, leaving or returning from a journey, performance of significant philanthropic activity, or recovery from an illness. An aversion to these limitations is why some orthodox Jews prefer smaller congregations.

The above procedure applies only to the Sabbath morning service. On weekday readings (i.e., Monday and Thursday) and on Saturday afternoon, the *parashah* is that of the coming Shabbat morning. But there are only three *aliyot* instead of seven, and each *aliya* is only a few sentences long. (There is a *halachic* minimum of three sentences per *aliya*.) The entire reading takes place near the beginning of the first of the seven subdivisions.

Five people are called to Torah on festivals. The Talmud[38] says that the number of people called to Torah corresponds to the number of words in each of the three sentences of the Priestly Blessing: 3, 5, and 7. This is a later rationalization of an already ancient practice whose origins were no longer remembered. On Yom Kippur, six people are called; on the intermediate days of festivals, four are called.

A better mnemonic for remembering the number of *aliyot* is: There are seven days in a week, and Shabbat is the seventh day, so there are seven *aliyot* on Shabbat. The Torah is read on three days each week, and this is to ensure that no more than three days ever elapse between readings, so there are three *aliyot* at these other readings. Between the numbers 3 and 7, are the numbers 4, 5, and 6. We assign these in accordance with the sanctity of the holidays. Yom Kippur gets the 6, festivals get the 5, and intermediate days of festivals get the 4.

Another way to look at this is to simply rank all the Jewish holidays in their traditional order of sanctity and importance:

Shabbat	7
Yom Kippur	6
Festivals	5
Intermediate days	4
Regular days	3

The sequence must begin at three to provide at least one *aliya* for each of the three religious groupings of the Jewish people (Priests, Levites, and Israelites). This will be explained more fully below.

MI SHE-BEI-RACH AND BIR-KAT HA-GO-MEIL

As noted earlier, *aliyot* are generally assigned to memorialize, celebrate, or reward events in the lives of individual congregants. After each *aliya*, a prayer is recited requesting a blessing for the congregant. This is popularly called a "*mi-she-bei-rach.*" "*Mi She-bei-rach*" are its first two words. The later words vary, depending on the reason for the aliya. So the community knows what's happenning with the individual and can react appropriately.

In addition to the "*mi she-bei-rach*" said for the honoree, there are often extra "*mi shebeirach*"s added for the benefit of others, usually absent sick people.

Traditionally, the "*mi she-bei-rach*" is chanted after summoning the next *aliya*'s honoree to the *bima*, but before the next honoree is ready to begin. This saves time. (At first, the summons and the "*mi shebeirach*" may sound to you like one rapid unbroken chant.) This is why honorees remain on the *bima* during the *aliya* following their own. They remain for their "*mi she-bei-rach*," and then can leave only between *aliyot*. On the way back to their seats, they are likely to be contacted appropriately by congregants all along the way.

Torah-Reading Procedure:
1. A new honoree is summoned. (Old honoree moves to side of reading desk.)
2. Divine blessing is requested for the old honoree (still present on *bima*).
3. New honoree is ready for *aliya*: says the benediction before.
4. Torah-reader chants the *aliya*.
5. New honoree says the benediction after.
6. Old honoree departs.
7. Repeat whole procedure

Many modern synagogues break the interlocked rhythm of the *aliyot* by stopping to explain, in English, what has just transpired, and to elaborate upon it. This makes the community's support much more explicit. It also can make each *aliya* into a small ceremony such as a baby-naming or a graduation.

After recovery from a dangerous situation, individuals append a brief extra benediction to the blessing that concludes their *aliya*. This is called "*Ha Go-meil*."

> *Baruch atah Adonai, Eloheinu melech ha-olam,*
> who bestows benefits on the undeserving,
> and has also bestowed all good unto me.

There is a congregational response, meaning:

> He who has bestowed all good to you,
> may he ever bestow all good to you.

Traditionally, situations requiring "*Ha Go-meil*" include journeys. So in traditional communities, one's reappearance at *shul* after an absence, whether due to vacation or illness, is often marked by an *aliya* featuring a "*ha-gomeil*."

The parent celebrating a child's attainment of legal majority (age thirteen for boys, age twelve for girls) also has an extra benediction:

> *Ba-ruch a-tah A-do-nai, E-lo-hei-nu me-lech ha-olam,*
> who has relieved me from [*halachic*] responsibility for this child.

The result of all the summonses, "*mi-she-bei-rachs*," and other blessings, is that the Torah-Reading Service is an important mechanism for social support and community bonding.

THE GABBAI AND YOUR HEBREW NAME

The person that functions as master of ceremonies at the Torah-Reading is called the *gabbai*. From the *bima*, the *gabbai* will chant the summons to each honoree in turn. After each summons, the *gabbai* chants the *"mi she-bei-rach"* prayer for the previous honoree, citing the reason for the honor. The *gabbai* may also insert additional prayers on behalf of people not present, who are sick or in need of other kinds of prayers. For all these prayers, the *gabbai* needs to know people's names. You may see people handing in slips of paper or whispering names for this purpose.

Jews are typically given just one name. For example:

> *Ya-a-kov*   (Jacob)
> *Riv-kah*   (Rebecca)

A full hebrew name is constructed by referencing one or both parent's names. For example:

> *Ya-a-kov ben Y'shai-a v'Cha-va*   (Jacob son of Isaiah and Eve)
> *Riv-kah bat Re-u-ven v'D'vo-rah* (Rebecca daughter of Reuben and Deborah)

For simple identification, the tradition is to cite just the father's name. But in petitionary prayers, the tradition is to cite just the mother's name. This pattern applies to both men and women, and is not limited to synagogue usage. This practice is in emulation of David in Psalm 116:16.[39]

Both types of usage will be needed by the *gabbai*. In a traditional synagogue, the *gabbai* will summon the honoree by the father's name. In the prayers requesting blessings for others, the *gabbai* will cite the mother's name. Usually the *gabbai* will chant a name however you provide it, including both parents' names if you so specify. In some modern synagogues, both parents' names will be expected.

If you don't know all the information needed to construct a Jew's full name, you use Abraham and Sarah as generic male and female names. Although only Jews may be called to the Torah, blessings may be said for anyone. For blessings on behalf of a non-Jew, you use *Noach* (Noah) and *Chava* (Eve) as generic male and female names. (Jews by choice choose their own names and become children of Abraham and Sarah.)

THE BA-AL K'RIYAT

The Torah will be chanted by a person called the *Ba-al K'riyat*, or *Ba-al Koreh*. Although any congregant may do this, it requires skill and advance preparation. Chanting the Torah is popularly called *"layning"* in Yiddish. The *Ba-al K'riyat* chants directly from the Torah scroll, which has neither vowels nor musical notation.[40]

The congregation follows along in the *Chumash*, and often joins in singing the last phrase of each *aliya*. The *Ba-al K'riyat* chants in accordance with the special musical notations, called "trope," imbedded in the *Chumash* text. He does not have recourse to the *Chumash*. Prompters on the *bima* (backed up by the congregation itself) will help if he gets into trouble. (Beware! Some editions have errors in the trope.)

Many Jews have some idea of how trope is read, even if they can't read trope fluently. This is because commemoration of one's attainment of Bar or Bat Mitzvah status usually involves chanting a portion of *Nevi-im* (The Prophets) from a *Chumash*.

Traditionally, Jews do not chant Torah for their own *aliya* even if they know how. The justification is as follows: If there were no *Ba-al K'riyat*, only the learned could enjoy the privilege of being called to the Torah. This would violate the democratic nature of Judaism. And if the Ba-al K'riyat were to chant only on behalf of the ignorant, that would constitute a public distinction between the ignorant and the learned. This is also contrary to fundamental Jewish ideals, which prohibit shaming a person in public.[41] So the honoree only recites a brief blessing before the Reading, and another after; and the Torah is chanted by the *Ba-al K'riyat.*

Originally, the first honoree said the blessing before, and the last honoree said the blessing after.[42] The other honorees were called up, but said nothing. But nowadays, each honoree says both blessings for each *aliya*. The underlying motivation for this change was to help pious Jews to reach the recommended goal of 100 blessings per day.[43] Blessings cannot be said in vain,[44] so this goal requires participation in the performance of 100 *mitzvot* (good deeds, commandments). The sages rationalized this change in procedure two ways. They suggested that latecomers and early-leavers might otherwise miss the opportunity to say *a-mein* to the single benedictions before and after, despite having fulfilled the mitzvah of hearing the Torah read. And they suggested that the change would prevent people from being misled concerning the status of *Kir'yat* Torah as a mitzvah,[45] as erroneous conclusions could result from not observing a blessing before and after.

One oddity of the blessing before the Torah-Reading is that it is preceded by the *Ba-r'chu.* The *Ba-r'chu* is the summoning of the community, the call to worship. It already occurred earlier in the service, at the beginning of the *Sh'ma* section (once the beginning of the service). This additional *Ba-r'chu* reflects the ancient origins of Torah-Reading as a separate event, with its own summons. The summons was retained when the Torah-Reading event was incorporated into the service. And it was replicated when the Torah-Reading Blessing later came to be repeated by each honoree.

The Case of the Angry Honoree

A congregant has made a large contribution to his synagogue. But he has long since forgotten what meager knowledge of Hebrew he did possess, so he asks the rabbi not to call him up to read the blessings when the Torah is read.

"Please," he says, "every eye will be on me. Some of my friends will be there and I don't want to appear like an ignoramus!"

On the following Saturday, what does the rabbi do? He promptly calls the man up to say the blessings.

Having no alternative, Howard Lieberman walks up. He is, of course, furious. The rabbi is standing next to him. Howard looks down at the blessings printed there and mutters, out of the side of his mouth: "Rabbi, what did you do to me? I specifically asked you not to call me up. I don't mind being an anonymous donor. But you have embarrassed me in front of everyone. I can't read Hebrew. Honestly, I'm really angry with you!"

At this point, the rabbi turns to him and sings out loudly, "Amen!"

from *What is a Jewish Joke?*
by Henry Eilbirt
published by
Jason Aronson Inc., 1991

PRIESTLY PRIVILEGES

A *Ko-hein* (often transliterated as "Cohen") is a descendant of Aaron, the brother of Moses. A *Ko-hein* is a priest under Jewish law. A *Lei-vi* (pronounced "LAY-vee"; often transliterated as "Levi" or "Levy") is a member of the tribe of Moses and Aaron, which served as the administration in the ancient social order. They are descendents of *Lei-vi* the son of Jacob (*Ya-a-kov*). They received no portion of land. They lived among, and were supported by, the other tribes.

The Torah-Reading section of the service is one of the few areas of Jewish life that still recalls these distinctions.[46] In the Torah-Reading Section of the service, the first *aliya* is reserved for a *Ko-hein* if one is present. The second is reserved for a *Lei-vi* if one is present. The remainder are for

Yis-ra-eil (Israel). Technically, all Jews are Israelites, but for the purposes of an *aliya*, the designation usually implies someone who is not Cohen or Levi.[47] Similarly, all *Kohanim* are from the tribe of *Lei-vi*, but "*Lei-vi*" is commonly used to imply a Levite who is not a *Ko-hein*.

Although people of Cohanic and Levitical descent seem to have a privileged status, it is understood to be purely hereditary and unearned. Ancient rabbinic law holds that "if the bastard is a scholar and the High Priest is an ignoramus, the learned bastard takes precedence over an ignorant high priest." This ruling is never actually applied to the order of *aliyot*, since Jewish law prohibits shaming a person in public. Therefore a *Ko-hein* and a *Lei-vi* are still honored by being called first, solely to avoid shaming these individuals by publicly suggesting (correctly or not) that the particular individuals in attendance are unworthy of this honor.

If *Kohanim* are present but there is no Levite, the *Kohen* given the first *aliya* remains on the *bima* for the second *aliya* as well. If there is no *Kohein* present, anyone can be given the first *aliya*. Then all subsequent *aliyot* (including the second) are for *Yis-ra-eil*.[48]

The remaining *aliyot* are identified by Hebrew numbers:

3 *sh'li-shi*
4 *r'vi-i*
5 *cha-mi-shi*
6 *shi-shi*
7 *sh'vi-i*

On the Sabbath, congregations may divide an *aliya* into smaller sections to provide more honors. An extra *aliya* is called "*ha-sa-fah*." The last of them is called "*a-cha-ron*." The points at which to divide the *aliya* are determined by those running the service, and are neither fixed by tradition nor marked in the *Chumash*.

HANDING OUT HONORS

In every synagogue, the honorees have to know who they are in advance, so the service can proceed smoothly. There is always someone who goes around quietly handing out the honors (or confirming earlier designations). In some synagogues, this is done verbally; others hand out laminated cards. Each card has the name of one of the various honors printed on it. These include opening the Ark, lifting the Torah, dressing the Torah, each of the seven *aliyot*, and so on.

So if a stranger appears by your seat and silently tries to hand you a card, feel honored and welcomed. Be brave and take it (if you are Jewish). Detailed instructions for performing these rituals are included below, so give it a try. (They might also be printed on the card.)

If, instead of handing you a card, the stranger furtively whispers the name of an *aliyah* (or the word "*Yisraeil*") as though it were a question, you are being offered an *aliya* subject to confirming whether you are a *Co-hein*, *Lei-vi*, or *Yis-ra-eil*.

If you are given a card, bring it with you when you go up to perform the mitzvah. Someone should collect it from you before you return to your seat.

THE STRUCTURE OF
THE TORAH-READING SECTION

The thrice-weekly Torah-Reading event was merged with synagogue services by appending it to the end of the *Sha-charit* (daily morning) service. On weekdays, this places the Torah-Reading at the end of morning services. On Saturday, there is still the Shabbat *Musaf* (Additional) Service to do. Synagogues may take a break between the *Shacharit* service and the Torah-Reading, or just before the Musaf Service, but this is rarely done.

Saturday Morning Services

[Preliminary Morning Service—described later]
Shacharit Service:
   Praise Section
   Sh'ma Section
   Amidah Section
   [Closing Section—described later]
Torah-Reading (Monday, Thursday, and Saturday)
Other miscellaneous community business
Musaf Service (only on Saturday and other holidays):
   Praise Section
   Amidah Section
   [Closing Section—described later]

There is a simple symmetry to the Torah-Reading section. The giving of the Torah at Sinai is represented in the liturgical rite by the reading of the Torah followed by the lifting (acceptance) of the Torah. This is the central event in the ritual, as it is the central transforming event in human history.

The processions of the Israelites from Egypt to Sinai, and from Sinai to Jerusalem, are also represented in the Torah-Reading ritual. They balance each other, one before and one after the reading and lifting.

The two halves of Numbers 10:35–36 are recited to link the opening and closing of the Ark, near the beginning and end of the Torah-Reading Section:

When the Ark set forth, Moses said:
Advance, Lord, let your enemies be scattered!
Let those that hate you flee before you!

And when it rested, he said:
Return, Lord, who are Israel's myriads of thousands!

Items that break this symmetry are later insertions and additions.

Torah Reading Section:
Open the Ark
　　Read Numbers 10:35
　　　　Remove Torah
　　　　　Procession
　　　　　　Read Torah
　　　　　　Lift Torah
　　　　　Procession
　　　　Return Torah
　　Read Numbers 10:36
Close the Ark

THE ARK IS OPENED

Someone in the congregation is discreetly notified that they are being given the honor of opening the Ark at the appropriate time. This honor is called *pesicha*. Often, the same person that opens the Ark has the honor of removing the Torah from the Ark and handing it to the reader. Other times, a second individual is given this honor. This honor is called *ho-tsa-ah*. As with all synagogue honors, the honor lies in being given an opportunity to participate in a mitzvah.

If you are the *ho-tsa-ah*, approach the Ark as the reader does, and then wait there. If you are the *pesicha*, approach the Ark as the reader does, and simply draw aside the curtain and/or open the doors. Then remain there.

On weekdays and Saturday afternoons, you open the Ark immediately. On Sabbath mornings only, *Ein Kamocha* is sung as the Ark is being approached. *Ein Kamocha* is an insertion from *gaonic* times (circa 800 c.e.).[49] You open the Ark only after *Ein Kamocha* is finished.

As the Ark is opened, the Torah is revealed. Everyone who is familiar with the service is standing by the time the curtain is drawn. The rest hustle to their feet immediately.

When the Ark is opened, we sing the biblical report of what Moses said in the desert whenever the Ark started out. The reader sings the beginning of Numbers 10:35, and the congregation sings the actual quotation of Moses (the rest of Numbers 10:35). This is followed by the last two phrases of Isaiah 2:3, followed by a line of praise to God for having given Israel the Torah.

> Reader: And when the Ark set forth, Moses would say:
> Congregation: Arise, LORD! Let Your foes be scattered!
>   Let those who hate You flee from before You!
>   [Numbers 10:35]
>   For from Zion will come forth Torah,
>   and the word of the LORD from Jerusalem!
>   [Isaiah 2:3]
>   Praised is the Giver of the Torah
>   to His people Israel,
>   in His holiness.

There is a meditation from *The Zohar*[50] (a classic book of Kabbalah, first published in the thirteenth century) that is inserted at this point. It is called *"B'rich Sh'mei"* (Blessed is the Name).[51] *B'rich Sh'mei* is written in Aramaic. It is a late addition to the service, added in the sixteenth century. *B'rich Sh'mei* is one of the many places in the service where a great cantor can improvise gloriously, although most congregations begin it silently. In either case, the congregation usually sings the ending. Be careful about repeated words and phrases. The most common tune has some very tricky repeats. One of these repeats takes you back to a point prior to the place at which you first began singing aloud.

THE READER TAKES THE TORAH

We have now reached a high point. The Torah is removed from the Ark. There are usually several scrolls in the Ark. If you are the *ho-tsa-ah*, someone should indicate which Torah scroll to pick. Simply reach into the Ark and pick up the Torah with one hand on the bottom left handle, and the other hand supporting the Torah's back. Turn yourself (not the Torah) around to face the reader, and let the reader take the Torah from you. Then remain there. On days when more than one scroll is needed, you may be expected to repeat the procedure with another Torah scroll; or another person may have been given this task as a separate honor.

On occasions when more than one scroll will be needed, a congregant may be given the honor of carrying a Torah. To carry a Torah, rest it on your right shoulder. Drape your right arm over it and support it from the bottom with your right hand. This emulates the physical expression of devotion described in Song of Songs 8:3.[52] Your left hand usually holds a prayerbook, but could also be used for additional support from beneath.

The same person that opened the Ark then closes it. If the Ark has doors behind a curtain, the person may be expected to just draw the curtain (to simplify reopening the Ark later).

On Shabbat morning only, the following insertion is made: The reader holds the Torah and turns to face the congregation. All the honorees at the Ark face the congregation along with the reader. The reader chants the first line of the *Sh'ma*, and the congregation repeats it: "*Sh'ma Yis-ra-eil, A-do-nai E-lo-hei-nu, A-do-nai E-chad!*" (Hear Israel, *HaShem* [is] our God, *HaShem* [is] One!) And then the reader chants: "*E-chad E-lo-hei-nu, Ga-dol A-do-nei-nu, Ka-dosh*

Sh'mo!" (One [is] our God, Great [is] our Lord, Holy [is] his Name.) And the congregation repeats that.

THE PROCESSION

The theme of Numbers 10:35 is now acted out in ritual! The Torah must get from the Ark to the reading desk. It does this in a very roundabout way. This recalls marching to battle in the wilderness, led by the Ark of the Pact. After inviting the congregation to join in a song, the reader carries the Torah up and down the aisles, ending up at the reading desk.

When the procession starts, everyone moves toward the nearest aisle. When the Torah goes by, you touch it with the fringes of your *tallis* (prayer shawl). Or you touch it with your prayerbook. Then you kiss the fringes, or the book. You don't touch the Torah directly.

The Torah (the Covenant evidenced by the scroll, not the ritual object itself) is thought of here as a powerful secret weapon. The Torah assures our survival through the millennia of dangerous encounters.[53] Like the Ark in the wilderness, it should stimulate our resolve, and enable us to triumph. In ancient midrashic exegesis, the word "strength" is sometimes treated as an allusion to the Torah.[54] Theoretically, the procession should feel triumphant and fearless.[55]

Now let's look at the texts of the procession. First, the reader and all honorees at the Ark turn and bow slightly toward the Ark, as the reader sings an invitation to the congregation (Psalm 34:4, *"Gadlu . . ."*). As the congregation responds by singing *"L'cha Adonai,"* the procession begins. *L'cha Adonai* consists of: I Chronicles 29:11, Psalm 99:5, and Psalm 99:9. There are several different dynamic melodies for *L'cha Adonai*. But they are related, and music may be interchanged phrase by phrase, so be alert when visiting a new congregation. Since these texts culminate in an exhortation to rise and exalt the holiness of God, it became the tradition on Shabbat morning (now followed only in some Orthodox congregations) for the congregation to respond by chanting a Hebrew paraphrase of the kaddish.

The honorees follow the procession away from the Ark. Once the Torah nears its destination they return to their seats, but they are not yet done. Generally, the same people that opened the Ark, removed the Torah, and carried the Torah, are expected to return to perform the corresponding functions when the Torah is put away.

TREATING THE TORAH
LIKE ROYALTY

The reader does not carry the Torah alone. The Torah is escorted like royalty, with a herald. This is not just during services. For example, if you happen to be at the synagogue when someone needs to remove a Torah from the Ark (to inspect it, or to position the scroll for an upcoming reading), you may be asked to walk with the person as they approach the Ark, and as they walk with the Torah.

The Torah scroll is tied shut with a strip of cloth called a "sash," and is covered with a mantle. A decorative breastplate often adorns it. And an ornate crown often fits atop its handles.

Once the Torah is at the reader's desk on the *bima*, it is always attended by no less than three people.

By standing in its presence, dressing it like royalty, and attending upon it, we transfer the symbols of human royalty to the Torah. This is another expression of *Malchut HaShamayim* (allegiance to the kingship of heaven).

CHANTING THE TORAH

The Torah is placed on the desk and undressed. At this point you can sit down, because the Torah is "sitting down." (You have been standing since the Ark was opened.) The congregation will follow the reading using a *Chumash*.

One does not leave or enter during the direct Torah reading. Do this between *aliyot*. You may notice that some synagogues station a person by the door during the Torah-Reading section, to detain people from entering until appropriate times. (Leaving is not controlled.)

The *aliyot* are named:
1   *ko-hein*
2   *lei-vi* (also called *shei-ni*)
3   *sh'li-shi*
4   *r'vi-i*
5   *cha-mi-shi*
6   *shi-shi*
7   *sh'vi-i*

One of these seven words will be imbedded in a summoning call from the *bima* before each *aliya*. You will see each honoree say their Hebrew name to the *gabbai* when the *gabbai* pauses for want of that information (if the name is unknown to the *gabbai*). Each honoree will go up in turn. Each will chant a blessing before their reading, then the *Ba-al K'riyat* will read the *aliya* for the honoree, and then the honoree recites another blessing after the reading. Most congregations sit through the entire process, and all congregations sit throughout the *Ba-al K'riyat*'s reading.

Between the *aliyot*, while the honorees are reciting their blessings, the Torah will be rolled shut and a decorative cloth (or the Torah's mantle) will be draped over it. This is a mark of respect for the Torah, so that it should not be open but ignored. Some congregations (or individuals) stand during the blessings and sit when the scroll is opened again for further reading.

WHAT TO DO IF YOU ARE GIVEN AN ALIYAH

To be given an *aliya* is a great honor. In an Orthodox synagogue, a (male) stranger appearing at *shul* is often given an *aliya*, the ultimate in hospitality. Here is the procedure:

When the person before you has finished the blessing after the reading, go up to the *bima*. Use the side of the *bima* nearest you. By taking the shortest route, you show eagerness to be near the Torah. Later, you will return to your seat using the opposite side. An alternate tradition is to always ascend on the right side of the *bima* and descend on the left.[56] (The previous honoree won't leave the *bima*, but will move aside. Like dominoes, this will bump the even earlier honoree off the *bima*.)

When the *gabbai* interrupts his chant on the word "*y'amod . . .*" and looks at you expectantly, state your Hebrew name. By repeating your name, the *gabbai* is imbedding your name in the summons being chanted.

Look on the desk for a big card with help text. Don't recite anything yet. It is traditional to recite the blessings by heart, but few do. To avoid embarrassment, there will be a large card lying on the desk. On it will be printed the blessings you need to know, including transliterations of them. The print will be large enough to read from a distance.

The *Ba-al K'riyat* points to the spot in the Torah scroll where he will begin reading. He uses a pointer called a "*yad.*"[57] The Torah is not touched directly. (*Yad* means hand. Traditionally, the pointer's tip is sculpted like a tiny pointing hand.)

Touch a fringe (*tsi-tsis*) of your *tallis* near the spot indicated, and then kiss the *tsi-tsis*. (It is healthier for the scroll if you touch in a margin.) If you have no *tallis*, use the cloth sash that is normally used to tie the scroll closed. The scroll will then be rolled closed and may also be covered with a decorative cloth or with its mantle.[58] In some congregations, people might then stand.

Hold onto the wooden rollers (called *eitz chayim*) of the scroll. Recite the *"Ba-r'chu"* (either from memory or from the card on the desk) as an introduction to the first blessing:

Ba-r'chu et Adonai Ha-m'vo-rach

Wait for the congregational response:

Baruch Adonai Ha-m'vorach l'olam va-ed

Repeat the congregational response. Then recite the first blessing:

Ba-ruch Atah Adonai, Elo-hei-nu Melech Ha-olam
A-sher Ba-char Ba-nu Mikawl Ha-amim
v'na-tan la-nu et Torato
Ba-ruch Atah Adonai, no-tein HaTorah.[59]

Do not be disturbed when the congregation interjects: *"Baruch sh'mo,"* and adds a final *"aw-mein."* (*"Aw-mein"* is Ashkenazic, *"a-mein"* is Sephardic.) The scroll will now be rolled open for reading. If people are standing they will sit.

The *Ba-al K'riyat* will chant the *aliya* on your behalf. Follow along quietly, watching the *yad* move above the scroll so that you can see where your *aliya* ends. The *Ba-al K'riyat* might remove the *yad* from above the parchment as soon as he's done, and you will need to know the spot. (If he realizes that you're not sure, he'll explicitly point to it.) Everybody will be very helpful through all of this. After all, you are being honored, not tested.

Touch the Torah with your *tsi-tsis* at the ending spot of your *aliya*, and kiss the *tsi-tsis* as before. The scroll is then closed and draped, and people may stand. Take hold of the rollers as before, and chant the second blessing:

Ba-ruch atah Adonai, Elo-heinu me-lech ha-olam
A-sher na-tan la-nu Torat emet
V'cha-yei olam na-ta be-to-chei-nu
Ba-ruch atah Adonai, no-tein ha-Torah.[60]

Remain on the *bima*, but move to the side of the desk to make room for the next honoree. The *"mi-she-bei-rach"* for your *aliya* is said after the next honoree is summoned, but before recitation of the *"Ba-r'chu."* This saves time. If the *gabbai* has forgotten your name, you may have to give it again.

When the next person has finished the concluding blessing, return to your seat. Use the side of the *bima* that is farthest from your seat. This reflects a desire to defer parting from the Torah. An alternate tradition is to ascend on the right and depart on the left. In either tradition, your descent is on the side opposite from your ascent. (If you sit on the right side of the congregation, you'll always match local custom even as you continue your own tradition.)

Expect people to congratulate you and shake your hand on the way back. They may say *"Ya-sher Ko-ach."* They are wishing you strength, as in "May you go from strength to strength." The appropriate response is *"Ba-ruch T'hi-yeh."* (If you forget, you can repeat *"Yasher Koach,"* or just say "Thank you.")

LIFTING AND DRESSING THE TORAH

Once we finish reading from the Torah scroll, it is lifted and then dressed. As a sign of respect for the Torah scroll, we do not leave it undressed for any length of time once we are finished reading from it. The lifting is a major signpost in your roadmap of the service. This occurs as follows:

The Torah is spread wide open, and lifted up high. This is tricky and requires strength. At least three columns of text should be visible. This lifting enables everyone present to fulfill, if only symbolically, the mitzvah of reading directly from the scroll. When it is lifted, the congregation sings Deuteronomy 4:44 and Numbers 9:23, as follows:

> *V'zot ha-torah*
> > *asher sam Moshe*
> *lif'nei b'nei Yisraeil, al pi Adonai*
> > *b'yad Moshe*

> This is the Torah
> > that was placed by Moses
> before the children of Israel; as per the LORD's command,
> > by the hand of Moses.

This wonderful ritual releases a bidirectional flow of honor and affection. It's a statement by every individual present that they are zealous for an *aliya* and are ready to fulfill this mitzvah. And it's an assertion by the community that everyone would be honored with an *aliya* if it were only practical. (On *Simchat Torah* we actually do that, despite the impracticability.)

The Lifting emulates Moses, as he displayed the tablets brought down from Sinai; and the congregational response emulates the acceptance of the covenant by the ancient Israelites. Ezra, our leader in late biblical times,[61] lifted the Torah before the Israelites to evoke this symbolism. Our lifting duplicates the practice of Ezra.

Then the Torah is dressed in preparation for its return to the Ark.

HOW TO LIFT A TORAH

The honor of lifting the Torah is called *hag'bah*. If you are invited to lift the Torah, there are two tricks that make it easier. First, keep it taut. Second, slide it off the desk. Here are details:

First, look around and make sure you know in advance where you are going to sit down with the Torah after you have lifted it. Second, look up to see if there is anything above you, like a low chandelier above the reader's desk, that might obstruct you. Plan ahead.

Open the scroll so that three columns are visible. (It is healthier for the scroll if a seam is also visible.) Spread the handles apart on the desk so that the scroll is taut, not slack. Don't try to lift the scroll off the desk with your arms. Instead, simply slide the scroll toward you until it is half on and half off the desk. Then bend your knees slightly and pivot the scroll about the edge of the desk into vertical position. This way, all the weight will be over your hands before you actually bear the weight.

Raise the Torah so that the congregation can see it. As you carry it, carefully balanced, keep the scroll taut, not slack. That way you are balancing one solid object with two hands, not two separate objects with one hand each. Keeping it taut may feel wrong—you may fear ripping it. But remember that a Torah is written on segments of cowhide that are sewn together—not on paper.

Turn a bit to each side, so the text is displayed to all present. After the congregation sings the response to your lifting, you can move to the seat and let the bottoms of the rollers come to rest on your thighs as you sit. Keep your hands on the bottom handles of the rollers, as someone rolls the scroll closed using the tops. (When the rollers come together, the roller on your right rests above the roller on your left.) Continue holding the Torah upright as it is being dressed. Once it is dressed, you can let it rest on your right shoulder, with your right arm wrapped around it and holding the bottom. The dressed Torah might be taken from you and set into a holder, or placed on a seat. But usually, it is held by you until it is time to return it to the Ark. Follow local custom.

(Everyone who sees a Torah fall to the ground fasts for forty days. It's only a big risk on *Simchas Torah*, when everyone is ecstatic and dancing wildly on chairs and tables, holding open Torahs high above their heads. I've never known anyone who's seen a Torah fall, although there have been close calls when those nearest have saved the day. But in case you do, the trick is to eat at night.)

HOW TO DRESS THE TORAH

Dressing the Torah is another honor given to someone in the congregation. This honor is called *g'li-lah*. The person that did the lifting will be sitting down, still holding the bottoms of the rollers that will now be resting on the person's lap. The front of the scroll will be facing the seated lifter; that is, facing away from you. You will then use the tops of the rollers to close the scroll tightly. The handle on your left goes above the handle on your right. (It is healthier for the scroll if you center a seam.)

Then you will tie (or buckle, or velcro) a sash around the scroll, fastening it at the front, which is the side away from you. It feels like tying a sash around someone facing away from you. Then you slip the mantle over from the top. As with the sash, the front of the mantle faces away from you. The tops of the rollers protrude through holes in the mantle.

The may be a breastplate to sling over both handles. There may be a *yad* to sling over one of the handles. Many congregations follow a tradition of always placing the *yad* on the *Bereishit* (Genesis) side, which will be on your left (the lifter's right). There may be a crown of precious metal to perch atop the handles, or separate finials for each of the handles.

It is like dressing royalty. People will be there to help you.

THE RETURN PROCESSION:
HODO AL ERETZ, AND HAVU L'ADONAI

The reader takes the Torah and sings an invitation to praise the divine Name (part of Psalm 148:13) and all sing the continuation of that passage, *"Hodo Al Eretz"* (Psalm 148: 13–14).

This is followed by a procession back to the Ark. The procedure is similar to the first procession. This emulates the wandering in the desert on the way to Jerusalem from the reading of the Torah at Sinai, with the Ark as a guide. During the procession, we sing *Havu L'adonai* (Psalm 29) on Saturday mornings, or Psalm 24 on weekdays (i.e., Mondays and Thursdays) and Saturday afternoons.

Psalm 24 is used because tradition says its final verses were used by King Solomon when the original Ark was brought to rest in the brand new Temple:

Lift up your heads, O gates!
Raise up, you everlasting entrances!
So that the King of Glory may enter!
Who is the King of Glory?
HaShem, Master of Legions!
He is the King of Glory! Selah!

Havu L'Adonai (Psam 29) is the Psalm that contains God's name eighteen times, cited in the Talmud as one reason for the *Shemoneh Esreh* being constructed as eighteen benedictions. Thus it is an appropriate response to the reader's invitation to praise the divine Name. Furthermore, the climactic ending of the Psalm is traditionally understood as a reference to Torah:

The LORD will give His people strength,
The LORD will bless His people with peace.

The dynamics of biblical parallelism operating in this poetry equates strength and peace. This is explained by regarding both as references to the Torah.

The honor of placing the Torah back in the Ark is called *hach-na-sah*. Usually, the same honorees that participated in removing the Torah from the Ark should proceed to the Ark during the return procession to assist in putting it away. Occasionally, the honor of placing the Torah in the Ark is separately assigned.

RETURNING THE TORAH TO THE ARK

The Torah is placed in the open Ark. A series of biblical passages is sung, starting with Numbers 10:36, which announces, and then quotes, Moses when he brought the Ark to its resting place:

> And when it [the Ark] rested, he [Moses] would say:
> Return, Lord—You who are Israel's myriads of thousands!

This is followed by phrases from later biblical books[62] that amplify the meaning. Thus the text is a precise parallel to the words we sang when the Torah was removed from the Ark (Numbers 10:35, see page 231). This is the culmination of the process that was begun then.[63]

The congregation usually joins in at the phrase "*Eitz Chayim.*" If they are already singing, some melodic cue will mark Eitz Chayim as a high point. We can compare the attitude of the Israelites when they first set out with the Ark (described above), to their attitude by the time it was rested. The contrast is dramatic. The central attitude of the entire Torah-Reading Service (and indeed a central theme of traditional Jewish life) is contained in the two lines that begin with "*Eitz Chayim.*" They say of the Torah:

> It is a tree of life
> to those who take hold of it,

and happy are those who support it.
Its ways are ways of pleasantness.
And all its paths are peace.

("*Eitz Chayim*" means "tree of life." The wooden rollers of the Torah scroll are also called "*eitz chayim*").
The Ark is closed. The Torah-Reading Section is over.

THE ACCELERATED CONGREGATIONAL KADDISH

As is usual with the major divisions of the liturgy, the end of the Torah-Reading is marked by a kaddish. This kaddish is an excellent signpost because it is a congregational kaddish. In Judaism, the study of Torah is thought to lead directly to righteous conduct. Hence, after reading Torah, the congregation joins in chanting much of the kaddish as an indication that it has gotten the message. (As opposed to the usual practice of the reader chanting nearly all of it.)

Furthermore, we accelerate this congregational kaddish so that we exclaim it as soon as we have fulfilled the mitzvah of hearing the Torah. We don't wait until after putting away the Torah. This shows how the experience of Torah-Reading transforms us. After hearing Torah, we rush to do good things (like saying kaddish) rather than doing them only when they become due, and we seek mitzvot rather than waiting for them to present themselves.

On some occasions, the kaddish after the Torah-Reading can't be accelerated. Accelerating the kaddish means that there will be nothing to delimit the end of the Torah-Reading from the start of the next liturgical event. Usually this is not a problem. But, as we noted earlier, the *Amidah* must always be immediately preceded by a kaddish. So if the Torah-Reading Section is followed by an *Amidah* Section, the kaddish can't be accelerated. This happens on Saturday afternoons at *Mincha*.

Torah Reading Section   (occurs Monday, Thursday, and Saturday mornings and Saturday afternoons)

Approach Ark	*Ein Kamocha*	(Shabbat A.M. only)
Open the Ark		
	Numbers 10:35	
	Brich Sh'mei	
Remove Torah	*Sh'ma* excerpt	(Shabbat A.M. only)
Procession	*L'cha Adonai*	
Read Torah	Summon next honoree	
	Mi She-bei-rach for last	
	honoree	
	Ba-r'chu	
	Blessing before	
	Chant Torah	repeat
	Blessing after	

Accelerated Congregational   (before Closing Section at
Half-Kaddish   weekday A.M. services and
                                                     before Praise Section of
                                                     Shabbat Musaf Service)

Lift Torah	*V'zot Ha-Torah* . . .
Procession	*Hodo Al Eretz*
	Havu Ladonai (Psalm 29)
	on Saturday A.M.,
	Psalm 24 otherwise.
Return Torah	
	Numbers 10:36
	Eitz Chayim
Close the Ark	

Unaccelerated Congregational   (before *Mincha Amidah* on
Half-Kaddish   Saturday afternoon[64])

COMMUNITY BUSINESS

The structure developed above occurs on Monday morning and Thursday morning. (And also on Saturday afternoon. The Saturday afternoon reading was inserted as a late addition, just before the *Mincha Amidah*.) This structure does not occur on Saturday mornings. On Saturdays, there is plenty of time. And since the original Saturday morning Torah-Reading was once a separate educational event that caused the whole community to assemble, it became customary to follow it with miscellaneous announcements and appeals of community interest. These now include a Prophetic Reading, a sermon (optional but customary), an exhortation to philanthropy, a prayer for the government, an announcement of the new month (when appropriate), a remembrance of martyrs, and so on. Nowadays, these events are sandwiched between the Torah-Reading Service and the *Musaf* Service. We shall now describe each of these events in more detail:

THE HAFTARAH

On Saturday morning, there will be a reading from *Nevi-im* (Prophets) after the Torah is read. The weekly prophetic passage is called the Haftarah. The word "Haftarah" comes from a root meaning "conclusion," and is unrelated to the word "Torah," which comes from a root meaning "instruction."

The particular prophetic passage is fixed for each weekly *parashah*, and bears some logical relation to the content of the *parashah*. The *Chumash* has the appropriate *Haftarah* printed after each *parashah*. (That's the primary attribute of a *Chumash*. Most Jews own a *Chumash*. Fewer own a *Tanach*.)

The practice of reading a selection from the Prophets was already well-established in *Mishnaic* times,[65] although the specific passages associated with each parashah had not yet been fixed.[66] Since the prophetic portions were chosen to complement the *parashah*,[67] the Prophets were never read in a cycle. Furthermore, the Haftarah portions do not cover the complete *Nevi-im*, or even a majority of it.

THE SERMON

Sermons were originally the stock-in-trade of itinerant Saturday afternoon preachers. They were attended as a popular entertainment. Today, they have been absorbed into the liturgy. They are an optional feature of congregational services, but are expected by congregations that support a rabbi.

The sermon is usually given by the rabbi of the synagogue, and traditionally is delivered on Saturday morning. Some congregations have the sermon immediately after the Haftarah. Others wait until the Torah is returned to the Ark.

In communities that have late (i.e., after-dinner) Friday night services, the sermon is sometimes delivered on Friday night before closing the service. This helps equalize the length of the Friday night and Saturday morning services. This is possible because people aren't awaiting their *Kabbalat Shabbat* home ritual (and Friday night dinner).

A Jewish sermon relates important current situations and issues to the text of the week's *parashah*. It regards Torah as a bottomless resource of relevant teaching on any current subject. Unlike a Christian sermon, which can cite scripture at the discretion of the preacher, Jewish sermons must be based on the current week's Torah portion. In Jewish tradition, there is an expectation that every Torah passage has something to say about every subject.

In modern times, the sermon might start with that week's *parashah* or Haftarah text, and extract a lesson. But a traditional (and more entertaining) way for a sermon to be structured is to start by raising a popular issue. Then work the subject toward the *parashah* text. This is done in three steps. First, relate the subject to a passage from *Ketuvim* (The Writings; the last of the three collections of books that comprise Jewish Scripture); then work the subject toward a passage from this week's Haftarah portion; and finally work the subject to arrive at this week's Torah portion.

Thus we go from Writings, to Prophets, to Torah. At its best, this is like watching a good Columbo episode on TV. You know exactly where he has to get to, but have no idea how he's going to get there. All along the way, references may be made to Talmud and other elements of oral Torah, thereby demonstrating the unity and sanctity of the complete tradition.

If your view of sermons comes from Christianity, you may find Jewish sermons rather different. Judaism is not about personal salvation, faith, purgatory, or resurrection. Judaism is about seeking mitzvot. We spend our days in search of one more opportunity to fulfill the special responsibilities that come with membership in this community, and that are evidence of our personal and communal relationship of partnership with the divine, in which both the Jew and God are dependent upon each other to do their part. This worldview is not usually the subject for a sermon, but it informs how the listeners relate to the sermon's content. Love for divine service, and a belief (especially for agnostics) in the importance of the mission, not personal salvation, and not reward, and not punishment, are what inform Jewish lives. This will be assumed by the rabbi delivering a sermon.

YEKUM PURKON:
IN PRAISE OF PHILANTHROPY

Yekum Purkon is a prayer for the well being of the Jewish community and its mainstays. It was instituted in the eleventh century, when the Babylonian academies had declined to the point of dependence upon European communities. *Yekum Purkon* was intended to stir up charitable donations, therefore it is written in Aramaic, the vernacular of the day. It incites contributions indirectly, since money is not handled or discussed on the Sabbath. It is now a standard feature of the liturgy, despite references to the *Exilarch* (political leader), academies, and judges of Babylonia. It has been reinterpreted, and is now said with reference to current leadership.

After two versions of its opening paragraph, one for the well being of the Jewish community's leaders and one for the community, *Yekum Purkon* concludes with a Hebrew prayer invoking blessings on philanthropists and philanthropic institutions. All this forms one liturgical unit. (The first paragraph is always recited. The last two paragraphs are skipped if there is no minyan.)

THE PRAYER FOR THE GOVERNMENT

Jews all around the world recite a prayer for the local non-Jewish government. Reciting the Prayer for the Government is an ancient biblical practice mandated by the prophet Jeremiah.[68] Jeremiah recognized that when any society enjoys well-being—when its citizens feel secure in their property, persons, and future—then everyone within that society benefits, even the oppressed minorities. He delivered the following instruction:

> Thus hath said the LORD of hosts, the God of Israel:
> To all the exiles whom I caused to be carried off from Jerusalem to Babylon:
> Build houses and dwell in them,
> plant gardens and eat their fruit,
> take wives and beget sons and daughters . . .
> and seek the welfare of the city to which I've banished you,
> and pray in its behalf to the LORD,
> for in its welfare shall you fare well.

The Prayer for the Government has sometimes served as a defense mechanism, although that is not its original intent. The Talmud[69] relates that Simon the Just cited this practice to Alexander the Great when Alexander reached the Land of Israel. (There are many fascinating ancient Jewish traditions about Alexander the Great.) A similar appeal was made to the Roman Emperor Caligula.[70]

Several rationalizations for reciting the Prayer for the Government (besides Jeremiah's) have been cited in later Jewish Tradition. Surprisingly, a very "Hobbsian" view is quoted in the Mishnah: "Rabbi Chanina ... says: Pray for the welfare of the government, for without it a man would swallow his fellow alive."[71]

The prayer's text and place in the service was fixed in the fourteenth century.[72] There was originally a place in it where the names of current rulers were filled in. In the nineteenth century, it was changed (or replaced, in the case of Reform and Conservative prayerbooks) to exclude references to individual royalty. Today, many American congregations make a point of saying this prayer in English, and many alternate versions are in use.

Some less traditional congregations omit the prayer for the Government except during special events (such as the recent Persian Gulf War). Of course this defeats the original significance and traditional intent of the prayer.

In modern times, most American congregations insert a Prayer for the State of Israel after the Prayer for the Government.

ANNOUNCEMENT OF THE NEW MOON

The new moon is a symbol of renewal, as well as the start of each Jewish month. It is a holiday celebrated particularly by Jewish women.[73] Chronologically, it is the first divinely established Jewish holiday—given while we were still slaves. The lunar cycle is about 29½ days long, so a new moon occurs every 29 or 30 days. This holiday is called *Rosh Chodesh* ("Head of the Month").[74]

About every fourth Sabbath, an announcement is made of which day of the coming week will start the new month. This tells everyone when to observe *Rosh Chodesh*. By fixing the start of the month, it also enables the other holidays to be determined.

In ancient times, determining the new moon was based on the tesitmony of witnesses before the Sanhedrin (Jewish Supreme Court). Once the new moon had been reliably sighted, signal fires were sent from hilltop to hilltop, at least as far as Babylon, and perhaps to Persia and beyond. Since this signal took time to propagate, it was possible for remote communities to get it too late. So the Sanhedrin decreed that we observe the festivals and Holy Days for two days outside The Land of Israel. (The exceptions are Shabbat, which doesn't depend on the moon, and the fast days, which would be unhealthy to observe for two days.) This is still the case, although we now calculate the new moons in advance.

The reader takes the Torah and the congregation stands during the announcement. This emulates the procedure used in the "Sanctification of the New Moon," a ritual which cannot be done due to the current absence of a Sanhedrin. The announcement is surrounded by extraneous prayers for a good month, added quite late to the service. These have given rise to the popular name for this part of the service: "Blessing the New Month."

THE COMMEMORATION OF MARTYRS (AV HA-RA-CHA-MIM)

Av Ha-Ra-cha-mim means "The Merciful Father." *Av Ha-Rachamim* is recited as a Commemoration of Martyrs. It was probably written during the first Crusade in 1096. Many of the worst moral abominations in history have been directed at us—from Vespasian, Hadrian, and Justinian; to the Crusades, the Inquisition, and the Holocaust. (Much of the time between these has also been difficult.) *Av Ha-Ra-cha-mim* is but one moving work of this kind, from a people that have had to write too many.

The Sabbath Peace is often experienced as a foretaste of the world-to-come. Reciting *Av Ha-ra-cha-mim* in such a context (and recalling divine promises of justice) has prevented us from becoming avengers and thereby coming to resemble the nations that have murdered, robbed, derided, and oppressed us.

Av Ha-ra-cha-mim is omitted on many Sabbaths, in accordance with a complex set of rules that varies from congregation to congregation.

AFFECTION FOR THE TORAH:
PARTING WITH THE SCROLL

There are two important principles that change the structure of the Torah-Reading Section that we developed above: affection for the Torah and respect for the Torah.

As a sign of our affection for the Torah, we are in no hurry to put it away. Therefore we do not return the Torah to the Ark until we have to. On Saturday afternoon, we must put it away immediately, because the *Amidah* follows immediately. On weekday mornings we must put it away in order to close the service. But on Saturday morning, the Torah-Reading Section is followed by all the miscellaneous liturgical events and then by the Praise Section of the *Musaf* Service. So we will delay its return.

The principle of parting with the Torah as late as possible caused the Torah to be retained through all the miscellaneous community events, which were regarded as short formalities. This makes it look like these too are part of the Torah-Reading Section. In fact, the parting from the Torah is delayed until after the *Ashrei* that comprises the Praise Section of the *Musaf* Service!

RESPECT FOR THE TORAH:
THE PRIMACY OF THE SCROLL

As a sign of our respect for the Torah, we don't permit anyone to read from *Nevi-im* (Prophets) in the presence of a Torah scroll, without having them first read Torah. But this is precisely the situation created when we delay returning the Torah to the Ark. Therefore the person reading the Haftarah begins with a very short *aliya*, called *Maftir*. Lifting and dressing the Torah must be delayed until we are done using the scroll—that is, after *Maftir*. Although the *Maftir aliya* is procedurally similar to the regular *aliyot*, it is *halachically* unrelated to Torah-Reading. *Maftir* is a late addition to the Haftarah-Reading, intended to avoid shaming the Torah by having someone read only from Prophets. (This is the same kind of logic that causes us to cover the *challah* while we say kiddush at home on Friday night.)

THE MAFTIR

Maftir means "the Concluder." The procedure and blessings are just like the earlier regular *aliyot*. The text for this *aliya* is just a rereading of the last few sentences of the seventh *aliya*. (The *Chumash* notes the starting place for the *maftir aliya*.) But after the normal *aliya* procedure, the person who "*daven*"s *Maftir* stays up on the *bima*. In a little while, this person will chant the blessing before the Haftarah, the Haftarah itself, and the blessing after the Haftarah. But first, it's time for lifting the Torah, another major signpost.

After two honorees have lifted and dressed the Torah, the *Maftir* chants the Haftarah from a *Chumash*, preceded and followed by blessings.[75] The blessings are in the siddur. (The only thing the siddur lacks is the Torah and Haftarah texts. These get inserted into the service from the *Chumash*.)

Technically, "*Maftir*" is the name of the *aliya*. But if you are ever asked to "*daven Maftir*," remember that this means staying up there and doing the Haftarah. And not just the Haftarah blessings. Usually, no one reads the Haftarah for you.

If you are in a Conservative or Orthodox *shul* on a Saturday, the *Maftir* will often be a boy that became a Bar Mitzvah[76] (an adult, *halachically*) that week. In larger congregations, two boys will sometimes share the readings; and the folks who get *aliyot* are their relatives. In most Conser-

The Saturday Morning Torah-Reading Service

Original Theoretical Structure:	Affection for Torah Causes This Change:	Finally, Respect for Torah Yields Actual Structure:
Torah-Reading Service:		
Open the Ark	Open the Ark	Open the Ark
Remove Torah	Remove Torah	Remove Torah
Procession	Procession	Procession
Read Torah	Read Torah	Read Torah
Accelerated Congregational Half-*Kaddish*	Accelerated Congregational Half-*Kaddish*	Accelerated Congregational Half-*Kaddish*
Lift Torah	Lift Torah	———
Procession	———	———
Return Torah	———	———
Close the Ark	———	———
Miscellaneous Community Business:		
The Prophetic Reading:	The Prophetic Reading:	The Prophetic Reading:
Haftarah	*Haftarah*	*Maftir*
. . .	. . .	Lift Torah
. . .	. . .	*Haftarah*
Sermon (optional)	Sermon (optional)	Sermon (optional)
Praise of Philanthropy	Praise of Philanthropy	Praise of Philanthropy
Prayer for the Government	Prayer for the Government	Prayer for Government
Prayer for State of Israel	Prayer for the State of Israel	Prayer for State of Israel
Announcement of the New Month*	Announcement of the New Month*	Announcement of the New Month*
Commemoration of Martyrs*	Commemoration of Martyrs*	Commemoration of Martyrs*
Praise Section of the *Musaf* Service		
Ashrei (Psalm 145)	*Ashrei* (Psalm 145)	*Ashrei* (Psalm 145)
. . .	Delayed Parting From Torah:	Delayed Parting From Torah:
. . .	Procession	Procession
. . .	Return Torah	Return Torah
. . .	Close the Ark	Close the Ark
Half-*Kaddish*	Half-*Kaddish*	Half-*Kaddish*
Amidah Section of the *Musaf* Service		

*(when appropriate)

vative synagogues, girls call attention to their attainment of
Bat Mitzvah status in a similar manner.

A groom gets an *aliya* or *davens Maftir* on the Shabbat
before his wedding. In Orthodox *shuls*, you may see the
women throw candy at him from the balcony while he does
this!

Learning to chant a particular Haftarah portion (and the
surrounding blessings) is a reasonable goal for one not flu-
ent in Hebrew. Some men keep their Bar Mitzvah *Haftarah*
portion in their heads their whole lives, by doing *Maftir*
every few years on the appropriate week.

Usually, a blessing's text is closely related to the mitzvah
performed. This is not true of the four blessings after the
Haftarah reading.[77] Their subject matter is far-flung. They
were originally an ancient divergent form of *Amidah*. Although they were not accepted in the official *Amidah* (can-
onized at Yavneh in the first century), they were incorporated here. This is yet another example of sages reconciling
divergent meritorious traditions in an inclusive way.

RULES OF ORDER FOR THE
TORAH-READING SECTION

We have seen that the Congregational Kaddish and the lifting are sometimes in different places in the various Torah-
Reading Services. There are even more variations when the
other holidays are taken into account, because sometimes
the *Maftir aliya* is from a different Torah scroll than the
Torah-Reading, and sometimes Haftarah is read at an afternoon service.[78] Furthermore, the observation of a flaw in a
Torah scroll may necessitate immediately changing scrolls
at any time, or using the flawed scroll in the most minimal
way. There are three simple rules that you can use to determine when the kaddish and the lifting(s) will happen under
any circumstances in any Torah-Reading Service:

1. The historical core of a service must always be immediately preceded by a kaddish. (Recall that this is the *Amidah* at *Mincha* and *Musaf*,[79] the *Sh'ma-Amidah* combination at *Shacharit*, and the *Sh'ma* at *Ma-ariv*.) Thus the kaddish preceding a core of a service can never be moved.
2. Except when prevented by rule 1, the kaddish at the end of the Torah-Reading Service is accelerated. It is recited immediately after fulfilling the mitzvah of Torah-Reading (and it becomes "congregational") to show how hearing Torah transforms us—we rush to do mitzvot.[80]
3. Except for the accelerated kaddish of rule 2, respect for each scroll calls for it to be lifted and dressed as soon as we are done using it.

The chart on the following pages shows the structure of Jewish services with the Torah-Reading Section added:

Weekday Services:

	Shacharit (morning)	Mincha (afternoon)	Ma-ariv (evening)
Preliminary Service			
Praise Section	Psalm 30 / Mourner's Kaddish prologue: Baruch Sheamar - texts - Psalms 100, and		Psalm 144 (Sat. only) Psalm 67 (Sat. only)
	- Psalms 145 (Ashrei) thru 150 - texts epilogue: Yishtabach	Ashrei (Psalm 145)	Psalm 134 (if no Mincha)
	Half-Kaddish	Half-Kaddish	Half-Kaddish (if no Mincha)
Shema Section	Barchu Yotseir (creation), for weekdays Ahavah Raba (revelation) Shema Ga-al Yisraeil - A.M. version		Barchu Ma-ariv Aravim (creation) Ahavat Olam (revelation) Shema Ga-al Yisraeil - P.M. version Hashkiveinu, for weekdays - with Baruch Adonai L'olam Half-Kaddish
Amidah Section	Shacharit Shemoneh Esreh: - avot, givurot - k'dushat hashem - 13 benedictions - Avodah, Modim - Sim Shalom Meditation Repetition: - avot, givurot - k'dushah - 13 benedictions - Avodah - Modim/Modim - Sim Shalom Tachanun Half-Kaddish	Mincha Shemoneh Esreh: - avot, givurot - k'dushat hashem - 13 benedictions - Avodah, Modim - Shalom Rav Meditation Repetition: - avot, givurot - k'dushah - 13 benedictions - Avodah - Modim/Modim - Shalom Rav Tachanun	Ma-ariv Shemoneh Esreh: - avot, givurot - k'dushat hashem - 13 benedictions - Avodah, Modim - Shalom Rav Meditation

Shabbat Services:

	Shacharit & Musaf (Sat. AM)	Mincha (Saturday afternoon)	Ma-ariv (Friday evening)	

Preliminary Service			**Kabbalat Shabbat:**
			
			- Psalm 95
			  (L'chu N'ran'na)
			- Psalm 96 and 97
			- Psalm 98 and 99
			- Havu L'adonai
			  (Psalm 29)
			- L'cha Dodi
			
			greeting mourners	

Praise Section	prologue: Baruch Sheamar
	- texts
	- Psalms 19, 34, 90-1,
	  135-6, 33, 92-3,
	- and Psalms 145 (Ashrei)
	  thru 150
	- texts
	epilogue: Nishmat-
	  Yishtabach
	
	Half-Kaddish
		Ashrei (Psalm 145)
		Uva L'Tsion
		
		Half-Kaddish
			- Psalm 92
			
			- Psalm 93
			
			- Mourner's Kaddish
			
			-Torah Study,
			  on candles
			- Kaddish D'Rabbanan	

Shema Section	Barchu
	
	Yotseir (creation),
	  for Shabbat
	Ahavah Raba (revelation)
	Shema
	Ga-al Yisraeil -
	  A.M. version
			Barchu
			
			Ma-ariv Aravim
			  (creation)
			Ahavat Olam (revelation)
			Shema
			Ga-al Yisraeil -
			  P.M. version
			Hashkiveinu,
			  for Shabbat
			- with Vishamru
			
			Half-Kaddish	

Amidah Section	Shacharit Amidah: - avot, givurot - k'dushat hashem - K Hayom-Vishamru - Avodah, Modim - Sim Shalom Meditation Repetition: - avot, givurot - k'dushah - shabbat - K Ha-yom-Vishamru - Avodah - Modim/Modim - Sim Shalom		Ma-ariv Amidah: - avot, givurot - k'dushat hashem - K Hayom-Vayichulu - Avodah, Modim - Shalom Rav Meditation Vayichulu Magein Avot R'tsei Vimnuchateinu	

Closing Section		Full-Kaddish	Full-Kaddish
Torah-Reading **(Mon., Thu.)**	Removing the Torah: - Zohar - Procession: L'cha Adonai 3 aliyot Congregational Half-Kaddish Lifting: V'zot HaTorah Returning the Torah: - Hodo Al Eretz - Procession: Psalm 24 - Return: Eitz Chayim ----------------		
Miscellaneous Community Business			
Praise Section			
Amidah Section			
Closing Section	Full-Kaddish		

Section				
Closing Section	Full-Kaddish			Full-Kaddish
Torah-Reading	Removing the Torah: - Zohar / Shema excerpt - Procession: L'cha Adonai 7 aliyot Congregational Half-Kaddish ---------------	Removing the Torah: - Zohar excerpt - Procession: L'cha Adonai 3 aliyot --------------- Lifting: V'zot Ha-Torah Returning the Torah: - Hodo Al Eretz - Procession: Psalm 24 - Return: Eitz Chayim Congregational Half-Kaddish		
Miscellaneous Community Business	Prophetic Reading: - Maftir - Lifting: V'zot HaTorah - Haftarah Sermon / Announcements Exhortations to Philanthropy (Yekum Purkon) Prayer for U.S. Government Prayer for the State of Israel Announce the New Month (when appropriate) Remembrance of martyrs (Av Harachamim)			
Praise Section	Ashrei (Psalm 145) * Returning the Torah: - Hodo Al Eretz - Procession: Psalm. 29 (Havu L.) - Return: Eitz Chayim Half-Kaddish			
Amidah Section	Musaf Amidah: - avot, givurot - k'dushat hashem - K Ha-yom (Yismechu) - Avodah, Modim - Sim Shalom Meditation Repetition: - avot, givurot - k'dushah - musaf - K Ha-yom (Yismechu) - Avodah - Modim/Modim - Sim Shalom	Mincha Amidah: - avot, givurot - k'dushat hashem - K.Hayom - Ata Echad - Avodah, Modim - Shalom Rav Meditation Repetition: - avot, givurot - k'dushah - K HaYom - Atah Echad - Avodah - Modim / Modim - Shalom Rav		
Closing Section	Full-Kaddish	Full-Kaddish		

* If a break is desired before Musaf, the ritual for returning the Torah to the Ark is performed before Ashrei.

Notes

1. c.f., page 125.
2. c.f., page 61.
3. c.f., page 165.
4. The Tanach is a library of twenty-two books grouped in three collections: *Torah* (The Five Books of Moses), *Navi'-im* (Prophets), and *Ketuvim* (Writings). *"TaNaCh"* is just an acronym for *Torah-Navi-im-Ketuvim*. Torah is the only part of Scripture that is traditionally regarded as the result of revelation, rather than prophesy or inspiration.
5. c.f., Sifre Deuteronomy Piska 306 "My doctrine shall drop as the rain . . ."
6. Two of these commandments were directly heard by all present at Sinai, while 611 of these commandments are known through the Torah only. The word 'Torah' has a numerical value of 611. (C.f., Exodus Rabbah 33.7 and Talmud Makkot 23b-24a.)
7. c.f., Sifre Deuteronomy Piska 45.
8. c.f., Exodus Rabbah 28.6.
9. The majority of recognized halachic decisors, not the majority of Jews. C.f., Yershalmi Sanhedrin IV, 2; Bavli Eruvin 13b.
10. c.f., Horaiyot 14.
11. c.f., Sifre Deuteronomy Piska 58.
12. I read this parable somewhere several years ago, and wrote this version of it from memory several weeks later in a private letter. I have been unable to find the original source for comparison and citation, and would welcome hearing from anyone who can attribute it.
13. c.f., Sifre to Numbers, CXII:IV:3.
14. Pesachim 22 (Akiva expounding the "et").
15. The effects of this tradition are evident even among secular Jews. Over 70% of American Jews are college educated, versus about 30% of Americans. The highest per capita consumption of books of any country in the world is in the State of Israel.
16. Kiddushin 33, Kiddushin 32.
17. Talmud Pesach 49a–b.
18. except for *lamed-vuvniks* and in Chassidic tradition.
19. On seeing a secular scholar:

Ba-ruch atah Adonai
Elo<u>hei</u>-nu <u>Me</u>-lech Ha-Olam
She-na-tan mei-<u>chach</u>-ma-<u>to</u>
l'va-sar va-dam.

On seeing a Torah scholar:

Ba-ruch atah Adonai
E-lo-<u>hei</u>-nu <u>Me</u>-lech Ha-Olam
She-cha-lak mei-<u>chach</u>-ma-<u>to</u> li-rei-av.

20. Pirke Avot 2:5–6.

21. c.f., Berachot 17; Y. Shabbat 1:2; Shabbat 31; Yebamot 109b.

22. c.f., Sifre Deuteronomy Piska 41 "R. Tarfon, R. Akiva, and R. Jose . . ."

23. c.f., Sifre Deuteronomy Piska 343.

24. c.f., Genesis Rabbah (Vayechi) XCVII:3.

25. See *A Torah is Written*, by Paul and Rachel Cowen, published by the Jewish Publication Society, 1986, for an outstanding introduction to the Torah Scroll.

26. c.f., Sifre Deuteronomy Piska 48.

27. c.f., Deuteronomy 6:7 and 31:13.

28. c.f., Deuteronomy 3:10–12.

29. c.f., Nehemiah 8:5–8.

30. c.f., Talmud *Baba Kamma* 82a; Rambam *Mishneh Torah* Laws of Prayer 12:1; Yerushalmi *Megillah* 4:1.

31. c.f., Talmud Meg. 3a.

32. c.f., Mishnah Meg. 4:4.

33. c.f., Talmud Meg. 31b.

34. c.f., Talmud Meg. 31a–b.

35. c.f., Talmud Meg. 54b.

36. c.f., Tosafot Meg. 4, 9.

37. c.f., Kitzur Shulchan Aruch 24:10.

38. c.f., Meg. 23a.

39. And may also be related to the fact that female prayer is traditionally regarded as more effective than male prayer.

40. Usually the *Ba-al K'riyat* is male, but this is not required by Reform or Conservative synagogues, nor in an Orthodox women's *tefilah* group).

41. c.f., Mishnah Bikkurim 3:7.

42. c.f., Talmud Meg. 21a–b.

43. c.f., Talmud Men. 43b.

44. c.f. Talmud Berachot 33a.

45. The Torah reading commandment is by Rabbinic enact-ment (except for two of the *parashot* which are in fulfilment of a biblical mitzvah).

46. The Diaspora (Greek for "Dispersion") or *Galut* (Hebrew for "Exile") are the names given to the condition of most Jews since the destruction of the second Temple. With the advent of the Diaspora, the ties between tribes and the fixed areas of land that had been possessed by them had been broken. Jews could no longer be certain of their lineage. Even if they felt cer-tain, they could never prove it. The sages of the Talmud were very much concerned with this issue. The halacha reached several conclusions:

Most of the system of tithes described in the Bible were tied to possession of the land, so the commandments regarding sepa-ration of produce naturally became void in the Diaspora. There was only one tithe that was not tied to the land. This was the per-sonal obligation to separate one's dough when baking bread and to give the segregated amount to a priest. Since we can not be sure who is a Ko-hein, the Talmud changed the amount to be set aside to a trivial bit, and directs us to throw it into the fire rather than worry about who to give it to. Thus we still perform the mitzvah of *challa*. In fact, the bread we eat on Sabbaths was renamed *challa* as a remembrance to housewives to perform this mitzvah while baking. The word for bread is *lechem*, not *challa*.

Nearly all priestly and Levite functions were tied to service in the Temple, and vanished with the destruction of the Temple. So one's lineage no longer has any special social function. But there are a few distinctions remaining. Jews have taken care to preserve the memory of Kohanic and Levitical lineages for thousands of years. A Jew whose last name is Cohen, Kahn, Katz, Kaplan, or Kagin is probably a Ko-hein. One whose first or last name is Levin, Levitt, Segal, Chagall, Levy or Levi (e.g., Asher Levy, or Levi Strauss) is prob-ably a Lei-vi. And one whose first or last name is Israel is probably neither of the above. These are all common Jewish names.

Some laws of ritual purity become impossible to observe without the Temple, so we are legally in a state of ritual impurity today. This status in turn affects the application of other laws. The net effect of all the Talmudic analysis is that the laws of ritual purity have been much watered down. (Pretty good pun there!) Orthodox Jews still wash their hands with a blessing before each meal, visit the *mikva* (ritual public bath) on a variety of regularly recurring occasions, etc. And there are a few laws of marriage and ritual purity still in effect for Kohanim (plural of Kohein) that distinguish their practices even today. A Ko-hein generally does not marry a Jew-by-choice, divorcee, or widow (although such marriages are legally in force after the fact). A Kohein does not visit an area where there is, or might be, a corpse, such as cemeteries. A dead body is the highest source of ritual impurity in Jewish law, and Kohanim do not go near them.

One biblical practice involving Kohanic distinctions which is still performed today is the *"Pid Yon Ha Ben"* (or *"Pid-Na-Ben"* in Yiddish). This is the "Redemption of the First Born." Anthropologically, this rite may reflect an ancient Jewish rejection of pagan practices of human firstborn sacrifice, or of firstborns constituting the religious or social administration. However, this is not the rationale presented in the Bible and bound up in Jewish law, which ascribes to it an educational value in remembrance of the slain Egyptians. Non-Kohanim still enjoy this ritual, and Kohanim still participate in the role of priests. (The "Presentation at the Temple" in Christian scripture was a *Pid Yon Ha Ben*.)

47. For this reason, the third *aliya* is thought of as the greatest honor.

48. c.f., Orach Chayim 135:10.

In the absence of a Kohein, the only *aliya* that may be given to a *Leivi* is the first. It need not be given to a *Leivi* even if one is present.

49. consisting of Psalm 86:8; Psalm 145:13; the first phrases of 10:16, 93:1, and Exodus 15:8; and Psalm 29:11.

50. Zohar Shemot 26.

51. *B'rich Sh'mei* includes a declaration of opposition to Christian dogma, through a pun that is not apparent in translation:

I am a servant of the Holy One,
Blessed be He,
and I prostrate myself before Him and the honor of His Torah
at all times.
Not in any man do I put trust,
nor on any angel do I rely;
but only on the God of heaven
who is the God of truth
whose Torah is truth
whose prophets are true
and who acts liberally with goodness and truth . . .
The Aramaic term for "angel" used here is *"bar e-la-hin,"* literally
"son of god." The Sh'ma excerpt which follows on Saturday mornings is an interesting juxtaposition. *B'rich Sh'mei* was added to the
service in the sixteenth century.

52. and perhaps Deuteronomy 33:2 as well.

53. This paragraph is taken, with adaptation, from *Ayn
Keloheinu* by Noah Golinkin, Shengold Publishers.

54. The last verse of Psalm 29 is one example.

55. c.f., Sifre to Numbers LXXXII:I to LXXXIV:V.

56. c.f., Talmud Zebachim 63a–b and Mishnah Middot 2:2.

57. c.f., Shulchan Aruch, Orach Chayim 147; Mishnah Yadayim
3:2, Zavim 5:12; Talmud Shabbat 14a, Megillah 32a.

58. Originally, the Torah-reading was accompanied by interpretive translation. So the covering clarified what was Torah and
what was interpretation. The translator was supposed to listen only
and not look at any text. This prevented people from thinking the
translation and interpretation was in the Torah and not knowing
the difference between oral Torah and written Torah.

Today, in some communities the scroll is not rolled closed but
honorees close their eyes or turn their face away from the scroll.
c.f., T. Soferim 13:8

59. c.f., Talmud Berachot 11b and 49b.

60. There are forty words in the two Torah-reading benedictions, corresponding to the 40 days that Moses spent on Sinai.

61. c.f., Nehemiah 8:5.

62. a variation on II Chronicles 6:41–42, Psalm 132:8–10,
Proverbs 4:2 and 3:18 and 3:17, and Lamentations 5:21

63. That is why the dedication of the Temple is the only event that the Bible dates with reference to the Exodus.

64. and at Yom Kippur *Mincha*

65. c.f., Mishnah Megillah 4:10.

66. c.f., Christian scripture, Luke 4:16–21.

67. There are minor differences between the Haftarah selections of Ashkenazic and Sephardic traditions. These will be noted in a modern *Chumash*, which should accommodate both.

68. c.f., Jeremiah 27:7.

69. c.f., Talmud Yoma 69a.

70. c.f., Josephus, *The Jewish Wars*, 2:10,4.

71. Avot 3:2

72. It includes phrases from Psalms 144:10 and 145:13, Isaiah 43:16 and 59:20, and Jeremiah 23:6.

73. c.f., Yerushalmi Ta-anit I,6.

74. There is a Torah-reading and a *Musaf* service on *Rosh Chodesh*. C.f., Numbers 28:2 and 10:10; Shulchan Aruch 419, 1.

75. c.f., Sofrim.

76. Under Jewish law, boys attain legal majority at age thirteen. Girls attain legal majority at age twelve. They are then a Bar Mitzvah (literally, Son of Commandment) or Bat Mitzvah (literally, Daughter of Commandment).

77. A mnemonic: The *Maftir* says a total of seven bendictions, the same as the number of *aliyot*. They are: one before and one after the *Maftir* Torah portion, one before and four after the Haftarah.

78. And on some occasions the *maftir* reading has the status of a mitzvah, such as on *Rosh Chodesh*.

79. and the *Nielah* service of Yom Kippur.

80. "Fulfilling the *mitzvah* of Torah reading" means that the prescribed number of honorees have been called up, as well as finishing all the required text. This is significant on occasions such as *Rosh Chodesh*, Yom Kippur, and whenever scroll defects are found.

The Closing Section

KADDISH SHALEIM

Just as each service has a praise section at the beginning, each has a closing section at the end. The "Whole Kaddish" (also called *"Kaddish Titkabal,"* or *"Kaddish Shaleim"*) is the basic ingredient of the Closing Section. This prayer was discussed earlier (on page 171). Depending on the service, other events may be appended to expand the Closing Section.

EIN KELOHEINU

Ein Ke-lo-hei-nu was composed during the early Gaonic period. It was added to the end of Sabbath and festival morning services. *Ein Keloheinu* is an extreme example of the sound of "nu" permeating the liturgy. Here is the text:

Ein kE-lo-hei-nu	*Ein* kA-do-nei-nu	*Ein* k'Mal-kei-nu	*Ein* k'Mo-shi-ei-nu
*M*i kE-lo-hei-nu	*M*i kA-do-nei-nu	*M*i k'Mal-kei-nu	*M*i k'Mo-shi-ei-nu
*N*o-deh lEi-lo-hei-nu	*N*o-deh lA-do-nei-nu	*N*o-deh l'Mal-kei-nu	*N*o-deh l'Mo-shi-ei-nu

Ba-ruch E-lo-hei-nu	*Ba-ruch* A-do-nei-nu	*Ba-ruch* Mal-kei-nu	*Ba-ruch* Mo-shi-ei-nu
A-tah hu E-lo-hei-nu	*A-tah* hu A-do-nei-nu	*A-tah* hu Mal-kei-nu	*A-tah* hu Mo-shi-ei-nu

You usually will not see it laid out like this in the siddur, as it usually appears as a running word-wrapped text. But this format shows what is really going on. Here is a translation:

None is like...	...our God	...our Lord	...our Deliverer ...our King.
Who is like...	...our God	...our Lord	...our Deliverer ...our King?
Acknowledge......	...our God	...our Lord	...our Deliverer ...our King:
[by saying:]			
Blessed be...	...our God	...our Lord	...our Deliverer ...our King.
You are...	...our God	...our Lord	...our Deliverer ...our King.

At first, this structure looks like a meaningless playful exercise. But notice that, logically, the first two stanzas are out of order. This is the key to noticing that *Ein Keloheinu* is an acrostic. The stanzas must be in this order so that the first letters of each phrase can spell a message. Here is the secret message of the prayer:

A	A	A	A
Mei	Mei	Mei	Mei
N	N	N	N
Baruch	Baruch	Baruch	Baruch
Atah	Atah	Atah	Atah

"*Amein*" is the last word of every blessing. *Ein Keloheinu* marked the end of the service. So the composer finished the service with "*amein*" in the form of an acrostic.

Each of the three Hebrew letters of *amein* are repeated four times. This has the effect of producing twelve verses of *amein*. *Ein Keloheinu* is sung on the occasions when the *Amidah* has only seven blessings (instead of nineteen).[1] According to Rashi, the twelve phrases of "*a-mein*" in *Ein*

Keloheinu can be thought of as augmenting the *Amidah* to bring the number back to nineteen.

"*Baruch Atah*" are the first words of every blessing. As soon as we have finished the grand "*amein*," we are right back to the beginning! Thus the real message of *Ein Keloheinu* is that Jewish service to God never ends. As soon as we finish one form of service, we are ready to begin another. Recall that "*avodah*," the word for (divine) service, is also the word for (earthly) work. Worship and deed are metaphorically one in Jewish thought.

This is reminiscent of the Torah-Reading schedule. We begin reading the next week's *parashah* at the Saturday afternoon service, the same day we read the entire current *parashah*. And on *Simchas Torah* we begin Genesis at the same service where we finish Deuteronomy.

Ein Keloheinu is followed by a study session of Talmudic passages.[2] They begin with a discussion of the ancient incense offerings in the Temple. The study session procedes to associate this with the seven Psalms of the Day, whose first lines are recounted. This builds to a midrash equating scholars and "teachers of children" with "builders of peace," and climaxes with a passage in praise of peace.[3] This section of study ends with a *Kaddish D'Rabbanan*. Non-Orthodox congregations tend to omit everything except the ending. (Note that we again see a climactic regard for peace, reinstated at the new end of the service.)

In the late Middle Ages, a sixth stanza was added to *Ein Keloheinu*. It means, "You are He to whom our ancestors offered fragrant incense." It is a very bad fit with the rest of the prayer, but it is still sung in most congregations. It is actually an introduction to the study section about incense offerings rather than a culmination of *Ein Keloheinu*. Strangely, it is often sung even by congregations that omit the incense study.

KIDDUSH

Kiddush is the basic procedure that Jews use to recognize the sanctity of time. It is a blessing said with the aid of wine. Kiddush is recited at the start of all festivals and Shabbat. Wine is a potent symbol of joy in Jewish tradition. Full cups (or diminished cups) are used in ritual to represent the fullness (or incompleteness) of our joy. ". . . and wine gladdens the heart of man" (Psalm 104:15).

Kiddush is said on Friday night before dinner, which traditionally occurs after returning from the synagogue. (In less traditional communities, synagogue comes after dinner. Kiddush still comes before.) Kiddush is also said at the "second meal" of Shabbat (the lunch after Saturday morning services). So our first taste on Saturdays is a full glass of wine.

In ancient Babylonia, travelers would be housed and fed in an annex to the synagogue. Since they could not travel after the start of Shabbat, on Friday nights they ate the Shabbat meal in this synagogue hostel right after services. Thus it became traditional to recite kiddush at the end of the service for their benefit. By the fourteenth century, Abudarham of Spain wrote: "As our predecessors have set up the rule, though for a reason that no longer exists, the rule remains unshaken."[4] Kiddush at services remains a custom throughout the Diaspora, but it never arose in *Eretz Yisroel* (The Land of Israel). (Kiddush is not included in the Sephardic version of the Friday night Closing Section.)[5]

In synagogues that have late after-dinner services on Friday night, kiddush is likely to be repeated afterwards with desserts being served. In traditional synagogues, the Saturday morning service may be followed by kiddush and food. Both traditions are based on the goal of delighting in the Sabbath (i.e., maximizing good feelings) known as *Oneg Shabbat*.

Review of the "K" Words

K'dushat HaShem	The third blessing of the Amidah
K'dushah	Replaces the third blessing in the repetition
Kiddush	Sanctification of time, usually said over wine
Kaddish	Aramaic: for mourners and throughout service
K'dushat HaYom	Replaces the Amidah's thirteen weekday petitions

ALEINU

Aleinu is the closing prayer at most services. It was composed in the third century c.e., by the Babylonian sage known as Rav.[6] In Talmudic times, it was used during the *Musaf* service of *Rosh Hashanna*. *Aleinu* became prominent during the Crusades, when it became the death song of the Jews as they were slaughtered for refusing to convert to Christianity. It is a solemn, dramatic, and defiant Jewish manifesto.

Aleinu makes extensive use of the poetic technique known as "biblical parallelism." Each verse has two halves. Although the second half seems to mirror the first, it actually modifies the first to develop, clarify, or intensify what is being communicated. So the effect is one of "heaving forward" even as it hearkens back. This creates a rhythm of great solemnity (totally different from the playful acrostic structure of *Ein Keloheinu*). This technique is common in the poetry of the *Tanach*.[7]

Aleinu has been used as the closing prayer of daily services since the thirteenth century. As a Jewish manifesto, it was the subject of repeated Christian attacks, and its present form is the result of Christian censorship. In its present use, it can express a mood of self-sacrificing dedication to, and joyful acceptance of, Jewish commitments.

Aleinu is sung while standing. The congregation bends slightly at the knee and hunches forward at *"Va-a-nach-nu Ko-r'im,"* which means "We bend our knees"; and straightens up at *"Lif-nei me-lech"* ("the Supreme King"). Usually, only part of the first paragraph is recited aloud. The rest of it is said "silently." But everybody joins in for the dramatic ending (Zechariah 14:9) to assert a shared vision of a united world under the "kingship of heaven."

ADON OLAM: AWE AND INTIMACY

Adon Olam is a majestic poem appended to the end of some Sabbath and festival services. It was probably written by Solomon ibn Gabriol in Spain in the eleventh century. Adon Olam is composed of ten lines, each containing twelve syllables. A single rhyme runs through every line. This structure gives Adon Olam the unusual property that it can be sung to almost any tune at all. (Try singing it to the tune of "Take Me Out to the Ball Game," or "Stairway to Heaven," or "Joy to the World" (!!!) or the first movement of Beethoven's Fifth Symphony! No problem!)

Adon Olam was originally written to be a bedtime prayer, used in conjunction with the Sh'ma and Hash-ki-vei-nu (see pages 143 and 158, respectively). But its ending is ambiguous enough to also be appropriate on arising. In the fifteenth century, Adon Olam was incorporated into prayerbooks at the beginning of the daily Preliminary Morning Service. (The Preliminary Morning Service is discussed later in this book; on page 291.) In the twentieth century, Adon Olam has become a popular addition to the end of the Friday night and Saturday morning services.

Placing Adon Olam right beside Aleinu enhances the drama and beauty of both. Adon Olam deals with the present, while Aleinu is futuristic. Adon Olam is a personal prayer while Aleinu is a collective prayer. Adon Olam reflects an individual's situation while Aleinu reflects national interest. Both end on a universal optimistic note, one for the human condition, and the other for the individual worshipper's human condition.

Adon Olam has two distinct sections. They are radically different in mood. The first half of *Adon Olam* explores the mystery of what it means to be outside of space and outside of time; to be Other than our material reality.

> Lord of . . . Eternity[8] . . . reigned . . . alone
> before . . . everything . . . void . . . alone.
> when . . . by will . . . all . . . was wrought
> his Name made known . . . sovereign
>
> And in the End . . . when chaos comes, and . . .
> all . . . ceases . . . to be . . .
> He still . . . will reign . . . awesome . . . alone . . .
> glorious . . . eternity.
> He was . . . He is . . . He will remain.
>
> He is Oneness . . .
> no other to compare . . . nor join with him
> no beginning . . . no ending . . .
> might . . . and mastery.

The second half celebrates the ability of the divine to be perceived simultaneously everywhere within material reality as needed. Nothing material can be everywhere at once, so this ability is a second mystery.

Both omnipresence (existence throughout reality) and transcendence (existence outside reality) are mysteries. Of course, these two mysteries can be combined to form a dichotomy that is in itself a mystery. *Adon Olam* does this by pressing its two halves together without any gradual transition. There is no change in the poetic form when the mood changes. *Adon Olam* presses these mysteries close together, and thereby celebrates the biggest mystery of all: that which is outside of space turns out to be right here!

Another way to look at this is that the first half of *Adon Olam* deals with "God and the Universe," while the second half deals with "God and the Individual." God is outside the universe, yet with each individual. This is the same mystical combination of simultaneous nearness and awe-inspiring transcendence that is expressed in the grammar of all the fixed prayers. The beginning of every benediction, *"Baruch Atah Adonai,"* is in the second person. But the ending of a benediction is always in the third person. For example: "Praised art Thou, LORD, . . . who returns His presence to Zion." or "Blessed are You, LORD, . . . who brings forth bread from the earth." Because there are prescribed fixed blessings for so many things, observant Jews say blessings fairly constantly, and have the opportunity to experience (or be reminded of) this intimacy and awe all day long.

In the second half of *Adon Olam,* God is portrayed as a personal "Rock" and "Protector." "I" and "my" (words with "ai" and "i" endings) occur frequently. This is dramatically different from the rest of the siddur. And the sound of "nu" is absent.

Although there are many different congregational tunes used for *Adon Olam,*[9] none of them actually sets the words of the poetry. They simply apply the poem to a preexisting melody. None of them make any distinction between the powerful dark mystical first half and the cheerful confident loving second half. (Great composers have written choral settings of *Adon Olam* that set the words to music carefully, but these are not generally sung by congregations.)

YIGDAL

When the great Jewish thinker Rambam (Rabbi Moshe ben Maimon, also known as Maimonides) was a young man, he was influenced by Aristotelian and Arabic philosophy. He attempted to systematize his Jewish faith by reducing it to thirteen axioms. They are listed in Rambam's commentary on the Mishnah.[10] They were challenged by his contemporaries, and have been rejected by many of the greatest Jewish thinkers since then.[11] Some disagreed with Rambam's principles, while others opposed the effort itself. Rambam never referred to them again during a long life of sage commentary and mature philosophy.

But those thirteen articles of faith became the basis for *Yigdal*, a poem written between 1100 and 1500, possibly by Daniel ben Judah of Rome about the thirteenth century. *Yigdal* has thirteen lines, paraphrasing Rambam's thirteen articles of faith. Every line has sixteen syllables, and all end with the same rhyme.

In some synagogues, *Yigdal* will be sung at the end of Friday night services, in place of *Adon Olam*. In the beginning of the Preliminary Morning Service (discussed later), *Yigdal* follows *Adon Olam*. (Both are relatively recent additions at the beginning of the day's liturgy.)

Rambam himself would probably be surprised by *Yigdal*, since he opposed the introduction of such poetry into the *Siddur*. He maintained that unacceptable doctrines would thereby be introduced.[12] Furthermore, the version of *Yigdal* found in most siddurim has a fifth verse that deviates from Rambam's fifth principle. This is either due to a very early scribal error, or due to the poet's own philosophy differing from Rambam's.[13]

As noted earlier (on page 93), all Jewish liturgical components were constructed as one (and only one) of the following: praise, petition, thanks, supplication, affirmation, or study. *Yigdal* is structured as a hymn of praise and located in the service where praise is appropriate, but with contents that are more approriately used as affirmation. It doesn't fit the traditional Jewish structural models of liturgy.

Furthermore, *Yigdal*'s preoccupation with systematizing and declaiming elements of faith is not typical of Judaism and makes many Jews uncomfortable.[14] No traditional authority has ever employed Rambam's formulation as a touchstone of Jewish commitment, and even prospective Jews-by-choice need not accept any creedal statement at all. The touchstone of one's Jewish commitment has always been behavioral—the observance of the commandments, especially kashrut and Shabbat observance, coupled with exemplary works and lifestyle.

Many congregations skip *Yigdal*; and siddurim that follow *Nusach Ari* (the variant liturgical rite employed by the *Lubuvitcher Chasidim*) omit it entirely. (Note that omitting *Yigdal*—for any of the above reasons—need not imply disagreement with the principles themselves.)

SHALOM ALEICHEM

Shalom Aleichem was introduced by *kabbalists* about 350 years ago. It is a song of peace and hospitality. *Shalom Aleichem* is traditionally sung Friday night upon returning home after services, and/or on the way home. It is sometimes sung in synagogue at the end of Friday night services.

It is based on a passage of folklore in the Talmud, which says that two angels accompany every person home from synagogue on Friday night. One is good and the other evil. If they find a beautiful table prepared and the family in harmony, the good angel says: "May the next Sabbath be as this one." And the evil angel is forced to say, "Amen." If, on the other hand, they find the house neglected and the family in disharmony, the evil angel says: "May the next Sabbath be as this one." And the good angel is forced to say, "Amen."

In traditional communities, strangers come to services to seek fellow Jews. On Friday night, travellers without a place to make Shabbat will be taken home from synagogue by members of the community. On those rare occasions when I travel on business and am out of town on Friday night, if I go to an Orthodox *shul* I can always count on invitations to dinner and good company.

Shalom Aleichem is therefore also associated with hospitality. The metaphor of welcoming angels also welcomes the Sabbath Bride and other guests into the home. Several wonderful tunes are popular.

(Shalom Aleichem is also the pen name of a beloved Yiddish writer, comparable in style to Mark Twain. Shalom Aleichem wrote the short stories that formed the basis for the musical play, "Fiddler on the Roof.")

THE PSALM OF THE DAY

In the ancient Temple, the Levites used to provide musical accompaniment to the daily offering, singing a specific Psalm for each day of the week.[15]

The Psalm of the Day

Sunday	Psalm 24
Monday	Psalm 48
Tuesday	Psalm 82
Wednesday	Psalm 94
Thursday	Psalm 81
Friday	Psalm 93
Saturday	Psalm 92

The Talmud[16] relates each of these Psalms' contents to divine activities on the corresponding day of creation. The exception is the Psalm for the Sabbath Day, which is related to future events; just as the Sabbath is a weekly foretaste of the world-to-come.

Today we recite the Psalm of the Day (followed by a Mourner's Kaddish) every day during the morning liturgy.[17] The Psalm of the Day has no fixed place. Each congregation inserts it somewhere between the major services of the morning liturgy. Some congregations put the Psalm of the Day at the conclusion of the Preliminary Morning Service, just before the Praise Section of the *Shacharit* service. Others put it after the Closing section of the *Shacharit* service. (On Saturdays, that puts it just before the Torah-Reading service.) Either position makes sense, since the Levites used the Psalm of the Day to accompany the daily *Shacharit* offering.

On Saturdays, some congregations put the Psalm of the Day at the end of the Closing Section of the *Musaf* service, at the end of the entire Saturday morning liturgy. This makes less sense historically, since the Levites used the Psalm of the Day to accompany the daily *Shacharit* offering. A completely different text was used by the Levites to accompany the *Musaf* offering. But it makes sense to some modern congregations, as it establishes a regular place for the daily Psalm at the end of the entire liturgy on any day of the week.

Reform congregations are an exception. They omit the Psalm of the Day entirely.

A-NIM Z'MI-ROT: THE HYMN OF GLORY (SHIR HA-KAVOD)

A-nim Z'mirot (I Will Chant Sweet Hymns) is the popular name for The Hymn of Glory (*Shir Ha-Ka-vod*). It is sung on Saturday and festival mornings in most congregations.[18] It is said standing before the open Ark, and is followed by a Mourner's Kaddish. *Anim Z'mirot* is attributed to Rabbi Judah of Regensburg (d. 1217 c.e.). It is usually sung fairly quickly, the reader and congregation taking alternate lines. It is a challenging tongue twister for those not familiar with it. Its allusive kabbalistic contents express the yearning for direct experience of the divine.

As a late addition to the liturgy, the Hymn of Glory is usually recited at the end of the Saturday morning liturgy, at the end of the Closing Section of the Shabbat *Musaf* service. But some congregations put the Hymn of Glory at the conclusion of the Preliminary Morning Service on Shabbat, just before the Praise Section of the *Shacharit* service. Others put it after the Closing Section of the Shabbat *Shacharit* service, before the Torah-Reading Section. (And some don't include it at all.)

This is identical to the placement options for the Psalm of the Day. But they are independent events. If a congregation inserts both the Psalm of the Day and the Hymn of Glory in the same place, the Psalm of the Day should come first.[19] And they are each followed by their own Mourner's Kaddish.

THE CONCLUSION OF SHABBAT: RETURNING TO WORK; HAVDALAH

The Talmud says, "Love work,"[20] and, "Torah study that is not combined with some trade must at length fail and occasion error."[21] The Talmud records that our sages had diverse jobs and businesses, including physically demanding labor. Until only two hundred years ago, Rabbis (and Jewish doctors) were compensated only for their lost wages or business opportunities. The Talmud says, "One should not use the Torah as a spade to dig with." This respect for work is reflected in the Saturday evening service, as we part from Shabbat.

On Saturday night, we insert Psalm 90:17 and Psalm 91 before the closing *Kaddish Shaleim*. According to a *midrash*, Psalm 90:17 is the blessing Moses gave the workers after completing the building of the Tabernacle, and Psalm 91 was written by Moses on the day the work was completed. The closing *Kaddish Shaleim* is followed by a collection of biblical verses, chosen to encourage the congregation when facing the new week of toil that follows the Shabbat peace. This is followed by Psalm 128, which emphasizes the dignity of labor.

And finally (before or after *Aleinu*, depending on whether the congregation is Ashkenazic or Sephardic), *Havdalah* takes place. Like *kiddush*, *Havdalah* at services is a duplication of a ritual that takes place in the home. *Havdalah* is a beautiful ritual that is about 2,400 years old. *"Havdalah"* means "separation."

In *Havdalah*, you exercise all your senses. You taste wine, smell spices, watch a candle, feel a flame, and hear yourself recite blessings. You light a special multi-wick braided candle (so that there are many dancing lights).[22] You say the blessing over wine. You smell the spices. You cup your hands around the candle. Light and shadow dance on your palms while you contemplate the distinction.

While doing this you express gratitude for the existence of differences, and for the ability to discern differences; and especially for the difference between the sacred and the profane (the not yet sacred), and the ability to discern this distinction. (These thoughts are also expressed in an extra paragraph inserted on Saturday nights into the fourth benediction of the *Amidah*.)

Although *Havdalah* is a sort of thanksgiving for the senses, it is very sad, because what we sense is loss. You spill out the few drops of wine left in the bottom of the cup . . . pick up the beautiful *Havdalah* candle . . . and extinguish it in the wine. Shabbat is gone.

The sadness is diffused a little bit as the congregation spontaneously sings any of several traditional songs about *E-li-ya-hu Ha-Na-vi* (Elijah the Prophet), and wishes each other a good week (*"Shavua Tov"* in Hebrew, *"a gute voch"* in Yiddish). Tradition says that Eliyahu will be the herald of the future redemption, and that the redemption won't occur on the Sabbath. So hope for a perfected world is renewed as Shabbat exits.

HAVDALAH AND THE ETHICS OF DIVERSITY

The ability to appreciate separation, as expressed in the *Havdalah* ritual, may be applied more broadly. Biblical narrative suggests that one can view God as the power that divides, separates, and makes distinctions—the force that runs counter to the physicists' entropy.[23] God appears as an ordering principle in a universe that normally is running down into blended uniformity. This force against entropy is active in both material and ethical spheres. Material examples: Creation divides void into light and dark, separates waters from waters (by sky). Ethical examples: God commanded ethnic diversity as a blessing;[24] distinguished Israel from the nations; prohibits working oxen and asses together,[25] wearing wool and linen together, planting different grains in the same field; men and women cross-dressing.[26] We are enjoined to recognize differences rather than to deny differences, and to enjoy rather than suppress diversity. We are to appreciate the goodness of the differences that distinguish each part of creation. Failing to regard these distinctions as boons, and failing to revel in their goodness, is akin to nullifying creation. (If Cheerios tasted the same as Corn Flakes— or vice versa—the world would be a poorer place. So give thanks with every bowl.)

THE DAILY SIDRA: ASHREI, PSALM 20, AND UVA L'TSION

There used to be a daily afternoon congregational Bible study session in which the Prophets and the Writings were read in Aramaic translation. At that time, Aramaic (and not Hebrew) was the common spoken language of the Jewish community. This congregational study session was called "the daily *sidra*." It included a recitation of *Ashrei* (Psalm 145). The daily *sidra* was one of the three daily recitals of *Ashrei*.

The daily *sidra* also included *Uva L'Tsion* ("A Redeemer Will Come to Zion"). *Uva L'tsion* contains words of comfort taken from Isaiah, Ezekiel, and Psalms, and an Aramaic translation of the *K'dushah*. This was inserted in response to persecution. The translation of the *K'dushah* is interpretive rather than literal. It was designed to negate the Church's association of "Holy! Holy! Holy!" with the Trinity. The translation says: "Holy in the highest heaven . . . Holy upon the Earth . . . Holy to all eternity . . . is the LORD of Hosts!" Reciting the *Sh'ma* or the *Amidah* had already carried a death penalty for some time.[27] The *K'dushah* had been permitted because the Church had confused it with an acclamation of the trinity. This translation of the *K'dushah* was "hidden" in *Uva L'tsion* when the Church finally forbade recitation of the *K'dushah*. Since Bible reading (other than the *Sh'ma*) was permitted when not accompanied by teaching, this version of the *K'dushah* was buried in *Uva L'tsion* on occasions of Bible study.

About 1,200 years ago, the daily *sidra* became no longer necessary. The study session was discontinued on weekdays for lack of time or interest. *Ashrei* and *Uva L'tsion* were incorporated into the end of the weekday morning service. They are regarded as Torah study, and are placed before the *Kaddish Shaleim*, where they can be thought of as establishing a return to the regular world after spending time in the world of prayer.[28]

On Saturdays, there is more time for study. *Uva'L'tsion* is combined with the *Ashrei* of the Saturday *Mincha* Praise Section, to introduce the Torah-Reading Section on Saturday afternoons.

So now our service looks like this:

Weekday Services:

	Shacharit (morning)	Mincha (afternoon)	Ma'ariv (evening)
Preliminary Service	*		*

Praise Section	Psalm 30 / Mourner's Kaddish
	prologue: :Baruch Sheamar
	- texts
	- Psalms 100, and
	
	- Psalms 145 (Ashrei)
	  thru 150
	- texts
	epilogue: Yishtabach
	
	Half-Kaddish
		
		Ashrei (Psalm 145)
		
		Half-Kaddish
			Psalm 144 (Sat. only)
			Psalm 67 (Sat. only)
			
			Psalm 134
			  (if no Mincha)
			
			Half-Kaddish
			  (if no mincha)

Shema Section	Barchu
	
	Yotseir (creation),
	  for weekdays
	Ahavah Raba (revelation)
	Shema
	Ga-al Yisraeil -
	  A.M. version
			Barchu
			
			Ma'ariv Aravim
			  (creation)
			Ahavat Olam(revelation)
			Shema
			Ga'al Yisraeil -
			  P.M. version
			Hashkiveinu,
			  for weekdays
			- with Baruch Adonai
			  L'olam
			Half-Kaddish

Amidah Section	Shacharit Shemoneh
	  Esreh:
	- avot, givurot
	- k'dushat hashem
	- 13 benedictions
	- Avodah, Modim
	- Sim Shalom
	Meditation
	
	Repetition:
	- avot, givurot
	- k'dushah
	- 13 benedictions
	- Avodah
	- Modim/Modim
	- Sim Shalom
	
	Tachanun
		Mincha Shemoneh
		  Esreh:
		- avot, givurot
		- k'dushat hashem
		- 13 benedictions
		- Avodah, Modim
		- Shalom Rav
		Meditation
		
		Repetition:
		- avot, givurot
		- k'dushah
		- 13 benedictions
		- Avodah
		- Modim/Modim
		- Shalom Rav
		
		Tachanun
			Ma-ariv Shemoneh
			  Esreh:
			- avot, givurot
			- k'dushat hashem
			- 13 benedictions
			- Avodah, Modim
			- Shalom Rav
			Meditation

Closing Section			

Shabbat Services:

	Shacharit & Musaf (Saturday AM)	Mincha (Saturday afternoon)	Ma'ariv (Friday evening)	
Preliminary Service			**Kabbalat Shabbat:** - Psalm 95 (L'chu N'ran'na) - Psalm 96 and 97 - Psalm 98 and 99 - Havu L'adonai (Psalm 29) - L'cha Dodi greeting mourners	
Praise Section	Psalm 30/ Mourner's Kaddish prologue: Baruch Sheamar - texts - Psalms 19, 34, 90-1, 135-6, 33, 92-3, - and Psalms 145 (Ashrei) thru 150 - texts epilogue: Nishmat-Yishtabach Half-Kaddish	Ashrei (Psalm 145) Uva L'Tsion Half-Kaddish	- Psalm 92 - Psalm 93 - Mourner's Kaddish -Torah Study, on candles - Kaddish D'Rabbanan	
Shema Section	Barchu Yotseir (creation), for Shabbat Ahavat Raba (revelation) Shema Ga'al Yisraeil - A.M. version		Barchu Ma'ariv Aravim (creation) Ahavat Olam (revelation) Shema Ga'al Yisraeil - P.M. version Hashkiveinu, for Shabbat - with Vishamru Half-Kaddish	
Amidah Section	Shacharit Amidah: - avot, givurot - k'dushat hashem - K Hayom-Vishamru - Avodah, Modim - Sim Shalom Meditation Repetition: - avot, givurot - k'dushah - shabbat - K Ha-yom-Vishamru - Avodah - Modim/Modim - Sim Shalom		Ma-ariv Amidah: - avot, givurot - k'dushat hashem - K Hayom-Vayichulu - Avodah, Modim - Shalom Rav Meditation Vayichulu Magein Avot R'tsei Vimnuchateinu	
Closing Section	**Full-Kaddish** **Psalms of the Day / Mourner's K.*** **Hymn of Glory / Mourner's K. ***			

Torah-Reading (only on Mon., Thu., & Sat.)	Removing the Torah: - Zohar - Procession: L'cha Adonai 3 aliyot Congregational Half-Kaddish Lifting: V'zot HaTorah Returning the Torah: - Hodo Al Eretz - Procession: Psalm 24 - Return: Eitz Chayim ---------------		
Miscellaneous Community Business			
Praise Section			
Amidah Section			

Closing Section	Half-Kaddish
	
	Ashrei
	Psalm 20 and
	  Uva L'Tzion
	
	Full-Kaddish
	
	Aleinu / Mourner's
	  Kaddish*
		Full-Kaddish
		
		Aleinu / Mourner's
		  Kaddish
			Half-Kaddish
			  (Sat. only)
			Psalm 91 (Sat. only)
			Atah Kadosh
			  (Sat. only)
			
			Full-Kaddish
			Tanach text (Sat. only)
			Psalm 128 (Sat. only)
			Havdalah (Sat. only)
			
			Aleinu / Mourner's
			  Kaddish

Torah-Reading (only on Monday, Thursday, and Saturday)	Removing the Torah: - Zohar / Shema excerpt - Procession: L'cha Adonai 7 aliyot Congregational Half-Kaddish --------------- --------------- --------------- --------------- --------------- ---------------	Removing the Torah: - Zohar - Procession: L'cha Adonai 3 aliyot --------------- Lifting: V'zot Ha-Torah Returning the Torah: - Hodo Al Eretz - Procession: Psalm 24 - Return: Eitz Chayim Congregational Half-Kaddish	
Miscellaneous Community Business	Prophetic Reading: - Maftir - Lifting: V'zot HaTorah - Haftarah Sermon / Announcements Exhortations to Philanthropy Prayers for U.S. / Israel Announce the New Month Remembrance of martyrs		
Praise Section	Ashrei (Psalm 145)† Delayed returning of the Torah: - Hodo Al Eretz - Procession: Psalm 29 (Havu L.) - Return: Eitz Chayim Half-Kaddish		
Amidah Section	Musaf Amidah: - avot, givurot - k'dushat hashem - K Ha-yom (Yismechu) - Avodah, Modim - Sim Shalom Meditation Repetition: - avot, givurot - k'dushah - musaf - K.Ha-yom (Yismechu) - Avodah - Modim/Modim - Sim Shalom	Mincha Amidah: - avot, givurot - k'dushat hashem - K Hayom-Ata Echad - Avodah, Modim - Shalom Rav Meditation Repetition: - avot, givurot - k'dushah - K.HaYom-Atah Echad - Avodah - Modim / Modim - Shalom Rav	
Closing Section	**Full-Kaddish** **Ein Keloheinu** **Talmud Study on incense** **Kaddish D'Rabbanan** **Aleinu / Mourner's Kaddish*** **Adon Olam**	**Full-Kaddish** **Aleinu / Mourner's Kaddish**	**Full-Kaddish** **Kiddush** **Aleinu / Mourner's Kaddish** **Adon Olam** **(or Yigdal)**

*The Psalm of Day (and the Hymn of Glory on Shabbat) can be inserted separately in any of these places.
†If a break is desired before Musaf, the ritual for returning the Torah to the Ark is performed before returning for Ashrei.

Notes

1. in Ashkenazic rite. In Sephardic rite *Ein Keloheinu* is recited more frequently.

2. Talmud Keritot 6a; Mishnah Tamid 7:4; Talmud Megillah 28b; Talmud Berachot 64a.

3. constructed out of fragments of Psalm 119:165, 122:7–9, and 29:11.

4. This information is from a note in the Birnbaum siddur.

5. Nor in *chassidic nusach*.

6. But see Kitzur Shulchan Aruch 25:6 where a tradition is reported ascribing *Aleinu* to Joshua.

7. Taken, with adaptation, from *Ayn Keloheynu*, by Noah Golinkin, published by ShenGold Publishers, 1989.

8. In biblical times, *"olam"* meant "ancient time" or "continuous existence." In later Hebrew, it means "world" in the sense that we might now say "universe." In other words, "everything that exists." Other prominent instances of the word are: *"Ahavat Olam"* and *"l'olam va-ed."* See the discussion of '*olam*' in the section beginning on page 72.

9. My favorite tune for *Adon Olam* is a *niggun*. A *niggun* is a kind of stirring cyclical chant. *Niggunim* come from the mystical side of Judaism. "You can't hear the grumble of an empty belly when you hum a *niggun*." Once launched, it is without beginning or end. A *niggun* can go on for a long time. It does not progress, but seems to suspend time. For this reason, the *niggun* seems to fit the opening mood of *Adon Olam*.

Another tune that you may encounter sounds like a great John Philip Sousa march. (It's actually based on a French folksong.) It's a stirring tune. (You'll know this tune by the fact that the congregation splits into two parts—one that would be brass and one that would be flutes and piccolos if this were a Sousa arrangement.) This tune does not express the mystical dark powerful feeling of the first half of the text.

And there are several other tunes that you may find in use. One of them sounds like a Russian drinking song, usually accompanied by much banging. This is fun for children, and for singing around the Sabbath table at home, but lacks the decorum that most nonChassidic Jews associate with congregational worship.

10. re: Sanhedrin 10:1

11. Including Ramban (Nachmanides), Crescas, the Shulchan Aruch, and Abarbanel. See also Joseph Albo, *Sefer Halkarim*.

12. c.f., *Teshuvot Ha-Rambam*, responsa 127 and 128.

13. At issue is the choice of a *lamed* or a *vuv*. Is it *"v'chawl no-tzar,"* as per Rambam's principles? Or is it *"l'chawl no-tzar,"* as found in most prayerbooks? One letter changes the meaning of the verse significantly.

14. e.g., Ba-ar Ha-tav (Shulchan Aruch Siman 46) asserts that the Ari did not say it, since according to kabbalah it should not be said. [My thanks to Oscar Tauber for calling my attention to this.]

15. c.f., Mishnah Tamid 7:4.

16. Rosh Hashannah 31a. See also *Avot d'Rabbi Nathan* I:XII.1 (using the verse numbering of Neusner's edition).

17. We also recite Psalm 67 during the *omer*, because it has 7 verses and 49 words. We also recite Psalm 27 during Elul and part of Tishrei.

18. Some congregations sing it only on festivals, or only on Rosh Hashanah and Yom Kippur.

19. There is a principle that the more frequent is placed before the less frequent.

20. c.f., Pirkei Avot 1:10.

21. c.f., Avot 2:2.

22. The kindling of lights (and the heating of spices) is forbidden on the Sabbath, so the *havdalah* candle is a clear demarcation of Shabbat's boundary. There is a story (c.f., Talmud Pesachim 54a) that God taught Adam to make fire on Saturday night. So *havdalah* can also be a commemoration of that aspect of creation.

23. The First Law of Thermodynamics is the definition of energy, a mathematically calculable function of observable measurable quantities so constructed as to remain constant throughout all observed reactions. The first law reflects a human choice to model the behavior of material reality by seeking transcendental constants (e.g., charge, strangeness, parity, etc.). The Second

Law of Thermodynamics is the definition of entropy, another mathematically calculable function of observable measurable quantities so constructed as to increase throughout all observed reactions. The Second Law of Thermodynamics is necessary to model the unidirectional nature of reactions allowed by the first law. Entropy's magnitude seems to correspond to our natural notions of disorderliness.

    24. Genesis 9:1 coupled with its fulfillment at 10:32.

    25. Deuteronomy 22:9–11 and Leviticus 19:19.

    26. Deuteronomy 22:5.

    27. These persecutions ended in 636 c.e. when the Arabs conquered the region from the Christians. The persecutions had begun with Constantine and reached a high point with Justinian.

    28. Depending on what day it is, they can be thought of as petitions appended to the *Shacharit Amidah* (Tuesday, Wednesday, Friday, Sunday), or as an adjunct to Torah-reading (as per the original daily *sidra*) when there is no *haftarah* (Monday and Thursday), or as the Praise Section of the *Chol HaMoed* or *Rosh Chodesh Musaf Amidah*.

    They can also be thought of as a device to enable latecomers to say the *K'dushah*. Or to enable late-comers to engage in Torah study (the Aramaic translation qualifying as "*gemara*").

The Preliminary
Morning Service

Every morning there is a preliminary service before *Shacharit*'s Praise Section. Its core consists of prayers that were originally intended to be said privately at home. Its contents reflect "first thoughts" upon waking up.

So many insertions and appendages have occurred over time, that the Preliminary Morning Service now looks like an endless series of conflicting "first wake-up thoughts" all vying with each other over the first slot. (And in fact, the addition of this entire service deemphasizes Psalm 30's pride of place at the head of the *Shacharit* Praise Section.)

To make any sense of this jumble, it is necessary to see how the service was built over time. There was no Preliminary Morning Service before the second century. Wake-up thoughts happened at home, the place where one woke up.

THE BLESSINGS UPON ARISING

The day originally began with a short prayer (*Elohai N'shama*), said upon regaining consciousness. This was followed immediately by a rapid sequence of fifteen one-line benedictions. There was one for opening one's eyes, one for stretching and sitting up in bed, one for dressing, and so on. The benedictions related each mundane act to a corresponding fundamental value, such as healing the blind, loosening the bound, clothing the naked, and so on. This was followed by a short prayer for starting the day (*Vihi Ratson*).[1]

The Blessings Upon Arising:
Elohai N'shama
Fifteen Morning Benedictions
V'hi Ratson

In ancient times, prayers were not written down; they were learned by heart. Different people would know more or less of the liturgy. Only the learned could maintain the complete oral tradition, including what was not regularly heard in synagogue.[2] (Hence the practical need for the reader.)

In the second century, a goal of the pious was to recite one hundred daily benedictions.[3] To facilitate this, some form of the morning wake-up benedictions were added to the morning service as an educational device. This was immensely popular. People heard the benedictions and said "*a-mein*," although the normal requirement of saying a benediction only immediately before fulfilling a commandment[4] was thus broken. And this has become the tradition.[5]

At some point, the short prayer upon regaining consciousness (*Elohai N'shama*) was also moved to the morning service, because the pious argued that it should not be recited prior to washing one's hands, since it contained God's Name.[6]

At some point, a similar process led to incorporating the prayer for defecating and/or urinating, normally said upon leaving the bathroom.[7] It was placed in the Preliminary

Morning Service just before *Elohai N'shama*. The same was done for the prayer for washing hands. This was inserted before the prayer for using the bathroom. These three prayers remain a logical unit as they obviously are "blessings upon arising." But the Fifteen Morning Benedictions have taken on a liturgical life of their own that generally ignores their origins as home rituals.

The fixed prayer for starting the day (*Vihi Ratson*), which marked the end of the fifteen blessings, was so similar to the personal prayer (*Y'hi Ratson*) that Judah HaNasi recited silently at the end of the *Amidah* (reported in Talmud Berachot 16b) that Rabbi Judah's prayer came to be viewed as related to *Vihi Ratson* and was added to the Preliminary Morning Service right after *Vihi Ratson*. (Note that *Y'hi Ratson* has the unusual feature of being in the first person singular, indicating its origin as a personal prayer.)

The Preliminary Morning Service:
Blessings Upon Arising:
Elohai N'shama
Handwashing Benediction
Bathroom Benediction
Fifteen Morning Benedictions
Vihi Ratson
Y'hi Ratson

Before examining the fifteen key morning blessings in their liturgical (i.e., nonhome) context, let's note more of the later additions to the Preliminary Morning Service.

THE BATHROOM PRAYER

The bathroom prayer expresses admiration and appreciation for the human body. It regards defecation as an occasion of pleasurable wonder.

There are strong elements within classical Christian tradition that associate spirituality with mind, and sinfulness
with body. These ideas are foreign to Judaism. Biblical
Judaism did not conceive of a dichotomy between mind and
body. There is only a whole person. In Jewish tradition, a
person is a body is a mind. The same biblical word is sometimes translated as "living creature," "soul," or "body," depending on context or on the philosophical predisposition
of the translator. In earliest Hebrew, there are no distinct
words for these later concepts.[8]

To be sure, Jewish thought ascribes to each individual
an evil inclination[9] and a good inclination. But these are
inherent to personhood, and neither is associated with mind
or body. Sex, eating, and other pleasures, are opportunities
to experience a boon. To abstain from them is to avoid an
opportunity to have a reason to praise God.

"If one forsakes his custom of drinking wine, he is a sinner."
Talmud Baba Kamma 91b (see also Talmud Nedarim 10a)

"A man will have a demerit in his record on Judgement Day
for everything he beheld with his eyes and declined to enjoy."[10]
Talmud Yerushalmi Kiddushin 4

"Isn't it enough that the Torah imposes prohibitions upon you?
But you wish to deny what is permitted to you?"
Talmud Yerushalmi Nedarim 9:1.

"In the World to Come a man will be asked to give an account
for everything appealing to eat, that he gazed at and did not
eat."[10]
Talmud Yerushalmi Kiddushin 4:12 (end).

"One who causes himself pain by abstinence from something
he desires is called a sinner."[10]
Talmud Nazir 19

Why does the Torah prescribe a sin-offering for a Nazirite? Wherein did he sin? He made a vow that it would be a sin for him to enjoy wine, and hence he castigated his soul. If a man who thus abstained only from wine is called a sinner, how much more so is one who vows to castigate his soul or body in matters far more important?[10]

Talmud Ta-anit 11.

Furthermore, the evil inclination is actually a good and necessary component of us. The Talmud says, "But for the evil inclination, no man would build a house, beget children, or start a business."[11] Our evil inclinations are controlled by ritual and Torah study. In this way they are harnessed to the good inclination.[12] One inclination is like an engine without a transmission, the other a transmission but no engine. The evil inclination is the power source that needs to be controlled. The good inclination harnesses it in order to move.

TALMUD TORAH (TORAH STUDY)

As noted in the Torah-Reading section, every Jew is required to study Torah daily.[13] Fulfillment of this obligation requires reading texts from the Tanach, Mishnah, and Talmud (or other later oral law).[14]

To allow pious poor people, who could not spare the time normally required for the luxury of study, to participate in this mitzvah, a brief Torah study session was incorporated into the Preliminary Morning Service. Like the lifting of the Torah, this is a symbolic fulfillment only. The "studied" texts are just a few sentences. And they are the same every day. The biblical text "studied" is the Priestly Blessing (Numbers 6:24), already familiar from the repetition of the last blessing of the *Amidah*. The Mishnaic text is a sentence from Peah 1:1. The Talmudic text is two sentences from Shabbat 127a. Both passages enumerate paramount Jewish religious obligations. The Mishnaic text cites supporting the poor, supporting the social administration, performing deeds of kindness, and the study of Torah. The Talmudic text cites honoring parents, performing deeds of kindness, providing hospitality to guests, visiting the sick,[15] bringing joy to a bride and groom, accompanying the dead to a proper burial, concentrating on the meaning of prayers, making peace between people, and the study of Torah, which is equivalent to them all.

Since this "study" is in fulfillment of a mitzvah, the "study" should be preceded by a blessing. In fact, it is preceded by a group of three blessings.[16] This can be understood in at least two ways. First, by associating the three benedictions with Bible study, Mishnah study, and Talmud study, respectively.[17] In support of this opinion, the last of the three (i.e., the one corresponding to the latest oral law) is the same as the blessing recited after an *aliya* (i.e., . . . who *gives* the Torah).

Alternatively, the three benedictions could represent three different types of blessings, reflecting three different understandings of Torah study: a blessing in preparation for the fulfillment of a mitzvah, a blessing recited over a pleasurable activity, and a blessing of thanksgiving for the Giving of the Torah.[18]

The complete Talmud Torah liturgical unit was inserted after the Blessings Upon Arising but before the Fifteen Morning Benedictions. At this point, the Fifteen Morning Benedictions have shed their original meaning and are now divorced from the idea of waking up. Figuratively, we wake up, study Torah, then go off to pray, and finish with the prayer for launching our regular daily activities:

The Preliminary Morning Service:

Blessings Upon Arising:	<—awaken
Elohai N'shama	
Handwashing Benediction	
Bathroom Benediction	
Talmud Torah:	<—study Torah
3 Torah benedictions	
Torah excerpt	
Mishnah excerpt	
Talmud excerpt	
Fifteen Morning Benedictions,	<—pray
Vihi Ratson and *Y'hi Ratson*	<—launch daily activities

THE MORNING SUPPLICATIONS

These are subtle texts, added in the fifth century c.e., during the persecutions in Babylonia, when it was unlawful for Jews to recite the *Sh'ma*. (Special government officials were posted in the synagogues to watch the services and ensure compliance.)

The Babylonian ruler was Zoroastrian, and Zoroastrians believed in a conflict between two opposing independent agencies, one good and one evil. The *Sh'ma* was seen as a challenge to this world view. (Judaism allows many different philosophical explanations for the appearance of evil in a world created good. But viewing evil as the result of activity by one of two opposing forces is definitely not one of them.)

The solution was for people to recite the *Sh'ma* at home in secret. The Morning Supplications were designed to publicize that strategy. They are extraordinary, moving texts. They were recited publicly in place of the *Sh'ma* Section.

They begin with veiled references to the need to arise early to recite the *Sh'ma* before leaving for synagogue. At the climactic point in the introduction, when we might expect the *Sh'ma* to commence, the text steps unexpectedly sideways into a magnificent prayer (*Ri-bon Kawl Ha-Olamim*) that was normally used for Yom Kippur. At one climax this prayer asks: "What can we say before you?" Later, it finishes by quoting the first line of the *Sh'ma*.

This prayer is then followed by one which provides veiled commentary on the persecutions and indicates acceptance of the duty of martyrdom. The end of *Ri-bon Kawl Ha-Olamim* is a natural bridge to this, since the *Sh'ma* is the dying words of Jewish martyrs. And the "duty to sanctify God's Name" has a double meaning here, as it is a euphemism for martyrdom as well as a reference to secretly reciting the *Sh'ma* twice daily. And finally, the section closes with a moving supplication for relief, also designed to remind one of the closing blessing of the *Sh'ma* Section (*Ga-al Yisraeil*).

When the Moslems conquered the country, the two hundred years of persecutions ended. This was in 637 c.e. The *Sh'ma* section was restored to the liturgy, but the Supplications were not dropped. After two hundred years, the emergency measure had become unalterable tradition.

The Morning Supplications are recited after the prayers for starting daily activity, as reciting the *Sh'ma* would be the first congregational activity.

The Preliminary Morning Service:
Blessings Upon Arising
Talmud Torah
Fifteen Morning Benedictions
Vihi Ratson and *Y'hi Ratson*
Morning Supplications

KORBANOT (OFFERINGS)

After the destruction of the Second Temple, the sacrificial service could no longer function. New mechanisms were needed to restore intimacy between individuals and their conception of the Divine. The Talmud[19] likens studying the laws of sacrifices to performing the sacrifices themselves, understanding them both to be ways of establishing humility and repentence. The Babylonian exile had set the stage for this development.[20]

The *Korbanot* section of the service is the most explicit example possible of study as a form of worship. Here, biblical excerpts related to sacrificial processes are studied and analyzed. While the Talmud Torah liturgical unit (described above, on page 212) symbolically fulfilled the halachic requirement for daily Torah study, the *Korbanot* liturgical unit engages in real Talmud Torah as a symbolic offering.

This is not symbolic study. The intent here is not merely to recite the texts, but to really learn something from them about the laws and significance of various offerings. The texts are extensive. When approached in the same spirit as a selfless ancient donor, seeking insight and a relationship with the divine, the effect on the worshipper could be as though one had actually offered a concrete expression of one's humility and repentance—a *korban*. The *Korbanot* section of the service is the alternative (or complimentary) process to the *Amidah*. It reflects ancient opinion that study (receiving divine insight) rather than prayer (expressing oneself) was the essence (or an equally crucial component) of the Service of the Altar.

The subject of all the biblical texts are the various communal offerings.[21] And if a particular offering would have been applicable to the occasion of this service, then the section of the text that describes that offering is followed by a short prayer expressing the hope that the recital can have the same effect on the worshipper as the ancient offering itself.

In order for study to be Talmud Torah, biblical texts must be studied with Mishnaic and later texts. So the *Korbanot* liturgical unit includes an excerpt from the Mishnah, and from *Sifra* (as a post-Mishnaic alternative to the Talmud itself). The first deals with details of the sacrificial laws; the second enumerates the thirteen logical principles that define how Jewish Tradition analyzes sacred text. Then a *Kaddish D'Rabbanan* (Scholar's Kaddish) completes the Korbanot unit. (*Kaddish D'Rabbanan* is the standard way to end communal Torah Study in any setting. It also appears in the Friday evening Praise Section.)

The *Mishnah* excerpt studied in the *Korbanot* section is Chapter 5 of the tractate *Ze-ba-chim*. Sacrifices are discussed in many places throughout the Mishnah, so why was this particular excerpt chosen? Because it is also a lesson in the value of peace between people. The Mishnah is a vast compilation of legal rulings, accumulated over hundreds of years. It records the minority opinions as well as the binding ruling of the majority. Chapter 5 of tractate *Zebachim* is the only chapter of the entire Mishnah in which there is not a single disagreement!

The *Korbanot* unit comes after the Morning Supplications, because it replaces the normal daily activity of the Temple, begun once the day is underway. Reform congregations omit the *Korbanot* Section. Most Conservative congregations include just its ending.

The Preliminary Morning Service:
Blessings Upon Arising
Talmud Torah
Fifteen Morning Benedictions
Vihi Ratson and *Y'hi Ratson*
Morning Supplications
Korbanot:
       Torah study re: *korbanot*
       Mishnah study re: *korbanot*
       Sifra study re: exegetical methodology
       Kaddish D'Rabbannan

THE ESTABLISHMENT OF
THE PRELIMINARY MORNING SERVICE

It is interesting to note that the Preliminary Morning Service has become like an abbreviated version of the complete service (but with the components out of order). We have an abbreviated *Sh'ma* Section (the Morning Supplications), a symbolic Torah-Reading section (Talmud Torah), an alternative Eighteen Benedictions (The Three Blessings Upon Arising, followed by the Fifteen Morning Benedictions), and a replacement for Temple rites (*Korbanot*)!

We can also view the daily morning liturgy as having an over-arching structure. The Preliminary Morning Service focuses on daily human renewal, the Praise Section on nature's daily renewal, and the Sh'ma Section on Israel's daily renewal. The Amidah, which is the heart of the service, climaxes in thoughts of the future utopia; and the Closing Section allows us to dwell on thoughts of the coming utopia as we prepare to return to earthly work.

Kavannah (intention) and *keva* (fixedness) coexist in Jewish tradition, but in an unstable way. When a spontaneous introduction to the service becomes thought of as statutory, the need for a spontaneous introduction becomes felt anew. We have seen how, as the *Sh'ma/Amidah* pair, and then the Praise Section, and finally the Preliminary Morning Service, became accepted as standard components of prayer, it was always felt necessary to add to the beginning of the service, to set the right mood for approaching prayer!

"One generation's *kavannah* becomes another generation's *keva*."

Jakob J. Petuchowski
in *Understanding Jewish Prayer*

Thus the following elements have been added to the Preliminary Morning service, *before* the "Blessings Upon Arising." These are the most recent extensions of the service.

MA TOVU

The morning liturgy now begins with a private meditation upon entering the synagogue (or upon settling into any other spot where one is preparing to pray). It is said first thing, before you put on a *tallis* (and *t'fillin* on weekdays). This meditation is called "*Ma Tovu*."[22]

In many synagogues, *Ma Tovu* is also used as a meditation upon entering the synagogue on Friday night before *Kabbalat Shabbat*. In some, it is sung aloud at the start of the *Kabbalat Shabbat* service rather than as a private meditation.

Ma Tovu begins with Balaam's blessing, "How goodly are your tents, O Jacob; your dwelling places, O Israel!" In this context, the reference is to the synagogue (or the site of the prayer service about to commence).[23]

Balaam, an ancient non-Jewish seer, had set out to curse the Israelites, but blurted out a blessing instead. An ancient midrash suggests what he saw that caused his exclamation: He saw that the Israelites all arranged their tents in distinctive formations so that they could not see into the tents of their neighbors. Everyone avoided being in a position to judge their neighbor's conduct.

OPENING HYMNS: ADON OLAM AND YIGDAL

Adon Olam and *Yigdal* were already discussed in detail during our discussion of the Closing Section for Friday night services (see pages 273 and 275), but *Adon Olam* was in use at the start of the Preliminary Morning Service much earlier. *Adon Olam* is now the beginning of the Preliminary Morning Service, unless *Ma Tovu* is sung aloud. *Yigdal* follows.

THE MEMORY OF THE PATRIARCHS: AKEIDA AND RIBONO SHEL OLAM

Before the Morning Supplications, the story of the Binding of Isaac (The *Akeida*; Exodus 22:1–19) is often recited. It is preceded by an appeal to the memory of the Patriarchs. It is followed by a meditation, beginning *"Ribono Shel Olam . . ."* ("Master of the Universe . . ."), on the same theme. On Sabbath and the festivals, the epilogue (and often the prologue also) is omitted by most congregations.

The story of the Binding of Isaac is an appropriate introduction to the Morning Supplications. Its popularity with important Kabbalists caused it to become a part of the service in most, but not all, congregations. In modern times, non-orthodox prayerbooks generally omit the entire section.

CONGREGATIONAL HABITS

Most of the Preliminary Morning Service is read silently, and many congregations skip parts of it. The only really reliable signposts are the Fifteen Morning Benedictions and the final *Kaddish D'Rabbanan.*

A common Ashkenazic practice is to expect everyone to begin silently and independently. The congregational service then begins with the Fifteen Morning Benedictions. The Morning Benedictions are recited standing.

The Preliminary Morning Service:
Meditation:
> Ma Tovu

Hymns:
> Adon Olam
>
> Yigdal

Blessings Upon Arising

Talmud Torah

Fifteen Morning Benedictions   <—many congregations
                                             begin aloud here

Vihi Ratson and *Y'hi Ratson*

Recalling the Merit of the Patriarchs:<—many congregations
                                             skip this

Introduction

The *Akeida* (The Binding of Isaac)

Epilogue: *Ribono Shel Olam*

Morning Supplications

Korbanot, ending with:	<—some congregations
Kaddish D'Rabbanan	abbreviate this
Psalm of The Day and	<—many congregations
Mourner's Kaddish	defer this
Hymn of Glory and Mourner's	<—many congregations
Kaddish	defer this

THE FIFTEEN MORNING BLESSINGS

As noted earlier, the original core of the Preliminary Morning Service is a rapid-fire sequence of fifteen one-line blessings from the Talmud. Even though they are no longer first in the siddur, they represent the true start of daily congregational prayer to many Jews. Some synagogues will begin with them. Others may sing the two opening hymns and then skip to the Fifteen Morning Benedictions.

They are very interesting. The first one thanks God for:

1. giving roosters the intelligence to distinguish between day and night!

This is a wonderful example of the Talmudic penchant for instantiation. The sages seldom talk about general principles or categories. Instead they deal with an example of the category, or discuss an instance of the general principle. It's up to you to figure out what the differences and commonalities are among the examples described, and what the larger issues are.

In the first benediction, we're primarily expressing gladness at having been awakened in time to show up for these services. That is:

1. —thank you for providing a means for me to ensure that I get here on time to fulfill this commandment.

But there are several other ways to interpret the "rooster" blessing. The rooster "foresees" the approaching day. Does it know? Or does it just feel? In either case, why does it crow? Some people use this blessing to express appreciation for nature's complex harmonious workings. In any case it's an appropriate start to an early morning service.

THE INFAMOUS BLESSING
AND WOMEN'S LIBERATION

Next in the sequence are three blessings that are often quoted out of context. They thank God for:

2. —not making me a gentile
3. —not making me a slave
4. —not making me a woman

Naturally, these have been the subject of protest and amendment over the years. Before tracing the changes, let's consider: What did they mean? Why only these three things? Why are they expressed as negatives?

The key is to recall that this is a Talmudic excerpt. There are 613 commandments in the Torah, 248 positive ones (i.e., "do this") and 365 negative ones (i.e., "thou shalt not . . ."). Of the 248 positive commandments, some must be fulfilled at a specified time (e.g., "dwell in a *sukkah*"), while others are independent of time (e.g., "love thy neighbor"). In the Talmud there is a stream of logic that concludes by exempting gentiles (non-Jews) from having to fulfill all but seven commandments out of the 613. There is another stream of logic that exempts Jewish slaves from the requirement of fulfilling most of the 613 commandments. There is a third stream of Talmudic logic which exempts Jewish women from having to fulfill most of the time-dependent positive commandments.

Thus Jewish men have more obligations than Jewish women, who have more obligations than Jewish slaves, who have more obligations than non-Jews. (More does not mean more important. In fact, it might appear that the more important obligations are the last to be given exemptions.) Praying communally in synagogue daily at the crack of dawn is one of the commandments that is only required of free Jewish men.

The Talmud doesn't mean that an individual can't adhere to a meritorious practice that is a law for others. It just means that one doesn't have to. The individual may gain personal satisfaction from doing things not required, but there's no external need for them to do so under Jewish law.

Note that the three blessings proceed in order of decreasing numbers of exemptions. This is key.

The intent of these blessings is to indicate enthusiasm for the service about to begin. They are said first thing in the morning at the start of daily prayer. (Only the rooster crowing has preceded them.) And the worship that is about to commence is being done in fulfillment of a commandment.

Therefore without these blessings, one might think that we were going to start the prescribed praying only because it is our duty. These prayers are put here to indicate that this is not so. They thank God for having put us in a condition such that we are commanded to do this.[24,25] In other words, these three blessings express the thought that we consider it a privilege, not a burden, to be subject to the commandment to be here praying at the crack of dawn. That is:

2. Thank you for not exempting me from nearly all commandments, including the requirement to be here.
3. Thank you for not exempting me from most commandments, including the requirement to be here.

4. Thank you for not exempting me from any commandments, thereby requiring me to be here.

CHANGES IN THE PRAYERBOOK

We now see that gentiles, slaves, and women are cited
together only because they have in common an exemption
from the obligation to be here. If a nonoffensive rewording were
to retain the original significance, it might thank God for:

—making me such that I am subject to all the commandments that are incumbent upon free male/female Jews.
(choose one)

I would love to see this in a siddur, but none of the
prayerbooks that I have seen makes changes in this way.
Some modern Conservative prayerbooks change the
meaning by stating the blessings in the positive. They may
also reverse the order, creating increasing specificity with
each blessing. They thank God for:

2. —making me in Thy image
   (i.e., human; avoiding male/female issues)
3. —making me free
   (like we say on Passover)
4. —making me Jewish

This makes the blessings appear to thank God for making us who we are, rather than thanking God for the commandments that we awoke to fulfill. This idea is lovely—we
should all be thankful for our selves. But these emendations,
while trying to eliminate an offensive expression, do not
preserve the nonoffensive underlying message.

By the fourteenth century women must have begun to
attend morning services, because prayerbooks changed to

provide alternate paths for men and women. Attendees now thank God for:

2. —not making me a gentile
3. —not making me a slave
4a —making me according to Thy will　　　(for women)
4b —not making me a woman　　　　　　　(for men)

This conceals the Talmud's original intent. The set of three blessings as recited by women look unrelated to each other, and unrelated to an appreciation of mitzvot. And the comparison of 4a with 4b looks (on the surface) more derogatory towards womanhood than does the men's original by itself. This formulation is asymmetric, but still in use in most orthodox prayerbooks.

THE CLIMAX OF THE WAKE-UP BLESSINGS

Remember that this all appears in the context of early morning awakening. After appreciation for nature awakening, and appreciation for our responsibility to be here, we express appreciation for: (Note: In some *Siddurim* the order is slightly different.)

5. —healing blindness
6. —clothing the naked
7. —setting captives free
8. —raising up those who are bowed down
9. —the existence of the world
10. —guiding history
11. —providing for our needs
12. —strengthening Israel
13. —honoring Israel
14. —giving strength to the weary

Thus we immediately begin the day by empathizing with the righteous and the defenseless. Similar thoughts are present throughout the siddur. Our prayers often mention strangers, the lowly, the humble, orphans, the poor, the ailing, the falling, widows, robbed ones, the hungry, the blind, slaves, the dumb, and captives.

The fifth and seventh blessings have often been interpreted metaphorically. They refer to ourselves. We can be blind to the sources of inspiration around us and to the potential for holiness. We can be enslaved to our evil inclinations, desiring to receive only for ourselves.

And then comes the climactic final blessing in the sequence, expressing appreciation for:

15. —removing sleep from my eyes
                        and slumber from my eyelids.

This imagery is important. It is used throughout Jewish tradition as a metaphor for sensitivity to the plight of others and an ability to perceive injustice.

It is a new day.
    We are awake.
        And there is work to do
            To redeem Creation.
                Time is a tool.

Weekday Services:

	Shacharit (morning)	Mincha (afternoon)	Ma-ariv (evening)
Preliminary Service	**Preliminary Morning Service:** Ma Tovu Adon Olam / Yigdal Blessings Upon Arising and Talmud Torah 15 Morning Benedictions** and Vihi/Y'hi Ratson Merit of the Patriarchs and Morning Supplications Korbanot / Kaddish D'Rabbanan*		
Praise Section	Psalm 30 / Mourner's Kaddish prologue: Baruch Sheamar - texts - Psalms 100, and - Ps.145 (Ashrei) thru 150 - texts epilogue: Yishtabach Half-Kaddish	Ashrei (Psalm 145) Half-Kaddish	Psalm 144 (Sat. only) Psalm 67 (Sat. only) Psalm 134 (if no mincha) Half-Kaddish (if no mincha)
Shema Section	Barchu Yotseir (creation), for weekdays Ahavah Raba (revelation) Shema Ga-al Yisraeil - A.M. version		Barchu Ma-ariv Aravim (creation) Ahavat Olam (revelation) Shema Ga-al Yisraeil - P.M. version Hashkiveinu, for weekdays - with Baruch Adonai L'olam Half-Kaddish
Amidah Section	Shacharit Shemoneh Esreh: - avot, givurot - k'dushat hashem - 13 benedictions - Avodah, Modim - Sim Shalom Meditation Repetition: - avot, givurot - k'dushah - 13 benedictions - Avodah - Modim/Modim - Sim Shalom Tachanun	Mincha Shemoneh Esreh: - avot, givurot - k'dushat hashem - 13 benedictions - Avodah, Modim - Shalom Rav Meditation Repetition: - avot, givurot - k'dushah - 13 benedictions - Avodah - Modim/Modim - Shalom Rav Tachanun	Ma-ariv Shemoneh Esreh: - avot, givurot - k'dushat hashem - 13 benedictions - Avodah, Modim - Shalom Rav Meditation
Closing Section			

Shabbat Services:

	Shacharit & Musaf (Sat. AM)	Mincha (Sat. afternoon)	Ma-ariv (Friday evening)
Preliminary Section	**Preliminary Morning Service:** Ma Tovu Adon Olam / Yigdal Blessings Upon Arising and Talmud Torah 15 Morning Benedictions† and Vihi/Y'hi Ratson Merit of the Patriarchs and Morning Supplications Korbanot / Kaddish D'Rabbanan*		**Kabbalat Shabbat:** - Psalm 95 (L'chu N'ran'na) - Psalm 96 and 97 - Psalm 98 and 99 - Havu L'adonai (Psalm 29) - L'cha Dodi greeting mourners
Praise Section	Psalm 30/ Mourner's Kaddish prologue: Baruch Sheamar - texts - Psalms: 19, 34, 90-1, 135-6, 33, 92-3, - and Psalm 145 (Ashrei) thru 150 - texts epilogue: Nishmat-Yishtabach Half-Kaddish	Ashrei (Psalm 145) Uva L'Tsion Half-Kaddish	- Psalm 92 - Psalm 93 - Mourner's Kaddish - Torah Study, on candles - Kaddish D'Rabbanan
Shema Section	Barchu Yotseir (creation), for Shabbat Ahavah Raba (revelation) Shema Ga-al Yisraeil - A.M. version		Barchu Ma'ariv Aravim (creation) Ahavat Olam (revelation) Shema Ga-al Yisraeil - P.M. version Hashkiveinu, for Shabbat - with Vishamru Half-Kaddish
Amidah Section	Shacharit Amidah: - avot, givurot - k'dushat hashem - K Hayom-Vishamru - Avodah, Modim - Sim Shalom Meditation Repetition: - avot, givurot - k'dushah - shabbat - K Ha-yom-Vishamru - Avodah - Modim/Modim - Sim Shalom		Ma-ariv Amidah: - avot, givurot - k'dushat hashem - K Hayom-Vayichulu - Avodah, Modim - Shalom Rav Meditation Vayichulu Magein Avot R'tsei Vimnuchateinu
Closing Section	Full-Kaddish Psalm of the Day / Mourner's K.* Hymn of Glory / Mourner's K. *		

†Most congregations begin aloud here.

Torah-Reading (Mon., Thu., & Sat.)	Removing the Torah: - Zohar excerpt - Procession: L'cha Adonai 3 aliyot Congregational Half-Kaddish Lifting: V'zot HaTorah Returning the Torah: - Hodo Al Eretz - Procession: Psalm 24 - Return: Eitz Chayim ----------------		
Miscellaneous Community Business			
Praise Section			
Amidah Section			
Closing Section	Half-Kaddish Ashrei Psalm 20 and Uva L'Tzion Full-Kaddish Aleinu / Mourner's Kaddish*	Full-Kaddish Aleinu / Mourner's Kaddish	Half-Kaddish (Sat. only) Psalm 91 (Sat. only) Atah Kadosh (Sat. only) Full-Kaddish Tanach text (Sat. only) Psalm 128 (Sat. only) Havdalah (Sat. only) Aleinu / Mourner's Kaddish

Torah-Reading
 	
(Mon., Thu.,
& Sat.)
	Removing the Torah:
	- Zohar / Shema excerpt
	- Procession: L'cha
	  Adonai
	
	7 aliyot
	Congregational
	  Half-Kaddish
	
	--------------- 	
	--------------- 	
	--------------- 	
	--------------- 	
	--------------- 	
	--------------- 	
		Removing the Torah:
		- Zohar excerpt
		- Procession: L'cha
		  Adonai
		
		3 aliyot
		--------------- 	
		
		Lifting: V'zot Ha-Torah
		
		Returning the Torah:
		-' Hodo Al Eretz
		- Procession: Psalm 24
		- Return: Eitz Chayim
		Congregational
		  Half-Kaddish	

Miscellaneous **Community** **Business**	Prophetic Reading: - Maftir - Lifting: V'zot HaTorah - Haftarah Sermon / Announcements Exhortations to philanthropy Prayers for U.S. / Israel Announce the new month Remembrance of martyrs		

Praise
Section
	Ashrei (Psalm 145)‡
	Delayed returning of the
	  Torah:
	- Hodo Al Eretz
	- Procession: Psalm 29
	  (Havu L.)
	- Return: Eitz Chayim
	Half-Kaddish		

Amidah **Section**	Musaf Amidah: - avot, givurot - k'dushat hashem - K Ha-yom (Yismechu) - Avodah, Modim - Sim Shalom Meditation Repetition: - avot, givurot - k'dushah - musaf - K Ha-yom (Yismechu) - Avodah - Modim/Modim - Sim Shalom	Mincha Amidah: - avot, givurot - k'dushat hashem - K Hayom - Ata Echad - Avodah, Modim - Shalom Rav Meditation Repetition: - avot, givurot - k'dushah - K HaYom -Atah Echad - Avodah - Modim / Modim - Shalom Rav	

Closing
Section
	Full-Kaddish
	Ein Keloheinu
	Talmud Study on incense
	Kaddish D'Rabbanan
	
	Aleinu / Mourner's
	  Kaddish*
	Adon Olam
		Full-Kaddish
		
		Aleinu / Mourner's
		  Kaddish
			Full-Kaddish
			
			Kiddush
			
			Aleinu / Mourner's
			  Kaddish
			Adon Olam (or Yigdal)

* The Psalm of Day (and the Hymn of Glory on Shabbat) can be inserted separately in any of these places, or together in either order.
‡If a break is desired before Musaf, the ritual for returning the Torah to the Ark is performed before returning for Ashrei.

Notes

1. c.f., Talmud Berachot 60b.

2. Because any writing would ultimately be destroyed, the early sages said, "One who writes down prayers is as one who burns the Torah."

3. In emulation of King David in II Samuel 23:1 (in which the Hebrew word *"al"* can be translated as "one hundred" rather than "on high"), or in fulfilment of Deuteronomy 10:12 (in which the Hebrew word *"mah"* can be translated as "one hundred" rather than "what"), or to negate the one hundred curses found in Deuteronomy (ending at 28:61). C.f., Talmud Menachot 43b, Kitzur Shulchan Aruch 6:7.

4. c.f., Talmud Berachot 33a.

5. The fifteen benedictions were themselves modified and expanded, producing what are now the second through fourth morning benedictions, which will be discussed below. C.f., Talmud Menachot 43b.

6. This left no rites for the home. So new home rituals were established and enlarged over time (e.g., Modeh Ani). C.f., Genesis Rabbah 78:1 and Talmud Sukkot 42a.

7. c.f., Berachot 60b and 24b; Y.Berachot 9:4, 14b; Orach Chayim 6:1. Its text is related by a *midrashic* pun to Deuteronomy 32:6. C.f., Sifre Deuteronomy Piska 312; and see also Talmud Bavli Hullin 56b.

8. Later on, *"guf"* and *"neshama"* acquire connotations of "body" and "soul," respectively.

9. The evil inclination is sometimes defined as "the desire to receive only for oneself," or "the desire to become larger."

10. translation taken from *The Talmudic Anthology—Tales & Teachings of the Rabbis*, edited by Louis I. Newman in collaboration with Samuel Spitz, published by Behrman House, 1945.

11. C.f., Ecclesiastes 4:4, Avot d'Rabbi Natan perek 16, Kohelet Rabbah on 3:11, Mishnah Berachot 9:5, Bereshit Rabbah to 1:31, Tikkune Zohar 132a, Midrash ha-Neelam I 138a, Kiddushin 30b, Sukkah 52b, Sifre Deuteronomy on 11:18.

12. Star Trek Fans: This bit of Talmud formed the basis for the episode, "The Enemy Within," in which a transporter accident

gives Kirk's good and bad inclinations independent bodies. The evil Kirk and the good Kirk are equally ineffective. One is like an engine without a transmission, the other a transmission with no engine. The evil inclination is the power source that needs to be controlled. The good inclination cannot move without harnessing it.

13. c.f., Talmud Kiddushin 30a, and Menachot 29a, and Shulchan Aruch Yoreh Deah 246:6.

14. c.f., Sifre Deuteronomy Piska 48, "By everything that procedes out of the mouth of the Lord . . ."

15. The trend, now prominent in less traditional American congregations, toward thinking of rabbis as the only people obligated to fulfill the paramount mitzvot of comforting the bereaved and visiting the sick is antithetical to Judaism. Congregations of individuals should not delegate these mitzvot. These are not traditional rabbinical functions.

16. c.f., Berachot 11b.

17. c.f., Abudarham, quoting R. Zechariah.

18. c.f., Rambam, Mishneh Torah, Laws of Blessings 1:4.

19. c.f., Talmud Menachot 110a, Megillah 31a, Taanit 27b.

20. c.f., Hosea 14:3.

21. Only the communal offerings are included, emphasizing the value of Jewish unity.

22. Ma Tovu is constructed from Numbers 24:5, Psalms 5:8, 26:8, 95:6, and 69:14

23. There are times when *Ma Tovu* can take on a special poignancy, as at an early morning minyan in the barracks at Auschwitz.

24. c.f., Tosefta to Berachot 6.18, which says: "[R. Judah: This is said daily,] for a woman is not obligated to perform all the commandments."

25. c.f., Judah ben Ilai, Tosefta Berachot 7.18.

Appendix A:
How to Put on T'fillin

This ritual is performed while standing. If you are wearing long sleeves, roll up the sleeve of your weak hand. Move any watches or jewelry to your other arm (or just remove them). Affix the heart/arm/hand *t'fillin* loosely, on the uppermost muscle of your inside arm, so it would point to your heart if your arm were at your side. (Lefties use their right arm, even though this lessens nearness to the heartbeat.) The edge of the base that is attached to the strap is placed closest to the shoulder.

Say the blessing and then tighten the strap. Then wrap the strap around the arm in a spiral, moving down the arm toward the wrist, with the black side out. Ashkenazic Jews wrap it so the strap comes toward you over the arm, and away from you beneath the arm. The strap may be wrapped several times above the elbow to stabilize the position of the box, but must be wrapped around the arm seven times below the elbow.

Before continuing with the hand *t'fillin*, we must free our hands so we can don the head *t'fillin*. Bring the strap under your wrist to the heel of the hand, and across the back of the hand to the space between thumb and forefinger, and wrap it around your palm until it is short enough to tuck in the end, so that your hands are free.

Put the head *t'fillin* on your upper forehead, centered between your eyes, with the edge of the base that is attached to the strap closest to the top of your head, and with that side of the box positioned at the hairline. Say the blessing (and associated text afterwards), fix the knot at the back of your head, and bring the straps over your shoulders so they hang down in front of you.

Finally, you finish donning the hand *t'fillin*. Unwrap the strap from your palm, until the strap is now wrapped between your thumb and forefinger but has not passed across your palm. Now resume wrapping, but instead of crossing your palm, bring it only as far as the space between your middle finger and ring finger, and wrap it three times around your middle finger, first near the palm, then near the tip, and finally in between (but still on the side of the knuckle toward the tip).

Recite Hosea 2:21–2 as you do this, establishing the betrothal metaphor, as though the strap were a wedding ring.

Now bring the strap across the inside of the ring finger near the palm, and then out between the ring finger and pinky. Take the strap over the back of the hand to the space between thumb and forefinger (where it makes a "V" with the part coming from the heel), then across the palm, and across the back of the hand (turning the "V" into a "*shin*"). Any excess length can be wrapped around the palm over the middle of the *shin*, and tucked in.

To remove the *t'fillin*, everything is done in reverse, also while standing.

All this is a lot easier to do than to describe. Ask someone to show you how.

Appendix B:
Concordance of Siddur
Page Numbering

FRIDAY NIGHT SERVICE

	Art Scroll	Birn-baum	Sim Shalom	Silver-man	Gates of Prayer	Hyman Segal	Ben Zion Bokser	Tehillat HaShem	Joseph Hertz
I. WELCOMING THE SABBATH (Kabbalat Shabbat)									
Psalm 95 (L'chu N'ra-n'na)	308	237	254	5	118	182	101	128	346
Psalm 96	308	237	254	6	119	183	102	128	348
Psalm 97	310	239	256	7	120	183	103	129	350
Psalm 98	312	241	256	8	121	184	103	130	350
Psalm 99	312	241	258	9	122	185	104	130	352
Psalm 29 (Havu Ladonai)	314	241	260	10	122	185	105	131	354
L'cha Dodi	316	243	262	11	123	186	106	131	356
II. THE MA-ARIV PRAISE SECTION									
Psalm 92 (Tsadik Katomar)	320	247	266	13	125	188	107	133	360
Psalm 93	320	249	267	14	127	189	108	133	362
Mourner's Kaddish	322	249	267	39	(629)	100	123	417	(399)
Mishnah Excerpt on Sabbath Candles	322	251	270	—	—	(203)	—	—	(390)
Kaddish D'Rabbanan	328	255	274	(49)	—	(205)	(11)	(418)	(237)
III. THE SH'MA SECTION									
Ba-r'chu	330	257	279	15	129	191	109	135	364
Ma-ariv Aravim	330	257	280	15	129	191	109	135	364
Ahavat Olam	330	257	282	15	130	191	109	135	366

	Art Scroll	Birn-baum	Sim Shalom	Silver-man	Gates of Prayer	Hyman Segal	Ben Zion Bokser	Tehillat HaShem	Joseph Hertz
The Sh'ma	330	257	283	16	130	192	110	136	366
Ga-al Yisraeil	334	261	288	18	131	193	111	137	370
Hashkiveinu	334	261	292	19	133	194	112	138	372
Vishamru	336	263	294	20	133	195	113	138	372
Half-Kaddish	336	263	294	20	(128)	195	113	134	(106)
IV. THE AMIDAH SECTION									
Avot	338	265	296	21	134	196	113	139	374
Givurot	338	265	296	21	134	196	114	139	376
K'dushat Ha-shem	338	267	296	22	135	197	114	139	378
K'dushat Ha-yom	340	267	298	22	136	197	114	139	378
Avodah	342	267	298	23	137	198	115	140	382
Modim	342	269	300	23	138	199	116	140	384
Shalom Rav	344	271	302	24	140	200	117	141	386
Elohai N'tsor	344	271	302	25	140	200	117	142	386
Va-y'chulu	346	273	314	26	(205)	201	118	142	(380)
Magein Avot	346	273	314	26	141	201	118	142	388
R'tsei Vimnuchateinu	348	275	314	27	(770)	202	119	143	390
V. THE CLOSING SECTION									
Full Kaddish	348	275	316	27	—	202	119	74	(206)
Kiddush	348	277	318	28	(777)	(215)	120	(146)	394
Aleinu	350	277	320	37	615	206	121	143	396
Mourner's Kaddish	352	279	324	39	629	100	123	417	398
Adon Olam	352	281	(6)	41	729	208	124	(13)	400
Yigdal	(12)	(11)	326	40	731	(8)	125	—	400
Shalom Aleichem	354	(283)	(722)	(358)	(270)	(209)	(348)	(144)	404

SATURDAY MORNING SERVICE

	Art Scroll	Birn-baum	Sim Shalom	Silver-man	Gates of Prayer	Hyman Segal	Ben Zion Bokser	Tehillat HaShem	Joseph Hertz
Ma Tovu	12	3	2	42	51	7	1	12	4
Putting on a Tallis	2	5	4	42	48	1	2	11	(45)
I. THE PRELIMINARY MORNING SERVICE									
Adon Olam	12	11	6	42	(729)	7	(124)	13	6
Yigdal	12	11	(326)	43	(731)	8	(125)	—	6
Blessings on Arising	12	13	6	44	284	9	4	6	6
Blessings of Torah (Birchot Ha-torah)	14	13	6	44	284	10	4	9	12
The 15 Morning Blessings	18	15	10	45	286	11	5	7	18
Akeida (The Binding of Isaac)	23	19	—	—	—	14	—	13	—
Morning Supplication	26	23	12	46	288	16	7	16	26
Korbanot (offerings)	30	27	—	—	—	19	—	18	34
Kaddish D'Rabbanan	52	45	20	49	—	28	11	26	(237)
Psalm of the Day	(488)	(415)	32	55	(125)	(262)	17	(76)	(215)
Mourner's Kaddish	(482)	(413)	(53)	(61)	(629)	(80)	(80)	(77)	(554)
Hymn of Glory	(484)	(419)	46	58	(364)	(299)	19	—	(361)
Mourner's Kaddish	(482)	(413)	(53)	(61)	(629)	(80)	(80)	(77)	(554)
II. THE SHACHARIT PRAISE SECTION									
Psalm 30	368	299	51	60	—	223	21	148/150	(234)
Mourner's Kaddish	368	299	53	61	(629)	223	80	(77)	(554)
Baruch She-amar (prologue)	370	301	54	62	290	233	22	158	50

SATURDAY MORNING SERVICE (CONTINUED)

	Art Scroll	Birnbaum	Sim Shalom	Silverman	Gates of Prayer	Hyman Segal	Ben Zion Bokser	Tehillat HaShem	Joseph Hertz
biblical texts	370	301	54	63	—	221	22	148	52
Psalms 19, 34, 90, 91	374	305	60	66	290	224	25	150	60–72
Psalms 135, 136, 33	382	311	68	70	291	230, 225	29	155	72–80
Psalm 92 (Tsadik Katomar)	388	317	76	74	292	233	33	158	80–
Psalm 93	388	317	78	75	(127)	234	35	159	82
Ashrei (Psalm 145)	390	319	80	76	294	235	36	159	84
Psalm 146, 147, 148, 149	392	321	82	77	—	236	38	160	88–96
Psalm 150	396	325	88	80	297	238	41	163	96
Biblical texts	396	327	90	81	—	239	42	163	98
Nishmat	400	331	334	84	297	241	126	165	416
Yishtabach (epilogue)	404	335	338	86	300	244	128	169	422
Half-Kaddish	406	335	338	86	300	245	128	(134)	422
III. THE SHACHARIT SH'MA SECTION									
Ba-r'chu	406	335	340	87	301	245	128	170	424
Yo-tseir Or	406	337	340	87	(315)	246	128	170	424
Ahavat Raba	412	343	346	91	302	250	132	174	434
The Sh'ma	414	343	346	92	303	251	133	175	438
Ga-al Yisraeil	416	347	350	94	304	253	134	176	444
IV. THE SHACHARIT AMIDAH SECTION									
The Silent Amidah:									
Avot	420	349	354	96	306	255	136	178	448
Givurot	420	349	354	96	307	255	136	178	450
K'dushat Ha-shem	422	353	358	96	(135)	256	137	179	454

SATURDAY MORNING SERVICE (CONTINUED)

	Art Scroll	Birn-baum	Sim Shalom	Silver-man	Gates of Prayer	Hyman Segal	Ben Zion Bokser	Tehillat HaShem	Joseph Hertz
K'dushat Ha-yom	424	353	358	98	309	256	138	179	456
Avodah	426	353	358	98	309	258	138	180	460
Modim	426	355	360	99	311	258	139	181	462
Sim Shalom	428	359	362	101	313	260	141	182	464
Elohai N'tsor	430	359	364	101	313	261	141	182	466
The Reader's Repetition:									
Avot	420	349	354	96	306	255	136	178	448
Givurot	420	349	354	96	307	255	136	178	450
K'dushah	422	351	356	97	307	256	137	179	452
K'dushat Ha-yom	424	353	358	98	309	256	138	179	456
Avodah	426	353	358	98	309	258	138	180	460
Modim	426	355	360	99	311	258	139	181	462
Priestly Blessing	428	357	362	100	—	260	141	182	464
Sim Shalom	428	359	362	101	313	260	141	182	464
V. THE SHACHARIT CLOSING SECTION									
Full-Kaddish	430	361	392	116	—	261	155	(74)	(207)
Psalm of the Day	(488)	(415)	(32)	(55)	(125)	262	(17)	182	(215)
Mourner's Kaddish	(482)	(413)	(53)	(61)	(629)	(100)	(80)	(77)	(554)
Hymn of Glory	(484)	(419)	(46)	(58)	(364)	(299)	(19)	—	(361)
Mourner's Kaddish	(482)	(413)	(53)	(61)	(629)	(80)	(80)	(77)	(554)

SATURDAY MORNING SERVICE (CONTINUED)

	Art Scroll	Birn-baum	Sim Shalom	Silver-man	Gates of Prayer	Hyman Segal	Ben Zion Bokser	Tehillat HaShem	Joseph Hertz
VI. THE TORAH READING SERVICE									
Ein Kamocha (Approaching the Ark)	432	361	394	117	417	263	156	—	472
Kuma Adonai (Opening the Ark)	432	363	394	117	418	264	156	183	472
B'rich Sh'mei	436	365	396	117	418	265	157	184	474
Sh'ma Excerpt	436	365	398	123	418	266	158	185	480
L'cha Adonai (The Procession)	436	365	398	123	418	266	158	185	480
Torah Blessings (Reading the Torah)	440	369	400	124	419	267	158	186	484-6
Congregational Half-Kaddish	(138)	373	408	125	(300)	(282)	160	(134)	(422)
VII. MISCELLANEOUS COMMUNITY BUSINESS									
Prophetic Reading:									
Maftir Aliya Blessings	440	369	400	124	419	267	158	186	484-6
V'zot Ha-Torah (Lifting the Torah)	444	373	410	125	419	271	161	187	492
Haftarah Blessings	446	373	410	126	420	271	161	187	494
Y'kum Purkon	448	377	412	128	—	274	162	188	500
Prayer for the Government	450	379	414	130	452	275	166	—	506
Prayer for the State of Israel	450	(789)	416	—	452	(550)	164	—	—
Announcing the New Month	452	381	418	129	453	277	166	191	508
Av Harachamim	454	383	420	131	—	279	165	191	510

SATURDAY MORNING SERVICE (CONTINUED)

	Art Scroll	Birn-baum	Sim Shalom	Silver-man	Gates of Prayer	Hyman Segal	Ben Zion Bokser	Tehillat HaShem	Joseph Hertz
VIII. THE MUSAF PRAISE SECTION									
Ashrei	456	383	420	132	(294)	280	167	192	514
Parting with the Torah:									
Hodo Al Erets (Taking the Torah)	458	387	422	133	423	281	168	193	518
Havu Ladonai (Psalm 29) (The Return Procession)	458	387	424	134	423	281	169	(131)	518
Eits Chayim (Returning the Torah to the Ark)	460	389	426	136	424	282	170	—	522
Half-Kaddish	460	389	428	137	(300)	282	171	(134)	(422)
IX. THE MUSAF AMIDAH SECTION									
The Silent Amidah:									
Avot	462	391	430	137	(306)	283	171	193	526
Givurot	462	391	430	138	(307)	283	171	193	526
K'dushat Ha-shem	464	393	434	138	(135)	284	173	194	530
K'dushat Ha-yom	466	395	434	140	—	284	173	194	530
Avodah	470	399	436	143	(309)	288	174	197	534
Modim	470	399	436	143	(311)	288	174	197	536
Sim Shalom	472	403	438	145	(313)	290	176	198	538
Elohai N'tsor	472	403	440	145	(313)	291	176	198	538

SATURDAY MORNING SERVICE (CONTINUED)

	Art Scroll	Birn-baum	Sim Shalom	Silver-man	Gates of Prayer	Hyman Segal	Ben Zion Bokser	Tehillat HaShem	Joseph Hertz
The Reader's Repetition:									
Avot	462	391	430	137	(306)	283	171	193	526
Givurot	462	391	430	138	(307)	283	171	193	526
K'dushah	464	393	432	139	—	284	172	193	528
K'dushat Ha-yom	466	395	434	140	—	284	173	194	530
Avodah	470	399	436	143	(309)	288	174	197	534
Modim	470	399	436	143	(311)	288	174	197	536
Priestly Blessings	472	403	438	144	—	290	175	198	538
Sim Shalom	472	403	438	145	(313)	290	176	198	538
X. THE MUSAF CLOSING SECTION									
Full Kaddish	474	405	507	156	—	292	199	(74)	(206)
Ein Keloheinu	476	407	508	157	—	293	200	198	544
Talmud Excerpts:	476	407	—	—	—	293	—	199	546
Pikum Ha-k'toret and Ha-shir									
Kaddish D'Rabbanan	480	411	(20)	(49)	—	295	(11)	200	(237)
Aleinu	480	413	510	158	615	297	201	200	550
Mourner's Kaddish	482	413	512	161	629	298	203	(77)	554
Hymn of Glory	484	415	(46)	(55)	(364)	299	(17)	—	(215)
Mourner's Kaddish	(482)	413	(53)	(61)	(629)	298	(80)	(77)	(554)
Psalm of the Day (Psalm 92)	488	419	(32)	(58)	(125)	(262)	(19)	(182)	(361)
Mourner's Kaddish	(482)	413	(512)	(61)	(629)	(298)	(80)	(77)	(554)
Adon Olam	(12)	423	514	162	(729)	301	204	(13)	556

Index

About the Author

Jordan Lee Wagner lives in Newton, Massachusetts, where he is an officer of his synagogue and an active volunteer in outreach to new Americans. His work has appeared in such publications as *The Journal of Chemical Physics, Soundwaves* magazine, *Byte* magazine, and *The Celator*. Mr. Wagner has served several congregations as administrator. He sings in various Jewish choirs and spends his time writing music, rehabilitating a Victorian home, and developing Jewish educational board games.